7-07

D1304847

A GOOD PLACE TO STOP

60 Seasons with Max and the Jayhawks

A GOOD PLACE TO STOP

60 Seasons with Max and the Jayhawks

By Max Falkenstien
with Matt Fulks and Doug Vance

Foreword by Kevin Harlan
Introduction by Lew Perkins
Afterword by Bill Self

P wer House
Marketing, Licensing, Publishing, Representation

Requests for permission should be addressed to **Power House, LLC**, Attn: Rights and Permissions Department, 10101 West 87th Street, Suite 100, Overland Park, KS 66212.

10 9 8 7 6 5 4 3 2 1

Printed in the United States of America

ISBN-13: 978-0-9767330-2-7
ISBN 10: 0-9767330-2-1

Library of Congress Cataloging-in-Publications Data available on request.

Design by Eddy Mora & IdentityBox

10101 West 87th Street, Suite 100
Overland Park, KS 66212

www.powerhousenow.com

Dedication

To all the wonderful fans who have been my faithful listeners, to all the magnificent (and not so magnificent) players whom I have come to know and love, and to that amazing lineup of successful coaches with whom I have worked, played and become a confidant and close friend.

Table of Contents

Acknowledgements

The authors would like to thank the following individuals — coaches, athletes, administrators, media, fans and others — who played a role in shaping the history of Kansas athletics over the past 60 years and helped us recall those many moments.

In addition to the people who were instrumental in helping shape Max's first book, *Max and the Jayhawks*, we would like to express our appreciation also to those who played a role in helping to make *A Good Place to Stop* a reality.

For taking time to be interviewed for the book: Gary Bedore, Bob Davis, Bob Frederick, Robert Hemenway, Drue Jennings, Jason King, Mark Mangino, Lew Perkins, Bill Self, Chris Theisen, Jerry Waugh and Roy Williams.

For transcribing tapes or serving as a source of information or encouragement: Rick, Amy, Brandon and T.K. Allen, Tim and Amy Brown, Elizabeth Eickhorst and Kathy Sutton.

For editing, along with guidance and assistance in putting this together: Jim Marchiony, Miles Schnaer and Bob Snodgrass.

And, to Fred and Sharon Fulks, and Libby, Helen, Charlie and Aaron Fulks.

Thank you, all.

Preface

As Bill Self strolled onto the court before KU's 2005-06 home finale at Allen Fieldhouse, he uncharacteristically walked straight over to press row, leaned down and said something to Max Falkenstien. The two laughed for a moment and then Self went to the Kansas bench.

That doesn't happen before each game. But this wasn't an ordinary game. It was "Senior Night." Really, though, it was Max Falkenstien's night. It was Falkenstien's last hurrah at Allen Fieldhouse after 60 years behind the microphone.

"I had a special gift for Max that I presented to him," Self said during the writing of this book. "It was something between Max and me that won't go any further.

"Really, it was an honor for me to be a part of Senior Night when Max was going out. He loves the guys so much and takes so much pride in the players at KU. That night was as much about Max and his 60 years as it was anything else, Self added."

Think about that number for a minute. Sixty. It doesn't sink in easily. After all, just living 60 years is a great goal for some, let alone being able to do something one loves at a place where he's adored for that long.

Sixty. It's a perfect number in terms of time. Sixty seconds in a minute. Sixty minutes in an hour. And, for KU fans, 60 years of memories from a Hall of Fame broadcaster.

During his 60 years, Falkenstien announced roughly 650 Jayhawk football games and 1,750 KU basketball games, including every men's basketball game played at Allen Fieldhouse from its opening in 1955 through the 2005-06 season.

In 1996, marking his 50th anniversary with KU, Max and co-author Doug Vance wrote a wonderful book, *Max and the Jayhawks.* In many ways it was the definitive source of KU's history through Max's eyes. *A Good Place to Stop* picks up where Max and the Jayhawks left off, covering Falkenstien's last decade with Kansas. Those 10 years included back-to-back trips to the Final Four, two bowl games and some interesting behind-the-scenes drama in the athletic department that resulted in the firing of an athletics director and a basketball coach leaving for his alma mater. We've also culled through Max's first book and picked out the best and most intriguing stories from his time of covering KU athletics.

During his 2,400-plus games, Falkenstien became a friend to every listener. Walking around Lawrence with him today is akin to walking around with a popular mayor. (Truth told, Max is more popular with KU fans than any mayor ever could be.)

Personally, Falkentien's is the voice — along with Bob Davis' — that I smuggled into my junior high and high school classrooms to listen to NCAA Tournament games, with the help of a transistor radio and an earplug. His is the voice that I would hear coming out of the "boom box" in my bedroom as I dozed off during late-night games from Alaska and Hawaii.

In fact, Max is one of the reasons that I'm writing today. My background, you see, is in radio, calling games for six years at Lipscomb University in Nashville, Tennessee. I guess I dreamed of becoming the next Max Falkenstien, Fred White or Denny Matthews. That work in radio eventually led me into writing. Obviously I wasn't destined to become the next Denny, Fred or Max. Not many are.

It's not often these days that a broadcaster becomes identified as a permanent part of the tradition of the university or team that he covers. Indeed, it's rare that broadcasters stay in one place for more than a couple decades, let alone long enough to become a part of the program's history.

Max told me one time: "I've been around for most of KU's sports history, but I don't know that I'm a part of it. It's certainly been great to be associated with it."

No, Max, for 60 years the pleasure's been ours.

—Matt Fulks
January 8, 2007

Foreword

There was a time in sports broadcasting when every game wasn't televised. In fact, most were not until the arrival of cable. The first great broadcast vehicle was radio. And while television has replaced it as the more common way to enjoy sports, unless of course you can actually be at the game, radio has had, and still has, a unique presence. Well-crafted words coupled with the listener's imagination — theater of the mind — can ignite images television cannot. The listener works to grasp the announcer's description, and if the right words come out of the broadcaster's mouth, it can be far more enriching and memorable. Certainly more riveting.

What a responsibility for the broadcaster to be totally in control of how the game is perceived through his impressions, his word choice and his passion. The rise and fall of a radio broadcaster's voice unlocks all kinds of emotions.

A radio sportscaster works with a blank canvas, coloring images through his words.

A TV broadcaster is a slave to the picture with the task of accenting what you already see. So if indeed a picture is worth a thousand words, think of the demands of a radio broadcaster and the clarity needed to report accurately. Now join that thought process with the importance and interest of the event to the listener. An interest that is so strong and so gripping, that the very fabric of their involvement hinges on your presentation of the event as they consume every word, visualizing, in the mind's eye, the play and result. Now you have a view of where a broadcaster like Max Falkenstien has placed himself in the minds and the memories of the Jayhawk Nation, with fans that are among the most passionate in all of college sports.

He has reported and broadcast Chamberlain and Manning, Sayers and Douglass, coaches Allen and Brown and Williams. He has been there for bowl games, great rivalries, tournaments, buzzer beaters, game winning catches and Final Fours. And even though TV has taken control of how we watch and digest KU, there needs to be a constant voice that accompanies and chronicles from a KU perspective, giving it meaning for us Jayhawks. And longer than any other for Jayhawk fans, that voice has been Max's. Multiple generations have followed the

Hawks through Max. He has stood the test of time in a way few have in this broadcast business. He was familiar and comfortable.

The voice of a university's sports teams is a special breed, having a relationship that's different with listeners than a professional team's announcer. The listener and fan of college sports have more invested because he or she went to that school, have sent their children to that school, have a family history with that school. It is part of their lives. Much of what they are today was formed by time they spent on that campus. They take pride in their school's accomplishments and anguish with each defeat. Their school is their shield. They are identified by their alma mater. This amplifies the person who delivers their Jayhawks to them. It's got to be someone who cares as much as they do. So through each win and loss, every coaching change and freshman phenom, through each season, there has been one voice associated with these events, players and coaches. And for KU that has been Max Falkenstien, with a career that has mattered to so many.

What a rich life he has had. Think of all the characters that have crossed his path. Imagine all the games he has prepared for, interviews he has conducted with coaches and players, and how they have colored his life. And then think of all the Jayhawk fans that have grown up with his voice accompanying them through the different phases of their lives. Whether you grew up on a farm in western Kansas and had his voice to keep you company as you bailed hay or fed livestock or drove a tractor, or slept with his voice under your pillow, hiding your transistor radio from your parents, Max was there to broadcast games courtside or from the press box. Listening on the Hill, in the stands, at the tailgate, or on the way home from the fieldhouse on a cold January night, his voice was your constant companion.

Everyone knows him. He is as famous as many of the players and coaches he has covered.

What will follow will be stories and events and names you will know. It'll be a trip through the last 60 years of Kansas Jayhawk sports history with the only person who has been a witness, who can say he was there. How lucky we are to have been participants in one of the truly compelling runs in college sports broadcasting.

I am a Jayhawk alum, and I am honored to have been asked to be a small part of a book that honors such an extraordinary and historic broadcast figure in our school's history.

Rock Chalk Jayhawk, KU!

— Kevin Harlan, CBS Sports, Class of 1982
January 2007

Introduction

What does Max Falkenstien mean to Kansas athletics?

Well, at how many other places do the fans crave the radio call of the games so much that the radio network buys equipment that attempts to synchronize the radio audio with the television video?

That's what Max Falkenstien has meant to Kansas athletics — and to the university as a whole. He is a friend who has given much more than he has taken.

During every conversation I have with Max, I learn something new about Kansas. I love that. I treasure the time I spend with him. Not to mention that walking around with him is like walking around with a beloved mayor. Everyone wants to say hi, introduce themselves to him, and tell him how much he has meant to them and their families.

This book is pure Max...great stories that span six decades as only Max can tell them. So sit back, relax and prepare to be entertained! This is a book that KU fans will read over and over again.

Thanks, Max. And Rock Chalk!

— Lew Perkins
Director of Athletics, University of Kansas

Chapter 1

A Good Place To Stop

It's time to resume my story. My story of (now 60 years) covering KU athletics. I want to start with the last, and later we'll go back to the beginning of the last decade. Does that make sense? Well, bear with me.

It was the basketball season of 2001, and we were sitting in the Denver airport, waiting for our departure. Assistant coach Joe Holladay said to me (as many others had done), "Max, how much longer are you going to keep doing this?" I said, "It won't be much longer." Joe replied, "You might as well go for 60 (years)." I told him probably not.

But the years inched along and athletic directors and staff changed, and Lew Perkins and Larry Keating and Jim Marchiony moved in to the KU hierarchy. Friends told me to watch out, because Perkins was coming from Connecticut and he would want his own people, and he was likely to let me go. It wasn't the first time I had heard that over six decades. Actually, nothing could have been further from the truth. There is no way Lew could have been nicer to me than he has been, and in fact his suggestion led to an unbelievable final year.

Marchiony and I had lunch one day at a hamburger restaurant. I was then in my 58th year of broadcasting KU sports, and I said to Jim, "I would like to go to 60 years, and that would be a good place to stop." He said that would be fine if that's what I wanted to do, which brings us to the late summer of 2005.

Lew and I went to one of our favorite places, Johnny's, for lunch. He asked me if I still planned on hanging it up after the up coming season. I told him I guessed so. He asked if I had any reservations. I told him I would certainly miss the close relationships with the coaches and players. He said that would be no problem — that I was free to sit anywhere I wanted, to go into the locker rooms, and to travel to any of the games I wished. And that they wanted me to remain part of the

"KU athletics team" as long as he was director of athletics. I felt like crying. And then I said I thought it would be best if I waited until the end of the basketball season to make the announcement, not to make it so far ahead. He said, "No, I want you to make it early, so that all season long people will be able to thank you and show you how much you have meant to them." I was wrong, and he was right. What a year it was!

Unfortunately, it started off on somewhat of a tough note.

Just a few days after I had announced that the 2005-06 season would be my final one broadcasting the Jayhawks, the football campaign opened with a win over Florida Atlantic. Two days later it was Labor Day, and Isobel and I were strolling downtown Lawrence looking for a place for lunch. After eating, I told her I didn't feel so good.

The next day, Tuesday, I went to the doctor. My good friend, Greg Schnose, scheduled me for a CAT scan of my abdomen. The technician couldn't find anything, but he told me if I didn't feel better that night to go to the emergency room at the hospital. I didn't, and I did. They ran that awful tube into my nose, and down into my stomach, and the next morning advised me I would have surgery immediately. They removed a golf ball-sized tumor from my small intestine, and I was on the sideline. (Although the tumor was malignant, all the follow-up tests showed no recurrence).

I was so very weak, and I missed the next three games, returning to the broadcast booth for the Kansas State game in Manhattan. I actually felt pretty good that day. I think coming back energized me, although the Wildcats won 12-3 in one of the worst, most boring games I can remember. I said to my buddies after the game, "I don't think either of these teams can win another game." I was wrong. KU won three of its last four regular-season battles behind quarterback Jason Swanson, and then copped a very satisfying victory in the Fort Worth Bowl.

There is no way I could have ever imagined the reaction of the listeners and fans to my absence. Immediately, they started coming in to the hospital, calling on the telephone, sending flowers and cards by the hundreds. I had to tell the nurses and my family that I didn't want to see anybody, or talk to anybody, but they tried anyway. Among the first to call were athletics director Lew Perkins, football coach Mark Mangino and basketball coach Bill Self. My room looked like the florist. It was a very warm reaction, which touched me greatly, and I believe certainly impressed my family.

Those were the only football games in 60 years that I missed due to illness. (I did miss two basketball games, one at Oklahoma in 1993 when I had a gallbladder attack, and another time in Colorado when I caught the flu after we had arrived there, just couldn't go, and watched the game from my Boulder hotel room. The team bus came by to get me after the game, and we flew home in a small plane. I sat next to Billy Thomas. I don't believe he caught it.)

There were times when I worked with a sore throat or a hoarse voice, but we always got through it. Sometimes both Bob Davis and/or I would have a big bottle of cough syrup on the table. There's nothing worse than a coughing attack when you're trying to talk!

During that terrific football season of 2005, KU broke Nebraska's long dominance dating back to the Orange Bowl team of 1968 with an amazing 40-15 win over the Cornhuskers. That night the phone rang and it was Coach Mangino wanting to know what I was going to be doing Sunday afternoon. He said they would like to have me come to the squad meeting at 3 p.m. in Hadl Auditorium. I said sure. When I arrived, Coach gave a little talk to all the players about how I was winding down 60 years of doing KU football, and he said they wanted me to have a little something. Believe it or not, it was the game ball from the tremendous win over Nebraska. I thought that was really nice of him to do that. I wished I knew more of the players well, but it's pretty difficult with football.

The recognition, or celebration, began with the Iowa State football game, KU's last home game of the season. It was a thrilling finish, a field goal to win in overtime, making the Jayhawks bowl-eligible. During a game timeout I still had my headset on, and Bob Davis said, "Stand up and wave. They're talking about you and you're on the video board." Sure enough, there I was. Public address announcer Hank Booth was reading a spiel on me, and everybody was cheering, so I stood up and waved out the window.

Later in the postgame interview, our partner David Lawrence said to Coach Mangino, "Congratulations, Coach. A great win and you got one more game for Max to do." Mark said, "That's right. One more for Max."

But you know, at that point, with the whole basketball season ahead of me, it really hadn't started to hit home yet. But, it would soon enough.

I was named Kansan Of The Year in 2007. I'm glad to see that Governor Kathleen Sebelius and her husband, Judge Gary Sebelius enjoyed my comments.
—Photo by Peggy Clark, Washburn University

Our first conference basketball game was at Colorado in early January. During a timeout while we were in a commercial, Bob Davis poked me and said, "Stand up! They're talking about you." So I took my headset off, and sure enough, the public address announcer was talking about Max Falkenstien making his last broadcast trip to Colorado after 60 years of covering the Jayhawks. And they congratulated me. I knew that Jim, Lew, and others must have arranged that. But little did I know that it would happen everywhere we went for the rest of the season, and that Dick Vitale, Jim Nantz, Billy Packer, Ron Franklin, Fran Fraschilla and others would be saluting me on national television.

When we went to Missouri for the next road game, I started to suspect that this was going to happen (at least at the schools where we had always traveled). I joked with the boys that if they introduced me at Missouri, I was sure to get a lot of boos. They did, and I didn't! It was a great ovation from the Missouri fans in a very tight game. Afterwards Missouri athletics director Mike Alden and coach Quin Snyder spoke to me personally. It was easy for them to do, since Missouri won in overtime.

At Texas A&M, more of the same, and coach Billy Gillespie presented me with an "Aggie Ball," signed by all the members of the team. Iowa State read the customary spiel, and another big ovation. Texas Tech mailed a bottle of Texas Wine — bottled in Lubbock, no less — to me. They obviously didn't know that I don't drink at all, neither wine, nor beer, nor alcohol. I'm not an alcoholic; I just have never liked the taste. But it was the thought that mattered!

The Oklahoma game in Lawrence was something really special. Just before tipoff, coach Kelvin Sampson walked across the court along with OU athletics director Joe Castiglione, and presented me with several T-shirts that they had made especially for me. The front said, "To The Max From Your Friends at Oklahoma," with my picture, and the back read "Two National Championships, 12 Final Fours, Over 1,750 Basketball Games, etc." That was really nice!

This shirt from Oklahoma and its former coach Kelvin Sampson was really special.

Joe had been a good friend way back to the days when he was at Missouri, and one of my dearest friends, former KU assistant coach Jerry Green, had joined the OU staff. Kelvin said Jerry was the best thing that had ever happened to OU basketball. Anyway, I don't know whether it was Joe or Jerry, or all three of them, but it was something they hadn't just put together overnight, and I thought it was great.

More of the same on our trip to Nebraska, and then we went to

Oklahoma State, and that's a story in itself. Two days before, one of my good friends, coach Eddie Sutton, was involved in an automobile accident and was charged with driving under the influence. I hated that, and I hurt for Eddie. Eddie almost came to Kansas. Phog Allen and Hank Iba recruited him, and Iba won out in a close one, although Eddie grew up in Bucklin, Kansas, way out in the southwest corner of the state. Eddie had told me that Phog had come to their home recruiting him, Eddie's mom had cooked Sunday dinner, and Dr. Allen stayed for hours visiting and telling stories. (No one could do that any better than Doc!) Anyway, Eddie ended up playing for Iba. On February 21, 1957, when KU played at Stillwater with Wilt Chamberlain, Eddie scored 19 points and the Cowboys won by two.

Eddie also has said often how growing up in Bucklin he used to listen to my broadcasts by putting a radio under his pillow at night. I said "Damn it, Eddie, don't tell people that. It makes me seem even older than I am." Incidentally, doesn't he have the most wonderful face? Especially during the games? I've said on the air several times: "Now there's a face that looks lived-in!" I'm getting like Phog Allen. One story leads to another!

But back to our Monday night "Big Monday" game. Interim coach Sean Sutton came by and said his Dad was really sorry he couldn't be here tonight, but that he was thinking about me. Then assistant coach James Dickey stopped by our broadcast table. He said coach Sutton wanted him to tell me how sorry he was that he couldn't be there for my last broadcasting trip to Stillwater. Coach Dickey formerly served as head coach at Texas Tech. He is a fine person and a good coach.

I said, "James, do you suppose there is any way I could talk to coach?" He said, "Well, let's just see. Follow me." And we went out into the hallway and he called coach on his cell phone and we had a good visit. Eddie said his back had been hurting him so badly that he just couldn't handle it. I felt bad, but wished him well. During the game, Steve Buzzard of their staff presented me with an Eddie Sutton bobblehead doll, autographed to me by Eddie.

When the Baylor Bears came to Lawrence February 21, they presented me with a handsome Baylor sweatshirt. It's in their school color green with the word BAYLOR in large gold letters on the chest.

Occasionally I will wear it around in public, and it is always interesting to notice the strange looks and comments I will get from people who know I shouldn't be wearing that! I just smile and move on.

I've thrown some people off by wearing this sweatshirt around Lawrence.

Then we went to Texas, and for the first and only time, no mention is made of Max. Texas athletics director DeLoss Dodds told me they just blew it, they forgot, and he was sorry. I had known DeLoss since he ran track at Kansas State a long, long time ago, and I believe him. Later, a beautiful set of Texas Longhorn bookends, made from Texas Limestone, arrived at my home.

During all this time, I was in awe of the reception I was getting, and all the well-wishers, but I was also becoming sadder all the time, realizing that I was close to the end of my career.

Among the avalanche of cards and letters I received as my last game approached was a particularly nice one from Raef LaFrentz of the Boston Celtics. He, of course, congratulated me, and said it wouldn't be the same without me, but he also said, "I miss those days at KU so much. This is so different! Those were the happiest days of my life." It's too bad that all the guys can't realize that until they've moved on. Of course, for the relative few, several million dollars a year for playing the game helps alleviate the longing!

I knew Kansas State would do something nice for me, and they did, although the timing was not good. Coach Jim Wooldridge (who was fired immediately after the last game) called me twice at home just prior to the game, but I missed him both times. Before the game at Bramlage Coliseum, I went to their locker room, and Jim and his assistant coaches were in there alone. I told him I had always enjoyed watching him coach, that his teams played hard, and that they were just snakebit, losing so many close games in the final minute. He thanked me and we shook hands.

They had told me that I would be taken out on the court at the 12-minute timeout of the first half, so I was ready. About 30 seconds before that timeout, the officials called a technical foul on Coach Wooldridge, and the K-State crowd was ticked off. And then here comes Max along with Wildcat athletics director Tim Weiser. Yes, sure enough, there were a few boos, which I could understand, but they were soon drowned out by a loud ovation. Tim presented me with a beautiful plaque commemorating the many KU/K-State games I had broadcast, and he also presented me with a handsome golf putter, emblazoned with the K-State logo. I used it a few times, much to the astonishment of my friends, but concluded it wasn't any better than my trusted old one, so it currently is on the practice squad.

At the Big 12 Tournament in Dallas, associate commissioner Tim Allen gave me a whole bunch of stuff, including a handsome Big 12 wristwatch, and I received still another big sendoff.

Now I've left out one game. Colorado at Kansas on March 1, 2006. My last game at KU, after broadcasting every single men's game ever played in Allen Fieldhouse. I knew there would be something big, but I didn't quite know what. My wife Isobel, my daughter Jane Hart, and my son Kurt, his wife Paula Martin, and my granddaughter Kate, all had special seats. They were all nervous because they were sure they would all be on television at halftime. Which they were.

I had done so many TV and radio interviews, and given so many interviews for specials in the papers that I was just about worn out. I had to decline all interview requests for that day, because there wasn't any way to be fair to everybody. I didn't even come out on the court early, because I didn't know what it would be like. Coach Bill Self had said that Max probably had been the greatest positive salesman for the

University of Kansas that there had ever been. So just about five minutes before air time, I walked out. There was a huge roar, and a standing ovation from most of the 16,300 fans who were there. *"The University Daily Kansan"* had published a huge insert with my picture and the inscription THANKS MAX, and they all held it up for me to see. It was something! And then we came to halftime!

My family and I walked out together, and I noticed that a lot of former athletes were gathering behind us at center court. My buddy Bob Davis emceed the halftime show, and gave me a big build up, after which Lew Perkins presented me with a bronze Jayhawk with a personal inscription. Then Bob directed everyone's attention to the south wall of Allen Fieldhouse, and with much fanfare a jersey FALKENSTIEN 60 was unfurled, right next to Nick Collison and joining the great basketball elite who had been honored by previous jersey retirements. I made a short speech, and it was over. Later I went on the floor to introduce the seniors for their speeches. I had done that for every senior night KU has ever had. The three seniors talked about how going out with Max was a terrific honor, and I really appreciated that. Isobel was extremely pleased when I told her that some people had asked me if that was my first wife! They thought she looked terrific that night.

Later, at a special night honoring the academic achievements of many KU student athletes, Lew Perkins presented me with a beautiful crystal Lifetime Achievement Award from KU athletics. And then he told me he wanted me to stay connected, and that I would bear the title of special assistant to the director of athletics.

Now that's enough about the end. Let's go back to the beginning of this 60-year journey. There's plenty to talk about!

Chapter 2

One-Take Max: My Early Influences

I guess it all started with my high school biology class and a woman named Mildred Seaman.

It was early in my junior year at Lawrence High School (then known as Liberty Memorial), and it was one of those warm September afternoons. My biology class took a field trip to KFKU, the University of Kansas' campus radio station, to participate in a classroom broadcast.

We students did some speaking on the air, and when the broadcast was over Mildred Seaman, the station's program director, singled me out and asked if I had ever thought about working in radio. She was impressed with the quality of my voice and encouraged me to consider broadcasting as a career. I thanked her for the praise and let it go at that. As far as I can remember, that was my first time behind a microphone.

Early in my senior year (1942), I learned of a job opening at WREN radio in Lawrence. I remembered what Miss Seaman had said, and I thought — what the heck — I might as well go to the station to see what this is all about.

I ventured downtown to the WREN studio and folks there agreed to give me an audition. The news editor tore some copy off the news printer and gave it to me to read. I remember there was a phrase about a French charge d'affaires somewhere in the world. I had taken a little French in high school, so that phrase didn't baffle me one bit. (I have always had the ability to read without stumbling over words. In fact, later in my broadcasting career a lot of people jokingly referred to me as "One-Take Max" or "One-Take Falkenstien," because I could read without flubbing.) I sailed through the audition and, to make a long story short, they offered me a job as an announcer at the station.

That was the start of my broadcasting career. I made $90 a month. In the real world, it would have been considered a modest wage. But it was pretty good at that time for a high school student. I worked mostly evenings and weekends; my schedule was built around my studies in high school.

I can remember the first time I ever went live on the air. It was around 8:15 a.m. on a Sunday, and there probably weren't more than 25 people listening. I was asked to read a promo regarding an appearance by Mrs. Franklin D. Roosevelt on a network program. I was so nervous. Somehow, I got through it okay in the allotted 28 seconds. My career in radio was underway!

Many people have assumed that my association with University of Kansas athletics began after I started my career in broadcasting. Actually, KU was in my blood long before I started calling games.

I was born in Lawrence on April 10, 1924, and my family lived in a little house at 1332 Massachusetts until I was 6 years old. We then moved to a three-bedroom house at 546 East 19th Street, where we had about six acres of land, including a small pond. I guess you could have called us suburban farmers.

My mom was of Scotch-Irish descent. Her maiden name was Gosper and she grew up on a farm near Frankfort, Kansas, one of six daughters. The family later moved to Lawrence, where my grandfather operated a dairy farm. When I was a little boy, I would sometimes go with Granddad Gosper on his dairy route. I really enjoyed that. We'd get up early in the morning to make the milk deliveries, putting the bottles in milk boxes on customers' front porches. But while it might have been fun for me, it had been a tough life for Mom when she was growing up. Everyone in her family worked hard, and there was not much money.

Dad was born in Onaga, Kansas. The Falkenstiens had moved to the Midwest from Pennsylvania, where my ancestors had emigrated from Germany. We have managed to trace our lineage to the 1400s. Back then, the Falkenstiens were land barons along the Rhine River and exacted a fee from river travellers wanting to pass through the family's territory. At that time, the surname was Falkenstein, the true German spelling of the name. In a family Bible a couple of hundred years ago, someone changed the spelling. In our branch of the family, Falkenstein became Falkenstien. Falkenstein, incidentally, means falcon rock. I have been to Germany and visited several of the Falkenstein castles and the town of Falkenstein, which is fairly close to Frankfurt am Main.

At about the same time my parents adopted my sister Sandra, when I was 12, my father left the banking business and took the position of business manager for athletics at KU. Phog Allen was the athletics director at the time, and he and my father had a very close relationship. I'm not sure when my interest in athletics started, but it was probably around that time, because my father would come home and talk about his job, the coaches and the athletes.

As business manager, my father directed ticket sales. He could remember everyone's seat location, whether it be football or basketball. He would get calls from fans on Sundays concerning their tickets, and he always remembered the exact location of everybody's seats.

It was a thrill for me, as a youngster, to attend Kansas basketball games. Like any other youngster, I had my favorite players. Guys such as Fred Pralle, Ernie Vanek and Doc Allen's son, Mitt, were all good players. When I tagged along with my dad, they always recognized me and spoke to me. I was really too little to be an athlete myself, but I loved to compete and play. My mom always said I could never stand to lose to anybody — be it Chinese checkers or any card game. My wife has observed that I would never even let our kids beat me in anything, if I could help it.

On the morning of December 8, 1941, we all sat in the Lawrence High School auditorium and listened to President Franklin D. Roosevelt ask that war be declared on the Empire of Japan, which had bombed Pearl Harbor the previous day. From that moment, we all realized our lives would change drastically from what we had planned. As I started at KU the following fall, the uppermost thought in my mind was: How long will I be able to stay in school before I have to go into the service?

It wouldn't be long — the following April, to be exact.

Graduation from high school came in 1942, and I continued to work at the radio station that summer. Because I had excellent grades and had been very active in high school, I fit the profile of what fraternities were looking for. It came down in my mind to whether I wanted to be a Sigma Chi or a Beta. I had a very good friend Dick Keene — who was a Sigma Chi, and he had recruited me hard. But I decided to be a Beta, and one of the hardest things I ever had to do was tell Dick of my decision. The Betas had always been the scholastic leaders at KU. My decision pleased my mom immensely, because she felt that being a member of Beta Theta Pi was the ultimate in the fraternity world.

Pledge training would be very tough. I did not live at the house like most of my pledge brothers. But I completed the pledge training, and in

January 1943, we were finally initiated and received our Beta pins. In the meantime, I completed the first semester of school with excellent grades, almost all As.

This was wartime, and we had all registered for the draft. It was becoming obvious that there was no way we were going to stay out of the service.

I decided to investigate my options. I had heard the Army Air Corps had a need for meteorologists, or "weather officers," so I enrolled in the Cadet Meteorology Program in April 1943, about halfway through the second semester of my freshman year.

At the time of my induction, I weighed 110 pounds. My duffel bag, I think, weighed about 97 pounds. It was full of all of my gear and everything that I owned.

I remember lugging that duffel bag on my shoulders through Union Station in Kansas City, Missouri, to catch a train for basic training in Greensboro, North Carolina.

Eventually, after a year of pre-meteorology training, we were transferred to the Army Signal Corps' radar division and sent to a Royal Canadian Air Force Base in Clinton, Ontario, for training.

I was there for one year, learning all the rudiments of radar. In the spring of 1945, we were sent to Fresno, California, for further training. While in California, we were trained on radar that would be used during the invasion of the Japanese mainland. Our equipment was needed ashore during the second wave of the invasion — a prospect that, very likely, would result in my death. Soon we had shipping orders for Seattle, where we were to embark for Japan for the invasion.

But the war ended when President Harry Truman ordered the dropping of the atomic bomb. As a result, the invasion — and the shipping orders — were cancelled.

I was in the service for 35 months but never did see combat. I was a staff sergeant when I was discharged in 1946.

I came home in mid-March at the age of 22, full of piss and vinegar, back in school at KU as a college freshman and back to WREN. Verl Bratton, the station manager who had hired me, was still in that position when I returned after the service. Right after I returned — I think it was the first week I was back — he searched me out.

"You know Kansas is in a big basketball tournament in Kansas City," he said. "How about you broadcasting the game?" I told him I didn't know anything about broadcasting games, but I would be willing to give it a try. I'm still not sure why he decided to give me this assignment.

It was probably because of my dad's association with the athletic department. To my knowledge, WREN had never broadcast any KU games until then. I'm fairly certain that I had never even heard a basketball game broadcast on radio.

It was a big game. It was Kansas against Oklahoma A&M, coached by the legendary Hank Iba, in an NCAA District 12 playoff game at Municipal Auditorium in Kansas City, Missouri.

The Aggies were led by the first of the great 7-footers in basketball, All-American Bob "Foothills" Kurland.

A&M won, 49-38, and went on to become national champion. Kurland was just too much for the Jayhawks, scoring 28 points. The

I'm probably the only guy who started his broadcasting career by calling an NCAA playoff game.

Kansas stars on that team, which finished the season with a 19-2 record, were Charlie Black, Ray Evans and Otto Schnellbacher.

Needless to say, the NCAA Tournament was a lot different then. It had been started in 1939, and interest was still building. But even if the tournament wasn't a headline-grabbing event, I was pumped up about doing the game. I had experienced a real adrenaline high and felt proud to have the opportunity.

My sportscasting career on radio was underway. I went to class the next Monday, and people kept coming up to me, telling me that they had listened to my broadcast. My mathematics teacher, Guy Smith, even mentioned it in class.

I'm probably the only guy in the history of the world that started his broadcasting career under those conditions — doing an NCAA playoff game in his very first broadcast. Never in my wildest dreams could I envision that I would call games for the next 60 years.

Chapter 3

Fam, Ray, Otto, and the Orange Bowl

The first football season that I spent broadcasting Kansas games also was George Sauer's first year as Jayhawk head coach. Sauer was a nice guy who was all business, and he had great success in his two seasons (1946-47) in Lawrence.

A former All-America fullback at Nebraska, he led Kansas to consecutive Big Six championships and the 1948 Orange Bowl. He left Kansas after the 1947 season to become head coach at Navy. He later became general manager of the fledgling New York Titans (later the New York Jets) and built the franchise into a Super Bowl winner.

Building on my basketball initiation to sportscasting, WREN decided in the fall of 1946 to carry the entire Kansas football schedule with me behind the microphone. We paid the athletic department some kind of a rights fee, which I think was $100 a game. It stayed that way for many years.

The season was set to open in Kansas City, Missouri, at old Blues Stadium with Texas Christian as KU's opponent. The Jayhawks were loaded with players who had come to KU from the Second Air Force football team. They chose Kansas thanks, in large part, to the efforts of Ray Evans. A talented all-around athlete who excelled in football and basketball, Evans had arrived on campus in 1941 and had led the nation in passing in 1942. His college career was put on hold during the War years while he served in the Air Corps. He was an All-American in football and a two-time All-America selection in basketball. He was selected for both the Helms Foundation college basketball and football halls of fame.

Evans was a "Pied Piper" for KU football and basketball during his days in the service, making friends and recruiting several talented athletes who arrived on campus after the War. The most influential and the one who stayed the longest was Don Fambrough. A native of Longview,

Texas, Fambrough would serve KU as a player, assistant coach and head coach, twice. Although he was undersized by today's standards (5-foot-10, 184 pounds), Fambrough was as tough as any to ever wear the Crimson and Blue.

With the return of standout players such as Evans, Otto Schnellbacher and Fambrough, expectations for the 1947 season were high. Sauer welcomed back an impressive collection of players. In comparison with today's rosters, members of the team were older, smaller and there were fewer of them. Most of the Jayhawks were experienced service veterans ranging in age from 23 to 28. The offensive line averaged just over 190 pounds, and there was just one player on the roster, 240-pound tackle Dick Channell, who weighed more than 215 pounds.

These were men in every sense of the word. They were rugged football players who had a passion for the game. Once again, KU opened its season in Kansas City at Blues Stadium against TCU. The contest was played at night in the backlash of a hurricane and in what might be the worst rain storm I've ever witnessed at a football game. It rained from the opening kickoff, and light bulbs on the grandstand began popping from the cold raindrops. Part of the game was played in semidarkness, and the quarters were shortened from 15 minutes to 12 minutes. On the field, which was almost ankle-deep in water, the players went about their business with an abundance of skids and splashes. As in the 1946 game, the teams battled to a 0-0 tie. It marked the last scoreless tie in KU history.

That season also produced an offensive record that still exists in the Kansas record book. Exploding off Sauer's standard T-formation, the Jayhawks defeated South Dakota State 86-6 in the fourth game of the season, establishing a record for most points in a game. As I remember, Sauer had a pretty good hunch we would beat South Dakota State. He started the second string! Kansas was tied by Oklahoma, 13-13, in its next game before reeling off five consecutive victories to conclude the regular season.

The Jayhawks ended the regular season with a trip to Tucson for a night game against Arizona. It was a little unusual to travel so far for a season-ending game in those days. The only mode of transportation for a lengthy trip was by train. We left Lawrence on a Wednesday and were somewhere near El Paso, Texas, when three or four cars derailed, leaving us bouncing along on the railroad ties. No cars tipped over, and I don't recall any injuries, but it was enough of a jolt to add an element of fear to the trip.

There was a player on the team by the name of Marvin Small, who was from Alabama and talked with a real deep southern accent. The accident really shook him up.

We were about seven miles outside El Paso and were in the diner having dinner. Food went flying everywhere. It scared the living daylights out of Marvin. He jumped up and started giving that Alabama chatter, and that scared everybody half-to-death. We got out of the dining car and walked to the depot in El Paso, where we waited for six or seven hours while they put the train back on the track. The rest of the trip, which would last a solid week, provided no more surprises.

Fambrough and Schnellbacher were team co-captains, and right before the Arizona game a telegram from KU athletics director E.C. Quigley was delivered in their name to the dressing room. The telegram brought the news that the Jayhawks had been invited to play Georgia Tech in the 1948 Orange Bowl in Miami. With that on their minds, the Jayhawks went out and beat Arizona, 54-28.

KU had won three of its last four regular-season games by coming from behind, finishing the regular season with an 8-0-2 record and capturing its second consecutive Big Six co-championship.

I was living a charmed life as a sportscaster. There I was still in college, and I had already broadcast an NCAA Tournament game and now, in my second year doing football, I was headed to Florida to witness KU's first appearance in a bowl game.

Not only would this represent the Jayhawks' first bowl game, it also marked the first time that any KU team would travel by air. The team chartered a four-engine, propeller-driven Lockheed Constellation from TWA. I didn't fly down with the team. Instead, I drove down to Miami with a group of KU students that included Robert Docking, a fellow from Arkansas City who would go on to be governor. (Prior to his successful career in state politics, Docking served several years as a clock operator at Allen Fieldhouse. Needless to say, he's probably one of the few governors in history to have that job on his resume.)

Because of the Orange Bowl's restrictions, I was not permitted to broadcast the game. I did, however, spot for Jim Simpson on NBC radio.

The ball game, as everybody knows, was won by Georgia Tech, 20-14. Kansas lost a fumble on the 2-yard line after a long drive in the final minute, and there has been an argument ever since about what happened.

Had KU scored, Fambrough would have been asked to kick the extra point to win the contest. There was controversy about whether Lynne McNutt, the KU quarterback, fumbled or had the ball stripped from his hands after he was already down.

Other voices from The Hill • Don Fambrough

The official didn't know where the ball was. He looked and he looked and finally, he pointed that finger and said, "Georgia Tech's ball." That was the game. I don't know what would have happened if we had scored. I would have been kicking the extra point for the win, and I probably would have fainted from the pressure. I was so dead tired; I could hardly lift my leg. But you know what? I would have kicked that damn point.

The 1948 Orange Bowl team included the unforgettable Evans and Schnellbacher, the first All-Americans ever at KU. Schnellbacher's pass-reception records and Evans' total-offense marks stood as Jayhawk team records for more than 20 years. Ray and Otto had great football and basketball careers for Kansas.

After the game, my dad invited me to fly back with the team. That was an unbelievable thrill, because it was my first airplane ride.

The trip home from Miami reminds me of one of the KU players, Don "Red" Ettinger, who used to enjoy having a good time a little more often than Coach Sauer could tolerate. Ettinger got in the sauce pretty frequently, not only before practice but before and after games. The morning we were loading the bus to go to the airport, Ettinger slammed a big sack of Orange Bowl oranges into a window of the bus and shattered it. Needless to say, that didn't make Sauer real happy.

Several days after we returned from Miami, there was a wonderful banquet to honor the team. Money was raised, and Sauer was presented with a new car. I think it was a Packard. The car had been bought by a number of alumni, and shortly afterward, Sauer resigned to accept the head coaching job at Navy. He kept the new car, using it as transportation to Annapolis. That ticked off a lot of the "givers" in Lawrence.

KU athletics director E.C. Quigley moved swiftly to fill the vacancy. He hired the tall Texan, J.V. (Jules Verne) Sikes. Sikes was an innovative coach who had spent several seasons as an assistant under Wally Butts at Georgia.

Next to Fambrough, I guess I felt as close to Coach Sikes as I did any football coach. I was just a young kid starting my career, and he was so passionate, so cooperative and so friendly. He helped me a lot in my radio career. I just loved the guy, to be quite honest.

Coach Sikes was extremely offensive minded. He really understood the passing game. He was somewhat profane in practice, (which some people thought led to his downfall at KU), but he had a heart as big as a bushel basket and would do anything in the world for his players. They all just loved him. Among the coaches that Sikes hired was Don Fambrough.

Sikes' pass-oriented teams of the late '40s and early '50s were among the nation's most exciting. He was probably years ahead of everyone else in the passing game. Fambrough has told me that the team worked on offense on Monday, Tuesday, Wednesday and Thursday. Then on Friday, when it was a short practice, they put in the defense.

One of the funny stories out of the Sikes era at Kansas involved Bud Laughlin and Galen Fiss, two fullbacks on the Jayhawk roster. Laughlin was a big, bruising runner. Fiss, who would spend 10 seasons as a linebacker for the Cleveland Browns, played both fullback and linebacker. Sikes loved a complete football player, a guy who would give you 100 percent in practice. That's why he loved Fiss. He was his fair-haired boy. Sikes had been critical of the running of Laughlin at practice one day. Finally, he told Laughlin, "Get out of there. You're just not doing it right. Take some laps." He put Fiss in the backfield to carry the ball. So they ran a play, and Sikes blew his whistle and yelled, "Fiss, damn it, you run just like Laughlin." Then he looked over at Laughlin and screamed, "Laughlin, you take more laps! Galen has been watching you, and he did the same thing you did!" So Laughlin kept running, and Galen stood on the field with his arms folded.

Other voices from The Hill • Don Fambrough

I remember a game one year against Colorado. They ran the single-wing offense to perfection. The score was something like 36-34, and Colorado had the ball. They were making three or four yards at a time. I was a young coach at the time and I wanted to do my part on the sideline. I was yelling, "Stop 'em. Stop 'em. Stop 'em." Sikes looks over at me and says,

"Hell, let them score so we can get the damn ball back." So I yell out, "Let them score so we can get the damn ball back."

Sikes was head coach at Kansas for six seasons. Three of those years, he won seven or more games, including 1951, when he guided the Jayhawks to a sparkling 8-2 record. He didn't have a losing record until 1953, when the team won just two of 10 games. Although he had tremendous respect from most of his players and was loved by many of those closely associated with the program, Sikes did make a few enemies.

Those enemies had significant power and influence, and they pushed hard for Sikes to be fired. Following the 1953 season, he was dismissed as head football coach at Kansas.

Word leaked out about the decision to fire Sikes during the final two weeks of the season. After the final game against Missouri, a 10-6 loss, Sikes was allowed to publicly resign.

Other voices from The Hill   •   Don Fambrough

Coach Sikes and Doc Allen were very good friends. Doc sincerely liked Sikes.

Coach Sikes decided he wanted Doc to address the team prior to the Missouri game to help inspire them. This was the final game of the year and the final one J.V. would serve as head coach. Doc accepted the invitation, and it was set up for him to deliver his inspirational talk just prior to the team's running on the field for kickoff. So, game day arrives. Coach Sikes tells me to stay in the locker room with the team. Sikes wanted me there to keep control of Doc. He said, "Doc will get started and he won't know anything about time, and we'll be late and get penalized for delay of the game.

"I don't want any other coaches in there but you. You stay in there, get out of sight, but keep track of the time. Make sure Doc doesn't keep them in there and cause us to get penalized." I wouldn't trade anything in the world for this experience. I was a big fan of Doc Allen. So, Doc starts out: "Young men, last week I had something happen to me that has never happened before in my career: I had the head football coach at the University of Kansas, J.V. Sikes, call me long distance — not a local call but long distance from Topeka — and say, 'Dr. Allen would you talk to my football team before the Missouri football game?' That may be the greatest honor I've ever had. It has never happened

*before. I told Coach Sikes I would be there. I got my hat and coat and went
down to my car and drove to Robinson Gym and went upstairs to my office
and got down on my knees to ask for Divine guidance to tell you fine young
men something before you go out and do battle against Missouri." With that
Doc Allen paused, and we all waited for this inspirational message:*
    "Now, go out there, and chew their nuts off"
    That was it. The kids were stunned.

There had never been such a groundswell of support for a coach who
was fired as we saw with Sikes. Except for those few powerful alumni,
everyone loved the man. One of the players' parents helped organize a
fund-raising drive for Coach Sikes once it was apparent he was finished as
head coach at KU. It started the week of the Missouri game.

During the last practice before KU faced the Tigers, it was planned to
have a surprise ceremony for Coach Sikes. Money started pouring in and
not only was there enough money to buy him a car, but they also bought a
fur coat for his wife Evelyn and gave them $3,000 or $4,000 in cash. They
cut off the fund-raising drive at that point.

KU had some outstanding football players during the Sikes era.
Among them was Mike McCormack, a 6-3, 230-pound offensive tackle
who made a name for himself in professional football. Cleveland Browns
Coach Paul Brown once called McCormack the "finest offensive lineman
I've ever coached." McCormack was inducted into the Pro Football Hall
of Fame in 1984. George Mrkonic earned All-America honors in 1951 as
a defensive tackle. Oliver Spencer was selected to the 1952 All-America
team and played in the NFL from 1953-1961. He served as an offensive
line coach for the Oakland Raiders for 19 seasons. Gil Reich earned All-
American honors in 1952 as a defensive back. Reich played defensive
halfback, as well as quarterback, fullback and halfback on offense. He was
also a starter on the 1952-53 KU basketball team. Another Sikes standout
was Charlie Hoag, a two-time all-conference selection at halfback, who
ranks in the Top 10 on KU's all-time rushing chart.

Sikes left Kansas and took the head coaching job at East Texas State.
Fambrough, somewhat bitter over the firing of Sikes, decided to give up
coaching football. But Sikes called Fam and invited him to be a part of
his coaching staff at East Texas. Fam rejected the offer at first, but later
changed his mind and joined Sikes. With Sikes out of the picture, KU

athletics director Dutch Lonborg surprised everyone by dipping into the high school ranks to select the next Jayhawk head coach.

Chuck Mather, who had compiled a 111-18-5 record and had won six state championships as a high school coach in Ohio, took over for Sikes. Mather drew attention because he had been innovative with the use of television and coaching. He had a TV set by the bench to monitor the plays. During his first season, when the team went 0-10, we were getting our brains beat out, and a fan yelled down to the sidelines, "Mather, you better switch to *The Lone Ranger*. This ain't working." Mather lasted just four seasons at KU, posting a combined 11-26-3 record.

In 1957, he was fired.

Chapter 4

Phog and Clyde Win a Title

Between my expanding broadcasting career and attending KU, I kept a fairly busy schedule. I did manage to squeeze in a social life and even found time for an occasional date. It was a custom back in my college days to double-date from time to time. I remember a night in 1947 or 1948 when Dan Kreamer, a pledge brother of mine at the Beta house, and I decided to double-date. I had arranged a date with a girl named Lynn Spencer, and Dan had a date with a girl named Isobel Atwood.

We went to a roadhouse somewhere between Lawrence and Kansas City to dance. I don't remember a whole lot about it. We danced a little, had some Cokes, and drove on back to campus. I do remember that I was attracted to Dan's date. I asked around and found out that Isobel had an older sister, Jane, and they were from nearby Olathe. They were known around campus as the Atwood sisters. Isobel was a very attractive young lady, and I decided to call her and ask her out - an invitation that ended up being delayed for several weeks while I was in the hospital with viral pneumonia.

She accepted, and we started dating on a regular basis. Our dates were not overly exciting by today's standards: dinner at the Dine-A-Mite, a little dancing, perhaps a movie. Neither of us drank, not even beer, so that wasn't part of our socializing. We went to a lot of movies. I remember one at the Pattee Theater, in the 800 block of Massachusetts. We decided to see a horror movie — Bella Lugosi in Frankenstein. It was too scary for us. We got up and walked out less than halfway through. (Today's kids can't have it gory enough! To them it's all a big joke. To us, it was serious.)

I graduated from KU at mid-semester in 1948 and continued to work for WREN, which had relocated its studios to Topeka. Isobel had left school and was working in Olathe. So for a period of time, we had a long distance romance. But we continued to date and, to make a long story short, we were married March 20, 1949, in Lawrence at Danforth Chapel on campus. As you might guess, we had to wait until the basketball season was over to schedule the wedding. Among the guests at the wedding was KU's basketball coach, Phog Allen.

Some of my fondest memories of Doc Allen are from my undergraduate days as a student at KU. Doc (I don't think anyone called him Phog or Coach) taught Coaching Basketball, Advanced Basketball Coaching and a class in Athletic Training. We called them Sports Stories 1, 2 and 3, because that's what we got out of it. Sometimes you would go from one class to the other, and they were the same thing. They just had a different label.

It was common for students to be strolling down a hall in old Robinson Gymnasium during the summer and pass a classroom in which Doc would be standing on a table in front of his class wearing nothing but his skivvies. Among those KU students who experienced a Phog Allen lecture was Bob Timmons, who later served as head track coach at KU.

Other voices from The Hill • Bob Timmons

This was around 1948 or 1949. Doc had a thing he called a foot-arch normalizer, which was little more than a glorified rolling pin. Doc always had glorified names for things. It was on gears and you took your shoe off and rolled it back and forth if you were trying to elevate your arch. In reality, all anyone really had to do was get a Coke bottle and roll your foot back and forth on it and achieve the same thing.

But this was the Doc Allen approach, and we understood that. The lecture about this foot-arch normalizer and its purpose took one hour. Demonstrating the use of this device was very important to Doc. As the class went on, more and more clothes came off. I have a theory why the clothes came off during the lecture. First of all, Doc had a great tan. He used to play golf with his shirt off. Also, Doc was getting along in years, and I think he wanted to show off the fact he was still in pretty good shape.

Like always, Doc would start out with a story that led to another story that led to still another story, and so on. Some of these stories you might really be interested in hearing, but Doc quite often never came back to the subject at hand.

I remember in this particular class, the door was open when the whistle sounded - the end of the hour. People were walking by the classroom.

There was Doc on top of the table. Shoes and pants off — nothing on but his under shorts and undershirt. All he had to do was take his shoes off to demonstrate the use of this contraption. That was his lecture. But it was fascinating.

When I had broadcast my first Kansas basketball game in 1946, Phog Allen's reputation as one of college basketball's outstanding coaches was firmly established. The colorful Allen was 60 years old and in his 36th season on the bench.

During the 1946-47 season, when WREN assigned me to call every basketball contest, Phog missed the last 14 games of the season because of a head injury he suffered in practice. As I remember, the team was running a drill, and one of the players collided with Doc, sending him hard to the floor. He suffered a concussion, and the university granted him an indefinite leave, allowing him time to recuperate.

He spent his time resting in California.

Howard Engleman, a two-time All-American at KU, was serving as assistant coach that year and was appointed interim head coach to finish the season. The Jayhawks concluded the year with a respectable 16-11 mark.

A healthy Phog Allen returned to the Jayhawk bench the following year, but his next few seasons were not typical of the Allen years at Kansas. The Jayhawks won just nine of 24 games in 1947-48 and were a mediocre 12-12 the following season.

These were tough times for Doc. He focused his attention on the rivalries with Kansas State and Missouri — two teams that were getting the better of the Jayhawks in those years. The KU alumni were not pleased to relinquish bragging rights.

Doc promoted each of those games. In particular, he and K-State's Jack Gardner would go after each other in the press and on the radio. In the days leading up to a Kansas State game, Doc would not be heard to say anything good about the Wildcats. He really indoctrinated players and others around him. He belittled K-State. He did all the things to get his players emotionally ready to play.

Coach Gardner irritated Doc. Gardner would frequently make derogatory remarks about KU or its basketball team, and then reporters would want a comment from Doc Allen. Finally he came up with a classic comeback: "If the mailman stopped for every dog which barked at him," said Allen, "he would never get his mail delivered."

Kansas won 22 consecutive meetings with Kansas State — a streak that ran from 1938 through 1947. During the 1947-48 season, the Wildcats won all three meetings with Kansas.

Doc no longer had a lock on the state's best high school players. Many suspected the legendary coach was at the sunset of his career. But Doc had an abundance of fire left inside, and it was obvious to me that his critics helped inspire him to re-establish his reputation as a coach. He wanted to bring a national championship to Lawrence.

One of the first major steps in lifting the basketball program out of the doldrums came in 1948 when Dick Harp, a former standout player at KU, was hired as the first full-time assistant coach. Harp came to Kansas after two successful seasons as head coach at William Jewell.

Other voices from The Hill • Clyde Lovellette

Doc Allen and Dick Harp were two completely different individuals. Doc was the captain and ran everything in the program. But he would designate Dick to do his thing, while Doc helped smooth things over if something got ruffled. Dick would serve as the buffer between Doc and the players. It was a great combination. Dick knew basketball, and Doc was the psychologist. Doc knew how to get you up from down and knew how to get you playing the way he wanted you to play.

Other voices from The Hill • Dick Harp

I remember the first day I came to work. Doc brought me into his office and said, "Now this is what I want you to do. There are three high school players I want you to go see play. I want you to see Bob Kenney, Bill Hougland, and Bill Lienhard. I want you to tell them that not only will they come to Kansas and win a conference championship, but we will be national champions and we'll go to the Olympics." I said, "You really don't want me to tell them that." And he said, "You're damned right I do." I took his orders and relayed that message. Of course, his prophecy came true for all three of those players.

Phog Allen wanted a national championship at Kansas and, with Harp at his side, charted a course for his program to achieve that goal. The Allen and Harp combination was a good blend. The pivotal step was to beef up recruiting efforts and find a centerpiece to build a team around. Doc adjusted his recruiting approach and got himself more involved.

Other voices from The Hill • Dick Harp

When Jack Gardner came along at Kansas State in 1946, it changed the whole business of recruiting for Doc. He never believed in recruiting as you know it now.

He believed that when a kid wanted to come to Kansas, he would provide him a job of some type and that was all there was to it. If a player didn't want to do that, fine, he could go somewhere else. And Doc was successful in doing it that way for a period of time. When Gardner came along, it became competition and changed the whole structure.

Doc was not about to stand still and let Jack Gardner have that success without giving it his full shot. He determined that he was going to get together a group of players that would be competitive for the national championship. He determined — and this is another part of his greatness — that things were going to have to change, and maybe he'd have to recruit differently. The players were not going to come by letter or a telephone call, they were going to have to come from what had been given the term "recruiting."

It was in 1948 that Allen was able to persuade Clyde Lovellette — a 6-foot-9, 240-pound high school star with a feathery outside shooting touch — to travel from Terre Haute, Indiana, and enroll at the University of Kansas. In those days, when airplane travel was not as common, Allen primarily stocked his roster with players from the Wheat Belt, home-grown talent raised with a good understanding of the Rock Chalk Chant.

Allen worked hard to lure Lovellette away from Indiana, which was also a hotbed of basketball success. Clyde had already told Hoosier coach Branch McCracken he would be in Bloomington that fall. But Doc could be very persuasive, and he was determined that Lovellette wear a Kansas uniform. Among other things, he sold Clyde's mother on the University of Kansas, convincing her that her son would be better served by attending KU. This was vintage Allen psychology and helped persuade Clyde to cast his lot with the

Jayhawks. Lovellette, who suffered from a light case of asthma, was told the hilly Lawrence landscape would improve his breathing problem.

"Up here on The Hill, a tall man can stand up straight and breathe the rarefied atmosphere," said Allen.

Other voices from The Hill • Clyde Lovellette

I had already made up my mind that I was going to Indiana. I had told Branch McCracken that I would enroll in the fall. Doc was very persistent, however, and continued to recruit me hard. I thought the world of him and didn't want to tell him no. Doc was scheduled to be in St. Louis, I think for a speaking engagement. I sent my brother-in-law to St. Louis with instructions to inform Doc that I would be attending Indiana.

When Doc got that news, he canceled his speaking engagement and immediately drove to Terre Haute and my house. I remember sitting on my porch with my dad. I believe it was a Sunday afternoon. I looked down the road and here comes this long car; and I knew immediately it was Doc Allen. I didn't have the courage to face him, so I jumped up and ran in the house. I told my dad to let Doc know that I was going to Indiana and to not let him come in the house.

Well, Doc pulled in and got out of the car. He walked up to my dad and said, "Mr. Lovellette, where is Clyde?" Instead of following my instructions, Dad said, "He's in the house." It was a chase, and I was on the retreat. I gave my mom the same instructions and ran out the back door. Doc came in the house and exchanged greetings with my mom. Once again, my plan failed, and mom identified my location outside.

I was finally out of places to hide. The backyard had a fence, so I was trapped. Doc came outside and found me. He talked to me for awhile, and I finally came to the conclusion that, if this man came this far to see me, I might as well just go to Kansas. So I packed a suitcase and left with Doc to enroll at Kansas.

The recruitment of Lovellette was significant in the Jayhawks' resurgence. He was essential, in Allen's mind, for the Jayhawks to achieve their destiny as an NCAA champion. Making his varsity debut in 1949-50, Lovellette would average 21.8 points and help Kansas to the conference co-championship and a No. 19 national ranking.

Allen had ventured to Indiana in search of Lovellette, but stayed within Kansas to stock the remainder of his lineup. With his star firmly in place, Allen filled other key spots with talented small-town Kansas products. Among those were 6-5 Bill Lienhard from Newton, Bill Hougland, a 6-4 forward from Beloit, and Bob Kenney, a 6-2 forward from Winfield.

Lovellette was a larger-than-life player for Kansas. He could shoot that soft right-handed hook shot with deadly accuracy and was a strong force inside with a bit of a mean streak at times. He really didn't have that hook shot when he came to Kansas. That's something he developed after he arrived. Off the floor, Clyde was blessed with a great sense of humor. He was a country music fan of sorts, and I helped set him up with his own radio show on WREN: Hillbilly Clyde and his Hound Dog Lester. The show was 30 minutes in length and aired each Saturday. We would tape the show, and it would air before the games. People would have those transistor radios to their ears before the game listening to Clyde. He would introduce himself as "Your country host, Clyde Lov-el-etty," mimicking the way many mispronounced his name.

Clyde attracted nicknames like he attracted honors. He was known as "Cumulus Clyde," "The Terre Haute Terror," "The Monster of the Music Hall," "The Leaning Tower of Kansas," "Peerless Percheron," "The Great White Whale" and "Mr. Highpockets."

Other voices from The Hill • Clyde Lovellette

There was one Halloween when a few of us decided to have some fun. Somebody worked it out with the manager of the Granada Theater in downtown Lawrence.

Wayne Louderback, the first team manager ever at KU, was just over 5 feet tall, dressed up as Igor, and I dressed up in a Frankenstein costume. At a certain point in the movie, the projector was shut off and the lights went out. At that point Igor and Frankenstein came out on the stage, and someone hit the spotlight. Well, you've never seen a theater clear so quick in your life. I had my arms out just like Frankenstein and there was screaming and everyone was scared to death. When the lights came back on it was just the spotligh, Igor, and I left in the theater.

It's December 1948 and Bob (Timmy) Timmons is still in school at KU. He's doing graduate work. Someone has decided that prior to the home opener at Hoch Auditorium, they are going to have a little fun. They dress Bob Timmons, who is about 5-4, up as a little old man. And they have an oversized baby buggy. It's a huge thing. They put a person in the baby buggy with a baby bonnet on his head.

He's wearing a gigantic baby diaper and some baby clothes. Now Hoch is packed with people. Timmy wheels this baby buggy out on the basketball court with this huge baby in it. He pushes this buggy down the floor to the top of the free-throw circle and out jumps this huge baby and someone throws him a ball and he takes a sweeping hook shot at the basket. He misses the shot, but the crowd goes absolutely wild. The baby is Clyde Lovellette. This was Clyde's freshman season and, of course, freshmen were not eligible. So this was his first exposure to the KU fans.

Kansas State, led by Ernie Barrett, was the dominant team in the Big Seven Conference during the 1950-51 season. The Wildcats won the conference title and finished with a 24-4 mark. There was no conference tournament at that time, so the league champion was the only team to qualify for the NCAA Tournament. KU had lost twice to the Cats that season, finishing second in league play. K-State had an outstanding team and advanced the finals of the NCAA Tournament to face Kentucky, which was coached by KU graduate Adolph Rupp. I was assigned by WREN to broadcast the title game, which was played in Minneapolis, Minnesota. After all of these years doing KU, it seems odd that my first NCAA championship broadcast featured Kansas State and Kentucky. The battle between the two Wildcat teams was won by the boys from the Bluegrass State, 68-58.

The summer of 1951 was a memorable one for me. But it's not a pleasant memory. WREN radio had completed its move to Topeka, and Isobel and I were living at 2112 Wayne Street in Topeka in a small but nice apartment. As the summer approached, it seemed like we had rain every day. Not just a shower but a downpour. The Kansas River, or Kaw as we called it, was rising rapidly at both Topeka and Lawrence, and downriver where it emptied into the Missouri at Kansas City as well.

Neither city had too much protection on the north sides of the river, and it began to surge higher each day. In those days, WREN signed off at midnight, which was customary. But as it began to be a dangerous situation, we started staying on all night.

Volunteers were working around the clock, trying to shore up the levees with sandbags, but it was a futile task. During this time, I was torn as to whether to stay at the station and give reports, or to go work on the river. I concluded I could probably be of more value by giving out vital information. Remember, this was in the pre-television days. It was touch and go, and finally the river surged over all barriers and tore into North Topeka and North Lawrence. It covered everything!

Our transmitter was located at Grantville, about eight miles east of Topeka, approximately a mile north of the river. The transmitter building itself was located on a knoll of ground slightly higher than the field where the transmitter towers were located. As the floodwaters surged over the Kaw River Valley to the north, our transmitter building became surrounded and was unreachable by car. Two of our transmitter engineers, George Egli, and Glenn Howard, were trapped. They couldn't get out, but they somehow kept the station on the air. The Air Force flew over their building and dropped food supplies to them.

At last, the waters receded, leaving a trail of destruction you couldn't believe.

And what a stench followed the flood. The damage was severe. At the building that housed the popular Tee-Pee night club far north of Lawrence, there remains a high water line marking the worst moment of the flood. It is about 15 feet high.

WREN received high praise for its outstanding coverage of the emergency situation. I always felt that really helped to establish our station as a vital link with and for the people of Topeka.

When the 1951-52 season got under way, Lovellette was well-established as one of the outstanding players in college basketball. (He had earned first team All-America honors as a junior, averaging 22.8 points.) The Jayhawks returned four regulars — Lovellette, Lienhard, Hougland and Kenney. Charlie Hoag, a standout on the football team, became a significant performer. Another recruiting class had brought in more Kansas high school products. Dean Kelley, a crafty guard from McCune, and John Keller from Page City, a little town in western Kansas that was so small the train didn't even slow down when it went through, became key players for the Jayhawks. Doc also found a backup center for Lovellette in B.H. Born from Medicine Lodge. B.H. hardly played at KU during the 1951-52 season but performed with distinction the following year.

Other voices from The Hill • Clyde Lovellette

With the exception of Charlie Hoag — who was from Oak Park, Illinois — and myself, it was a team made up of guys from small Kansas towns. They were almost too good, too nice. They were all great guys. They couldn't say a bad thing about anyone if they had to. All the guys were unselfish, and they had talent and played within that talent. It was basically a seven-man team. We had a nucleus of guys who believed they could accomplish anything. It was a bunch of guys who wanted to play basketball for the fun of basketball.

There were a couple of other notable players on the KU roster: La Vannes Squires, a Wichita sophomore and Kansas' first black player, and guard Dean Smith, from Topeka.

I first saw Dean Smith play at Topeka High School. At that time, WREN was broadcasting some of the local high school games. He wasn't a great player, but he always worked hard. It is a trait that has served him very well indeed at North Carolina.

Dean later told me that his father kept a recording of my broadcast of the state championship game between Topeka High School and Lawrence. Dean scored 20 points and made six free throws down the stretch as Topeka won.

When he told me this, I asked, "Did I make you sound good?" "You sure did," he told me. "That's why Dad kept it all those years."

Other voices from The Hill • Dick Harp

Dean could play the game and never hurt you. He was an average player. An intensely average player. What I always did was let him run the other team's offense in practice, and he always had no trouble with that. He was very inquisitive and very much a learner. He saved a lot of the stuff we gave the players. In retrospect, if I had to do it over, I would have seen that he played more.

The Jayhawks opened the year with seven straight wins before they entered play as a favorite that year in the preseason Big Seven holiday tournament at Municipal Auditorium in Kansas City, Missouri. The Jayhawks exploded past Colorado, 76-56, in the first encounter of the tournament, setting up a semifinal clash against rival Kansas State. The Wildcats again were formidable.

Playing before a howling mob of 10,200, the Jayhawks prevailed in overtime, 90-88, as Lovellette scored 27 points and Kenney contributed 22 points. (The Wildcats would later hand KU its first defeat of the season.) KU moved into the finals of the holiday tournament against rival Missouri.

The game, as with most of the Missouri battles through the years, was very physical from the outset. The Tigers stayed close throughout the encounter, but the game is legendary for an incident involving Lovellette and Missouri's Win Wilfong. In the first half, there was a collision on the floor and Wilfong fell on his back behind the goal. Clyde was stumbling at the same time and, as he attempted to regain his balance, he went over Wilfong and stepped right on his stomach. The officials called a foul on Clyde.

The crowd just erupted. All of the Missouri fans just went crazy, screaming and booing. It was starting to get out of hand. After a minute or two of this intense booing, Sparky Stalcup, the Missouri coach, grabbed the public-address microphone and said, "Folks, please settle down. This is no big deal. These are good young men and tempers may have got a little short, but this is a fine ball game and we don't want anything to ruin it." The crowd quieted down, and the game resumed.

Other voices from The Hill • Clyde Lovellette

Smaller people shouldn't come after the big people. They should let us keep to ourselves to do our own battles. They shouldn't try digging into your arms and those kinds of things. Win Wilfong kept doing that. I just got tired of it and when he hit the ground, I thought about stepping over him, but I shortened my stride and stepped on him. I didn't put all my weight on him, though.

I was really sorry after it happened because it shouldn't be in any contest. If you can't keep your cool enough, you shouldn't be on the floor because those things will happen in the course of the game. Doc took me out and reprimanded me, and sent me to the locker room. I can't tell you the humiliation I felt.

Kansas went on to win the game, 75-65, and capture its first Big Seven preseason tournament championship.

From that point on, Phog and Sparky became very good friends. Sparky would make frequent appearances at KU basketball banquets in spite of the heated rivalry between Kansas and Missouri.

That tense moment in Kansas City is memorable, partly because traveling with that team was ordinarily a lot of fun. Part of that fun revolved around Clyde and Charlie Hoag, who loved to try to outfox their head coach and spend their spare time on the road at any handy pinball machine.

Other voices from The Hill • Clyde Lovellette

Charlie was a rounder anyway. Kind of a wild man. We would always try and find something to do on the road, and when we stayed at the Boulderado Hotel in Boulder, Colorado, we would always end up at the pinball machine. Charlie and I would play pinball for hours and hours. We were in good shape as long as Doc didn't catch us. He wanted us off our feet and in the room resting. Sometimes Doc would come down from his room, and we would have to quit playing. When he went back up to his room, we would sneak back down and continue playing. Doc might come back down and catch us again. He would scold us, and we would retire back to our room. We'd stay up there awhile, then slip back down after Doc left and play some more.

Kansas finished the year with an 11-1 conference mark, falling only at Kansas State. Oklahoma A&M, then of the Missouri Valley Conference, was responsible for the other regular-season defeat. KU finished with a sparkling 22-2 record heading into NCAA play.

The Western Regionals had been played in Kansas City for the previous 12 years, but the NCAA altered the tournament format for 1952. For the first time, the semifinalists wouldn't playoff at the regional site. Four teams would advance to the final, and the Final Four was born.

Lovellette had never scored fewer than 20 points in a game at Municipal Auditorium, and he extended that streak with 31 points as Kansas beat

Texas Christian, 68-64, in the regional semifinal. The next night, Clyde pitched in 44 points in a 19-point victory over St. Louis. The win earned the Jayhawks a trip to Seattle and the Final Four.

Disaster almost struck the Jayhawks before they played their first game in Seattle. Killing time the day prior to the semifinal contest, Lovellette called an old Sigma Chi roommate who was serving with the Coast Guard in Seattle. "His name was Fig Newton and he was captain of a Coast Guard cutter that was afloat in Puget Sound Bay," said Lovellette.

"When I called him, he asked me if I'd like to have dinner on the boat and go on patrol with them that evening. He said we'd be back in plenty of time to meet curfew."

While out on the boat, a thick fog rolled into the bay, and the cutter had a lot of trouble returning to the dock. In fact, Lovellette was stranded for several hours out on the boat. It was after curfew when Clyde finally returned to the hotel, and he had to endure a tongue-lashing from Doc as a result of his escapade.

Somehow it was only fitting, considering the joke that Clyde had played on his head coach on the flight to Seattle.

Other voices from The Hill • Clyde Lovellette

Doc was an individual you could have fun with if you caught him off guard. The plane (to Seattle) had a belly, and a passenger could come downstairs from the main cabin and there was additional seating. Whenever we traveled and Doc sat down, he usually fell asleep. So he's down there in the belly of the plane asleep. There were artificial flowers all around the windows in the plane. So when Doc went to sleep I went around and gathered up a bunch of flowers and laid them all around him. His hands were folded across his chest so I stuck a few in the grip. I woke him up at that point and said, "Doc, we're going down and you're ready."

KU's semifinal opponent, Santa Clara, was playing the role of Cinderella in the tournament. It had knocked off favored UCLA and Wyoming to reach Seattle.

The Broncos' good fortune ran out against third-ranked Kansas, which advanced to the finals with a 74-55 win. It was happening just as Phog Allen had envisioned five years earlier. St. John's, which had upset Kentucky in the Eastern Regionals, surprised second-ranked Illinois to reach the finals.

But the Redmen were no match for Kansas. Lovellette was spectacular, scoring 33 points and leading the Jayhawks to an 80-63 victory and the coveted national championship. Clyde, the Most Valuable Player of the tournament, became the first — and remains the only — player in NCAA history to win a national championship and lead the country in scoring.

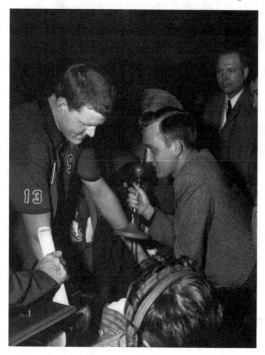

I did many live, on-the-air interviews, such as this one with Clyde Lovellette after the Jayhawks won their first NCAA championship.

More than 5,000 people welcomed the team upon its return to Lawrence the following night. A parade was formed in the wee hours of the morning, and the players were positioned on fire engines to ride downtown. The street was lined with screaming fans. I remember Clyde drove the lead fire truck with the fire chief's white helmet perched on his head.

Kansas had won the title, but its season wasn't over. There was one more important item on the Jayhawks' shopping list. Phog Allen wanted to win the Olympic playoffs, which would make him the coach of the U.S. Team. Four days after winning the championship in Seattle, Kansas was back at Municipal Auditorium in Kansas City against Southwest Missouri in an Olympic playoff game. The Jayhawks easily disposed of the Bears, 92-65. The next day, KU flew to New York for a semifinal game with La Salle, the NIT winner. The Jayhawks beat La Salle to reach the finals against the Peoria Caterpillar Diesels, the Amateur Athletic Union champion.

At that point, the Olympic team had been selected. Seven Jayhawks — Lovellette, Hougland, Kenney, Lienhard, Keller, Kelley and Hoag — combined with six players from Peoria to form the squad. The playoff winner, however, would determine the head coach.

Peoria jumped out early in the game, leading by 15 points in the first half.

KU fought back and had an opportunity to win it at the end. With the score tied 60-60 and the clock winding down, Lovellette stole the ball — just ripped it out of the hands of a Peoria player — and went in for an easy lay-up way ahead of everyone else. He proved to be human, however, and missed the shot. Peoria grabbed the rebound, went the length of the floor, and scored the winning points with 5 seconds remaining.

As a result, Phog served as an assistant to Warren Womble as head coach of the U.S. team.

The United States swept through its Olympic competition, earning a gold medal in impressive fashion.

Phog Allen had proved to he a prophet in forecasting a conference title, an NCAA championship, and an opportunity to win a gold medal while recruiting the stars of the 1951-52 team. Clyde and a group of small-town boys had given the legendary Kansas coach one of his proudest moments.

Meanwhile, Isobel and I were the recipients of our own special prize that spring. On June 13, 1952 — just a few days prior to Father's Day — Janie was born in Topeka. *The Topeka Capital-Journal* did a big Father's Day feature and included a picture of Janie and me.

For one of the few times in my life, I had trouble finding the proper words to express how proud I felt.

Chapter 5

The Twilight Years of Phog Allen

Nutrition and health remedies had a great influence on Phog Allen and his approach to coaching. He was legendary for the various treatments and medications that were a part of the daily routine in his dealings with the Kansas players.

Doc may have been ahead of his time in terms of nutrition. He was so big on yeast that he would eat it just as a snack. He thought it was good for the body and would help fight bacteria. After every practice, each player would return to the locker room for a cup of a mixture called Glycolixer (the players called it Glyck for short), two yeast tablets, followed by a little lemonade with Dextrose in it. The Glycolixer was a tonic of some type that was intended to replenish vitamins — and I'm told it tasted horrible.

Doc also had a unique approach to the pregame ritual. The players always were on their own for lunch. Then they would check in at the Eldridge Hotel at 3 p.m. and take a nap. They would meet in the lobby around 5 p.m. and walk as a team around the block. The walk was supposed to bring their energy back after the nap. Then the team would get on a city bus and ride over to the old Jayhawk Cafe.

Doc didn't believe in putting much in a player's stomach — just enough to take some of the hunger pangs away. First of all, each player had honey and toast. There was also celery. Doc always said celery was good for the nerves, and it was good for the eyes. The players were also served Ovaltine.

After that it was off to the game.

Graduation in 1952 took a heavy toll on the Jayhawks. Gone were starters Clyde Lovellette, Bob Kenney, John Keller and Bill Lienhard, along with top reserve Bill Hougland. An early season football injury shelved Charlie Hoag from the basketball team.

The cupboard was not completely empty, however, and the 67-year-old Allen had some quality players left on his roster when he started his 36th season at Mount Oread. Senior guard Dean Kelley was the most experienced player returning. But there were a lot of question marks. The 1952-53 Jayhawks were picked to finish no better than fourth or fifth in the conference.

Phog's most important task was replacing Lovellette and his point production. Allen's obvious choice for that assignment was a 6-foot-9 string bean named B.H. Born had learned his basketball while serving as practice fodder for Lovellette the previous two seasons. It was obvious to both Allen and Dick Harp that Born had the ability to fill the void. But B.H. had averaged only 1.6 points the previous year and certainly had a lot to prove.

Born hadn't seen a lot of playing time in the championship season, but he and Lovellette had some tough battles in practice. Born was about 30 to 40 pounds lighter than Clyde, which meant that he took a pretty good beating each day in practice.

Other voices from The Hill • B.H. Born

He literally tried to kill me. He broke my nose one time. He bloodied my lip. He knocked me out one time. And this is all in practice! I put him on my all-opponent team one year. But he toughened me up and made me a better player from then on. As far as positive aspects, he probably prepared me for the next year.

Other voices from The Hill • Clyde Lovellette

I always thought B.H. was a wimpish kind of person. In the back of my mind I may have thought he was trying to take my job away. I wasn't going to let him do that. Every time we would get in practice, when I got the opportunity, I would punish him a little bit. There was one time I really clubbed him good and Doc comes over, looks at me and says, "You, in the dressing room, now." He sent me off the court, out of practice, and that really hurt me. I sat down there in the locker room and wondered why he had punished me. I was just playing my normal game. Whenever B.H. got close to the basket, I would have my knee in him or my elbow in him. I worked him over real good.

The 1952-53 squad featured just two seniors — Kelley and Reich.Reich had just one year of basketball eligibility remaining after earning All-America honors on the 1952 KU football team. An important addition to the roster was junior-college transfer Harold Patterson, who also played football in the fall of 1952. The 6-foot-1 Patterson, from tiny Rozel, Kansas, also excelled in track and would be a three-sport letter winner at KU.

Three weeks into the season, though, the defending national champions didn't resemble a title contender. After back-to-back losses to K-State and Oklahoma, the Hawks boasted a 5-3 record on January 5.

I'm not sure what turned it around for the Jayhawks, but after the Oklahoma defeat, KU played much better. The Jayhawks won 11 of their final 13 regular-season games.

They reached the NCAA Tournament where they cruised past Oklahoma City and Oklahoma State. The Jayhawks then took the NCAA Western Region crown with an upset win over Washington.

The Jayhawks, for the second consecutive season, moved into the finals of the NCAA Tournament in Kansas City. Their opponent would be Indiana, which was coached by Branch McCracken. McCracken had plenty of incentive to beat the Jayhawks. Five years earlier, Phog Allen had crossed the Indiana border to take away prep standout Clyde Lovellette. McCracken was probably still having visions of what might have been if Lovellette had gone to Bloomington.

The game loomed as a battle between a pair of 6-9 centers — Born and the Hoosiers' top performer, three-time All-America center Don Schlundt.

Kansas stayed even with Indiana throughout the first half, although Born was slowed with an illness.

At halftime Born reported to trainer Dean Nesmith that his throat was clogged and he need something to clear it out. "So he got some alum water, which was one of Doc's things. Alum water is not the most pleasant stuff to try to gargle," Born later reported.

Born stood in the back of the locker room, trying to gargle the alum water, when Doc spotted him. Born was not performing the act of gargling to Allen's satisfaction, so the head coach decided to give his star center a demonstration on the way it's supposed to be done.

Try and picture it — it's halftime of a national championship game and the coach is taking 10 minutes to teach his center how to gargle, telling Born to throw his head back and gargle deeper in his throat.

Finally, Dick Harp grabbed some chalk and, during the last three minutes of the break, gave instructions.

The second half was just as close as the first. Kansas led by as many as six points on two occasions, but Born fouled out with five minutes left in the game.

With 27 seconds remaining, Hoosier guard Bob Leonard hit a free throw to break the game's 14th tie and give Indiana a 69-68 lead. KU's Jerry Alberts got off a desperation shot from the corner, but it hit the rim and bounced off as the buzzer sounded. It marked the first NCAA Tournament championship game decided by a single point.

Born had scored 26 points in the game and was named the tournament's Most Valuable Player. It marked the first time someone from the runner-up team had earned MVP honors.

The fact that Allen and the Jayhawks had come within one basket of back-to back national championships meant that expectations were again high in 1953-54.

Just two players — Kelley and Reich — were gone. Born was back after gaining All-America honors as a junior. Allen Kelley, Dean's brother, and Patterson, both starters, also returned. In addition, Allen was counting on sophomore Dallas Dobbs to add scoring punch to the lineup.

By most standards, it was an outstanding season. The Jayhawks won the conference holiday tournament and were Big Seven co-champions. Born averaged 18.9 points and was named to the all-conference team. KU tied Colorado for the title that season. Although the Jayhawks were 16-5 and the Buffs 11-11, CU was chosen the league representative to the NCAA tournament. And that's another interesting story.

The league decided to let an up-and-coming television sportscaster, Jay Barrington of WDAF-TV in Kansas City, draw the tournament team from the hat. Jay drew Colorado. Doc was furious, and the players were crestfallen. Later, Doc said the players didn't deserve to go anyway (they had lost the season finale to Missouri). Bill Mayer of the *"Lawrence Journal-World"* wrote that Phog should have been more supportive of his players and not belittle them.

At the basketball banquet, Mayer was sitting up front, and Doc blasted him, calling him a "pusillanimous, pencil-pushing, purple piss-ant!" Mayer, dumbfounded, blurted out, "Why purple?"

Even Doc broke down laughing.

Born was taken in the third round of the 1954 NBA draft by the Fort Wayne Pistons but never played for them. Instead, he accepted a job with Caterpillar Tractor Co. in Peoria, Illinois, after graduating from KU.

The mid-1950s would prove to be a transition period for Kansas basketball. Both its leader and its home court were at the end of long and storied trails.

Kansas had called Hoch Auditorium its home court for 28 seasons. There were numerous complaints about the building, the floor, and its strange design for basketball. The curved walls at the east and west ends of the court were distracting to visiting players, and it showed. The Jayhawks won 204 of 242 games in "The Opera House," for a sparkling .843 winning percentage.

The Jayhawks struggled to find success on the court during 1954-55. KU finished the season with an 11-10 record.

The highlight of the season came in the final home game of the regular season when the Hawks welcomed a new basketball palace on the south portion of campus. Built at a cost of $2.6 million, Allen Fieldhouse was dedicated March 1, 1955, when KU played host to K-State. An announced crowd of 17,228 was on hand to witness the Jayhawks' only conference home win of the season, 77-67 over Kansas State.

The *University Daily Kansan* had conducted an informal poll regarding a name for KU's new basketball arena. Phog Allen was the unanimous winner, pulling in 924 votes. The Board of Regents was of the same mind, voting to name the building, the second-largest college basketball facility in the country, in honor of the renowned coach.

The dedication ceremony was a great tribute to Doc.

A total of 103 letter winners, representing teams from the first year of Kansas basketball through 1953, attended the game, and Allen was the focus of a halftime ceremony. One thing I remember vividly is that first scoreboard. You say the video board today is spectacular? That first scoreboard had a Jayhawk painted on it and was wired so that the Jayhawk would wink each time KU scored.

In the spring of 1955, Doc reportedly got a phone call from an eastern newspaper reporter. The reporter said he had heard that Wilt Chamberlain would be enrolling at the University of Kansas the next fall.

"That's great news," Doc supposedly replied. "I hope he goes out for basketball."

I will always remember Wilt Chamberlain's arrival in Lawrence in the summer of 1955. Why is that memory so vivid? Because our son, Kurt, was born in August of that year. We were elated to be lucky enough to have both a daughter and a son.

Back on campus, Kansas now had one of the country's largest basketball arenas and one of the biggest players in the game. The 7-foot-1 Chamberlain couldn't play as a freshman, but his debut at Allen Fieldhouse that year gave a tantalizing hint of what was to come. A crowd of 14,000 gathered to watch Wilt's freshman team play the varsity. Chamberlain scored 42 points in the contest — an 81-71 victory for the freshmen.

That night was significant for another reason — it was Allen's 70th birthday. The coach who had guided Kansas for 39 years and more than 1,000 games had reached the state's mandatory retirement age.

Doc appealed the university administration's decision all the way to the Board of Regents, even offering to relinquish his teaching duties if he could keep his coaching job. But the state stood firm, and Doc coached his final game March 10, 1956, against Colorado in Boulder. The Jayhawks lost 75-67.

Phog Allen had amassed a 590-219 record with 24 conference championships and one NCAA title. He was a special individual who left a lasting imprint on the University of Kansas and the many athletes who had the opportunity to be a part of his teams. I grew up watching Doc Allen's teams and feel fortunate that I had the opportunity to be a part of his final seasons as head coach at KU.

Dick Harp had been at Doc's side since 1949 and had been an important component in the team's success. I think it's safe to say that Dick didn't receive his due for all of his contributions during the early 1950s when KU made its two runs in the NCAA Final Four. He was an outstanding coach and the natural choice to replace Doc.

Unfortunately, Dick was in a very tough situation. It was an overwhelming challenge to follow a legend, and it became even more difficult because Doc wanted to stay on as head coach. It wasn't a warm, fuzzy feeling that greeted Dick when he took over as head coach. There were people who had wanted Doc to continue and actually hoped that Dick would fail. Having Wilt Chamberlain on the roster also added considerable pressure. Fans had been talking about an NCAA championship since the first day Wilt stepped on campus.

It was a period of adjustment for Kansas basketball and, as both a broadcaster and friend of the program, I eagerly waited to see what was going to happen.

Some of Phog's famous lines:

"They stood around like Christmas trees, and out of season at that." (After his team played badly)

"They're a bunch of quadrennial, transoceanic hitchhikers, who don't own a hurdle." (Referring to the AAU)

"It was a transitional, stratified, man-to-man with zone principals." (Explaining a Jayhawk defense)

"He is so provincial that when he gets as far as Philadelphia, he thinks he's on the Lewis and Clark expedition." (Referring to a New Yorker)

"They're still taller and fairer than the Chinese but not nearly as progressive. " (Referring to Easterners in general)

"He's just like a big turkey gobbling up all the grain." (Describing Clyde Lovellette)

Chapter 6

Dick Harp and The Big Dipper

On a chilly evening, December 3, 1956, to be exact, Dick Harp, wearing his finest suit and tie, strolled briskly onto the Allen Fieldhouse court and positioned himself in a seat that someone else had occupied for 39 years.

From my perspective, high off the floor in the media section, it was both exciting and appropriate to see the 38-year-old Harp in Phog Allen's courtside location on the Jayhawk bench for that first game of the 1956-57 season. The previous season, Allen had protested before yielding his seat after reaching the mandatory retirement age of 70.

Even beyond the absence of Phog Allen on the bench, however, the pregame ritual that night was anything but routine, and it had everyone in their seats early. The lay-up drill included a peculiar sight – a basketball player who stood more than five inches taller than any other player on the floor. His name was Wilton Chamberlain.

The paint in Allen Fieldhouse was still fresh that season, the second year the building served as home of the Jayhawks. In those early years, the portable wooden court was elevated about 18 inches above the floor. Fans in the first few rows looked up to watch the game.

I can only imagine how towering the seven-foot Chamberlain appeared that night from the perspective of those viewing the action from courtside. His size and agility made him an entertaining oddity from the pages of "Ripley's Believe It or Not" for many of the wide-eyed Kansas faithful, fans who were still getting accustomed to the concept of a black man on the floor. Racial indignities were prevalent throughout the country, and the colossal ebony presence of Wilt was too much for many of the traditionalists.

Coupled with his enormous talents was the fact that K-A-N-S-A-S was stitched on his shirt, making Jayhawk fans more than willing to expand their capacity for acceptance. Chamberlain, the tallest player in KU basketball history, was well established as a basketball legend before his appearance that night.

He had averaged 37 points over his three-year career at Philadelphia's Overbrook High School. Twice during his prep career, Wilt had scored an amazing 90 points in a game.

Measuring 101 inches from fingertip to fingertip, Wilt was a man of mammoth proportions. He had a standing reach of nine feet, seven inches.

Harp had a well-documented legacy in Kansas basketball. He had served as co-captain of the Jayhawks' 1940 NCAA Tournament team, which lost in the national finals to Indiana. He had been at Allen's side as an assistant coach in 1952 when KU won the NCAA title and the following year when the Jayhawks again made it to college basketball's championship game.

After being elevated to head coach, Dick made a wise decision and hired Jerry Waugh as his assistant coach. Jerry was a classmate of mine at KU and had been serving as basketball coach at Lawrence High School. I'm not sure if any of the star systems were visible over Lawrence that December evening. But I can assure you that the "Big Dipper" — Wilt's preferred nickname — was in clear focus in Allen Fieldhouse.

The head coach and star pupil passed their first test. Wilt put on a performance that few of the 15,000 fans in attendance could ever have imagined, scoring 52 points and pulling down 31 rebounds in an 87-69 victory over Northwestern. Both scoring and rebounding marks obliterated the school records.

Wilt Chamberlain's career averages of 29.9 points and 18.9 rebounds a game are easily the best in KU history.

Everyone expected Wilt to move the Kansas basketball team out of the mud with as much ease as he could push his car. An aura of invincibility surrounded Chamberlain. It probably didn't help matters when Phog, still bitter about being forced into retirement, suggested that Chamberlain could win a national championship with four cheerleaders as teammates. It was a flip remark, but it increased the pressure on Harp as he guided the team.

As if the burden of following a legend wasn't enough to carry on his shoulders, Harp was coaching a player considered among the best in college basketball.

Harp had been hired as head coach at Kansas for $7,500. He would earn every penny of that salary.

The Jayhawks actually were talented aside from the presence of Wilt. KU returned three proven seniors in guards Maurice King and John Parker, and forward Gene Elstun. The Jayhawks also had bench strength in 6-7 senior Lew Johnson and a trio of sophomores: Ron Loneski, who earned a starting role on the team; 5-11 Bob Billings; and Monte Johnson.

King had become the first black starter for a Big Seven team two years earlier. Fortunately, Maurice, who had averaged 14.0 points as a junior, had a Jackie Robinson temperament, because he was subjected to outrageous racial insults on a regular basis.

KU dominated its opponents, winning its first 12 games of the 1956-57 season. The only close encounter during that stretch came against Iowa State during the Big Seven Holiday Tournament in Kansas City. The Cyclones slowed the tempo of the game, but the Jayhawks took a narrow 58-57 decision.

Kansas spent much of December and early January ranked No. 1 in the country. Looking for any method to throttle the surging Jayhawks, gimmick defenses and slow-down tactics were commonly used by KU opponents. Slowing the game could be effective against the Jayhawks. The gimmick defenses also began to frustrate Chamberlain, who was anxious to move up and down the floor.

The Hawks suffered their first loss of the season in unlucky Game Number 13 against Iowa State at Ames. The Cyclones slowed the tempo, held Wilt to just 17 points and came away with a 39-37 win. Panic didn't set in with the defeat, but a combustible situation was building.

The defenses teams employed frustrated Chamberlain, and his response to the situation did the same to his coach. It didn't help matters that Wilt wasn't the most dedicated performer in practice.

The relationship between Harp and Chamberlain was becoming strained. I think Wilt harbored some ill feelings from the start, because he had expected to play for Doc Allen.

Chamberlain was forced to tolerate more than the constant public pressure and the gimmick defenses. Along with Maurice King, Wilt was often peppered with racial insults from leather-lunged fans. The hostile climate was unfortunate for two young black players traveling around the country playing before predominantly white audiences. It was a sign of those times, but I doubt that many of us recognized the potential scars inflicted by such cruelty.

Both Maurice and Wilt handled themselves with dignity, unlike the adults and students who dished out the verbal punishment.

Following the Iowa State defeat, the Jayhawks had only one bump in the road before the NCAA Tournament. At Oklahoma State, on February 21, the Cowboys slowed down the game and won 56-54.

Two weeks later, though, KU needed just one victory in its final two games to secure the coveted conference title and earn a trip to the NCAA Tournament.

Clinching the championship in Manhattan was an appealing prospect, and the Wildcats were no match for Kansas that night. Chamberlain lived up to his All-America selection, which had been announced earlier in the afternoon, as he scored 24 points and pulled down 17 rebounds in a 65-57 victory.

The Jayhawks wrapped up the regular season with a win over Colorado and moved into NCAA regional action, playing against SMU in Dallas. The racial tension seemed to reach a boiling point in the Lone Star state. The Jayhawks were treated as second-class citizens from the moment they arrived in Texas.

Other voices from The Hill • John Parker

None of us could have imagined the atmosphere awaiting the team at the 1957 Midwest Regionals. The tournament hotel refused to accommodate blacks, so we stayed at a dingy motel miles away in Grand Prairie. No restaurant would serve us, so we took all our meals together in a private room.

Our first game was against our hosts, the fifth-ranked and all-white SMU Mustangs. SMU was undefeated in its new field house, and it was easy to see why.

Their crowd was brutal. We were spat upon, pelted with debris, and subjected to the vilest racial epithets imaginable. The officials did little to maintain order. There were so many uncalled fouls, each more outrageous than the last, that Maurice and Wilt risked serious injury simply by staying in the game. And, incredibly, they responded with some of the best basketball of their lives. We escaped with a 73-65 overtime win.

Naively, I thought the worst of our crowd problems were over. But the next night SMU fans adopted our opponents, the all-white Oklahoma City Chiefs. Their flamboyant coach, Abe Lemons, encouraged the support, and soon emboldened OCU players were throwing themselves on the floor, trying to take blacks out of basketball - permanently. Our ordinarily mild-mannered coach had a few choice words for Lemons, and the two nearly came to blows.

Before long, however, we were winning easily, and OCU's frustration became desperation. Wilt in particular appeared at the free-throw line over and over again.

Infuriated fans hurled food, seat cushions, and coins at the court, and the field house rocked with racial slurs and threats.

The Jayhawks escaped Dallas with an 81-61 victory over Oklahoma City as Chamberlain responded to the intimidation by scoring 30 points and hauling down 15 rebounds. The atmosphere was dangerous as armed police officers escorted the team off the court and all the way back to the airport.

Charges flew back and forth following the trip to Dallas. Lemons punctuated the insults by claiming the referees were "protecting" Chamberlain. Referee Al Lightner, who also served as sports editor of the *Oregon Statesman*, had a different opinion.

"The real trouble seemed to be that Chamberlain and guard Maurice King were dark-skinned," said Lightner. Lightner went on to say that OCU players were "deliberately dumping Chamberlain." He also said Lemons had warned of trouble "if that big nigger piles onto any of my kids." Lightner told of Oklahoma City players referring to "those niggers."

Lemons denied Lightner's charges. "You can ask my boys, and I know they never made a statement like that. I've never called a colored boy a nigger in my life."

The victories in Dallas propelled KU back home to the NCAA finals at Municipal Auditorium in Kansas City. The Jayhawks faced defending national champion San Francisco, while No. 1- ranked North Carolina was paired against Michigan State.

Playing in an arena just 40 miles from the KU campus, the Jayhawks enjoyed a near home-court advantage. Kansas had added incentive because three starters were Kansas City natives.

Just prior to the tournament, the Kansas Turnpike Authority announced, in a strange news release, that in checking license plates and travel habits it had determined that basketball fans spent $16,150.50 in tolls that year to see Chamberlain and the Jayhawks play in Lawrence. Those who traveled to Kansas City for the NCAA finals would also get their money's worth.

Chamberlain scored 32 points and Elstun chipped in 16 as KU easily dumped San Francisco, 80-56, to earn the opportunity to play for the national championship.

North Carolina survived three overtimes and advanced to the final game with a 74-70 win over Michigan State. The Tar Heels were coached by Frank McGuire, a native of Brooklyn who was finding happiness in the South.

The national championship game would feature the two top-ranked teams in college basketball. By playing in the title game, Kansas became the first team in the tournament's history to reach the finals four times. Chamberlain was obviously the star for KU, but the Tar Heels also had a standout performer in 6-5 Lennie Rosenbluth, who averaged 28.3 points an outing.

McGuire devised a special defense against Chamberlain: a collapsible zone with one man in front of the KU center. Anytime the ball came off the boards, McGuire would have four players ready to box out Chamberlain and one to go for the ball.

The crafty Carolina coach also started the game with a gimmick. He sent 5-foot-10 guard Tommy Kearns out for the opening tip against Chamberlain. It was just a ploy designed to confuse Wilt and start him thinking about what other tricks the Tar Heels might employ.

Other voices from The Hill • John Parker

Emotions were running high, perhaps too high. We fell behind early, and only Wilt's incredible ability kept us from digging our own graves. We spent all of the first half and much of the second playing catch-up, but with two minutes to go we were ahead by five. Then, inexplicably, we went into a slow-down game, completely at odds with our usual run-and-gun style. The score was tied 46-46 when the buzzer sounded. Both teams began playing nervously and cautiously; no one wanted to make a mistake that could cost a national championship. Each team scored only once in the first overtime, and in the second, neither scored at all.

By this time, the crowd noise was deafening, the court was blanketed in thick cigarette smoke, and the tension was almost unbearable. The pace picked up. With six seconds left in triple overtime, we led 53-52, and Carolina's Joe Quigg was called to the free-throw line. He sank both shots, and Carolina was up by one.

With the game on the line in the final moments, KU's strategy was obvious.

Get the ball inside to Chamberlain. How to maneuver a pass through the teeth of the Tar Heel defense would be a challenge for Harp and company. We all anticipated that Carolina would double-or triple-team Wilt and blanket Elstun, the team's second-leading scorer.

Harp figured that Loneski would be free and could take advantage of his six foot-six frame to pass the ball over the Carolina defense in Wilt's direction.

Other voices from The Hill • John Parker

I took the ball out of bounds at mid-court and had little trouble passing in safely.

But North Carolina's defense, playing on pure adrenaline, trapped Ron out of position. He was forced to make a shaky pass inside, and somehow, unbelievably, horribly, the ball landed in Carolina hands. The buzzer sounded, and the game was over.

What is now considered the greatest college basketball game ever played had for us deteriorated into a nightmare. Stunned, we watched Carolina celebrate, and somehow we made it through the awards ceremony dry-eyed. But as soon as we passed through the locker room doors, we all broke down. The long bus ride back to campus was completely silent.

Harp and Chamberlain had finished their inaugural season with a 24-3 record and had advanced to the NCAA championship game — by most standards, highly significant achievements for a rookie head coach and player in his first varsity season. Not all agreed, and many so-called "loyal fans" quickly condemned Harp and the Jayhawks for failing to bring home a title.

About a month after the season, rumors surfaced that Wilt would skip his final two years of college and sign a contract to play for the Harlem Globetrotters. The source of the rumor, in fact, was Doc Allen. "It would appear that Phog knows more about my business than I do," said Chamberlain in response to Allen's prophecy.

Just like Clyde Lovellette, Wilt and I did a 30-minute radio show together at WREN. We called it *Flippin With The Dipper* and it was a lot of fun. Wilt would arrive at the radio station and pick out some music he enjoyed, and we'd play it and talk a little basketball. I remember him inviting Monte Johnson as a guest to play the spoons. Monte was one heck of a spoons player.

Off the court, Wilt was a bona fide giant! Here, Isobel and I greet Wilt and R.A. Edwards.

Basketball season was over, but the multitalented Chamberlain continued to compete as a Jayhawk in track. Wilt won the conference outdoor high-jump title and was second at the Kansas Relays. He was also third in the Kansas Relays in the triple jump.

In addition to the long- and triple-jump competition, Wilt had competed in the shot put as a freshman. He was quite a sight at the Kansas Relays, sprinting down the jump runway wearing a freshman "beanie" on his head. One intriguing tale concerning Chamberlain and his strength is a product of his track involvement.

During Wilt's time at Kansas, Lawrence High School product and Jayhawk All-American Bill Nieder was working up to becoming the world record holder in the shot put. His magic goal was 60 feet. Chamberlain and Nieder used to meet regularly in Allen Fieldhouse to arm wrestle. Neither could put the other down. After hearing versions of the following story for years, I finally got a chance to ask Nieder about it during the fall of 2006.

According to the story, a bunch of the boys were whooping it up one night, and Wilt said he could probably throw the shot 60 feet. So, Bill said he could beat Wilt in the shot throwing left-handed. He was so confident, in fact, that he offered a $10 wager.

As advertised, Bill put the shot out there left-handed and it went about 56 feet. (Sixty feet was about as good as anybody could throw it back in those days.)

Then, it was Wilt's turn. He took the shot in both hands, bent down and threw it backwards over his head with a two-handed throw. He beat Bill by a few inches.

Bill didn't say if he paid Wilt the $10 or not, but that's one of the more intriguing stories in KU lore and another example of Wilt's incredible athletic ability. It seemed that whatever sport Wilt attempted, he was highly successful.

You can credit Wilt for breaking the color barrier in Lawrence restaurants. He walked into the Dine-A-Mite, a popular campus hangout that was run by Roy and Mary Borgen — two great KU fans — and he sat down and ordered. They served him, and history was made. There was virtually no social life for a black student in Lawrence in those days, so Wilt spent a lot of time in Kansas City. In fact, he was driving on the turnpike before it opened.

Chamberlain returned for the 1957-58 season, and the Jayhawks once again got off to an impressive start, winning their first 10 games. The Big Dipper, however, suffered an injury midway through the season, and the winning streak was ended with a pair of two-point losses to Oklahoma State and Oklahoma.

The Jayhawks won six of their next seven games, but their conference championship hopes fell apart in consecutive losses at Nebraska and Iowa State.

Other voices from The Hill • Dick Harp

After the season, Wilt decided he wanted to play for the Globetrotters. I was outside in the yard working when he came by the house to tell me. He had everything packed up in his car. He just stopped by on his way out of town, and we talked for a little while. He thanked me and drove away. That was it.

Kansas was 42-8 in the two years that Chamberlain played. The eight losses were by a total of just 21 points, or an average of 2.6 per game. Three of those defeats were in overtime, and two were inflicted with Wilt out of the lineup.

Without Wilt in the lineup for the 1958-59 season, KU encountered a murderous menu of games with no one over 6-foot-6 on the roster. Kansas was not ready for the challenge. After two wins to open the season, the Jayhawks lost seven consecutive games. The team would continue to falter and conclude the season with an 11-14 mark.

Along the way, however, the play of 6-5 sophomore Bill Bridges gave Jayhawk fans a degree of excitement. With Bridges returning to the lineup and a talented sophomore class coming up, Jayhawk fans approached the 1959-60 season hoping for improvement. KU had lured another plum from Overbrook High School in Philadelphia (the same school that had produced Chamberlain) in the form of Wayne Hightower. During his first varsity season, Hightower averaged 21.8 points a game for an improved Jayhawk squad. The team reached the NCAA Tournament where it defeated Texas, 90-81, behind Hightower's career-high 34 points. Then, the next night, top-ranked Cincinnati and its star Oscar Robertson proved to be too much for KU. Kansas finished the season with a 19-9 record.

It was a rewarding season for Harp. It sent a message to those critics who had questioned Harp's ability to win without Chamberlain. Dick was a good coach.

Harp opened the 1960s with a new assistant coach. Ted Owens had been hired to replace Jerry Waugh, who decided to leave the coaching profession and enter private business.

Visions of another conference title and more were on everyone's minds when the Jayhawks opened the 1960-61 basketball season. But, it wasn't to be. The season in which the Hawks finished with a 17-8 record, ended on a sour note as the Jayhawks were defeated, 79-76, by Missouri in a nationally televised game that was marred by a bench-clearing fight.

The ugly incident spurred athletics director Dutch Lonborg to suggest that the teams discontinue their rivalry.

Bridges, however, set a KU career rebounding mark with 1,081 for a 13.9 average and earned All-America honors for his performance. He would enjoy an outstanding professional career, playing 13 seasons at the next level.

Dick Harp coached three more seasons at Kansas. With Bridges gone and Hightower deciding to skip his senior season, the Jayhawks dipped to 7-18 in 1961-62.

The following season, the Jayhawks won seven of their first 11 games and concluded 1962 with a dramatic, 90-88, four-overtime win over Kansas State when seldom-used Jay Roberts, a walk-on from the football team, tipped in the winning basket. One day later — New Year's Eve — KU sports information director Don Pierce was killed in a car accident.

The Jayhawks won just five more games and concluded the 1962-63 season with a 12-13 mark. The following year, Harp's final season, Kansas finished with a 13-12 record.

Other voices from The Hill • Dick Harp

It was late in the year and after one particular defeat, I called my wife, Martha Sue, and told her I would be late. I went up and sat down on the grass under the Campanile Memorial. I was looking around and praying a little bit and probably crying a little when it started to rain. I thought, "OK Lord, I recognize what you want me to do now." So I got up and went home and told Martha Sue that I'd decided to resign. She wasn't particularly happy with that decision, but it was my decision.

No one loved the University of Kansas more than Harp. It was a special place for him, and he preached its importance to his team.

Other voices from The Hill • Al Correll

To Dick Harp, wearing the Kansas uniform has a special significance. One night we had finished practicing, and we were not doing very good. It was my senior year and I was the last one out of the locker room. As I was leaving, I looked out on the floor. The whole court was dark and there was one light on above the big scoreboard and it shined down on the big K on the floor. Coach Harp was sitting there in a chair by himself on the big K with that light over his head. It was kind of an eerie thing, and I walked out to check on him. I looked at him and asked, "Coach, are you all right?" He said he was fine, but he just couldn't understand why a player wouldn't give his all and realize how important this game is and what it means to wear a Kansas uniform. He was real serious. I don't think I've ever felt as strange as I did at that moment. It really hurt him.

Assistant coach Ted Owens replaced Harp, whose teams had a 121-82 record over eight seasons, winning two conference championships and finishing as national runner-up once. Dick left Kansas to become a top official with the Fellowship of Christian Athletes, a position he held for 13 seasons.

In 1986, North Carolina Coach Dean Smith invited Harp back to the coaching ranks as a volunteer coach for the Tar Heels. Dick was back in basketball and a contributor at one of college basketball's great programs.

During his years in Chapel Hill, Harp was impressed with the skills of young Carolina assistant Roy Williams. Dick and I traded phone calls on a regular basis while he worked for Coach Smith, and he kept telling me about Williams and what a great candidate he would be for Kansas if Larry Brown ever left the job.

Showing my insight, I told Dick that Kansas would never hire an unknown assistant for the position.

When Brown resigned, Harp called one of his former players, KU director of athletics Bob Frederick, and recommended Williams. Dick and Martha Sue Harp came back home to Lawrence in 1989.

On March 18, 2000, Dick, whose health had been declining, died at Lawrence Presbyterian Manor. He was 81.

Chapter 7

Mitchell, Hadl, Sayers —Fun Years

It cost just $20 to buy a season football ticket at Kansas in 1960. With a roster that included future Jayhawk legends such as John Hadl, Curtis McClinton and Bert Coan, that price was a definite bargain.

Jayhawk football swooped into the '60s like a twister through a Kansas wheat field. The Jayhawks played football with pizzazz. They operated in a fast and furious manner and reflected the aggressive, cocky style of their leader, an unbending optimist named Jack Mitchell.

General Jack — as he had become known during his playing days at OU — blew into town, quite appropriately, on Thanksgiving Day 1957, when KU Director of Athletics Dutch Lonborg introduced him as KU's new head football coach. It was obvious from the start, however, that this coach was no turkey. Mitchell — a flamboyant, cigar-smoking, tobacco-chewing bundle of energy — recruited blue-chip players, charmed the fans, and ignited hope at a school eager to earn a spot among the football elite.

The ambitious Mitchell arrived in Lawrence following the dismissal of Chuck Mather, who was canned after losing seasons in four of his five years at the helm. It was reported in the *Lawrence Journal-World* that Mitchell had been given a five-year contract at $15,000 per year.

Mitchell, a former Oklahoma quarterback and native Kansan who had excelled as a high school player at Arkansas City, had served two years as head coach at Wichita University and three years as the head man at Arkansas. He was the 27th head football coach in Kansas history.

Those eventful Mitchell years are full of moments I will always remember.

Jack was a charismatic charmer who had an instinct for entertaining KU football fanatics off the field and exhibiting exciting teams on the field. He was a salesman who excelled as a showman and master recruiter.

Other voices from The Hill • John Hadl

The recruiting process for me began my junior year at Lawrence High School, when Chuck Mather was head coach. Chuck was a nice guy, but I had been watching that program firsthand, and I knew things were bad. I went down to Oklahoma on a visit during my senior year and actually committed to Bud Wilkinson. Bud just asked me if I'd like to come to Oklahoma. I didn't have to think about it. I said YES. Chuck Mather had just been fired at the time and Jack Mitchell was the new KU coach. I got back from Oklahoma about 10 p.m., and there was a call waiting from Jack Mitchell.

Mitchell insisted on my coming over for a talk. By the time I left his house, around 2 a.m., I didn't even remember having said I was going to Oklahoma.

I was going to Kansas.

The 1959 season marked the debut of Hadl and McClinton in the Jayhawk backfield. McClinton operated at right halfback, and Hadl played left halfback. Lee Flachsbarth played quarterback, and KU had a break-even season, winning five of its 10 games.

Hadl brought a new dimension to the Jayhawk attack — something that was evident in his first varsity game against TCU. John, who started on defense and offense, picked off a Horned Frog pass in the second quarter and sprinted 98 yards for a touchdown. It marked the longest interception return in school history, a standard that still ranks first in the school record book.

In his second varsity game, versus Syracuse, Hadl etched his name in the school record book once more, this time with an electrifying 97-yard kickoff return.

Mitchell was not giving Jayhawk fans an instant winner, but he was making autumns more interesting in Lawrence. He brought a new attitude to the table, and his teams reflected a cocky confidence. Off the field, Mitchell dazzled the alumni.

He was the best I've ever seen at influencing the sensitive Jayhawk faithful. People would come up with harebrained suggestions, and Jack was so full of it, he would laugh and always tell them it was a great suggestion.

Misfortune often brought out the best in Mitchell after games. Following one of those discouraging defeats to Nebraska, Jack made the long, lonely climb to the Memorial Stadium press box for the post-game radio show. Jack wanted everyone to know the full magnitude of such a difficult defeat. In his mind, it would take generations to recover.

"I'm so embarrassed and ashamed of the way we played today. I know our players are going to be embarrassed and ashamed about this. Their kids are going to be embarrassed and ashamed about it, and their grandchildren are even going to be embarrassed and ashamed about it."

There was nothing to be ashamed about when the Jayhawks entered the 1960 season. Mitchell recognized the talent on his roster and hinted that the season offered promise.

"It's possible for us to have one of the finer teams Kansas has ever had," he said during a preseason media gathering.

The Jayhawks were scheduled to open the football season September 17 against defending Southwest Conference champion TCU, and the inauguration for KU's new chancellor was set for two days later. Chancellor Clark Wescoe was not shy about issuing a challenge to the football team.

"I certainly want to be inaugurated undefeated," said Wescoe in a speech during a preseason banquet.

Although fully aware of the pressures and expectations surrounding his team, Mitchell seemed comfortable in that environment.

Needless to say, Jack was good at blowing more than just cigar smoke. His optimism helped sell Kansas as a football powerhouse, and the Jayhawks were ranked seventh nationally in the first Associated Press college football poll that season. The multitalented Hadl returned for his junior season along with McClinton, a big, fast, powerful and punishing runner. KU's offense also featured Doyle Schick, considered one of the best blocking fullbacks in school history, and sophomore Bert Coan, a TCU transfer who combined impressive size (6-4, 210) and speed (9.4 seconds over 100 yards).

Against the Horned Frogs, a team that featured All-America tackle Bob Lilly, Kansas quickly erased any doubts about its potential. On the Jayhawks' second offensive play, Hadl bolted 52 yards on a quarterback sneak for a touchdown.

KU prevailed, 21-7, and Mitchell was able to attend the inauguration of a new chancellor feeling somewhat secure in his job.

Kansas rolled over outmanned Kansas State, 41-0, in its second outing. The Jayhawks were then matched against Syracuse in one of the biggest games in Lawrence in many seasons. It was Band Day on the KU campus, with 72 high school bands converging on Memorial Stadium on a warm September afternoon for the nationally televised game. Kansas had moved up to fifth in the weekly football poll. The Orangemen arrived in Lawrence ranked No. 2 nationally, the winners of 18 consecutive games. All-America halfback Ernie Davis led Syracuse into sold-out Memorial Stadium.

Syracuse rushed for more than 300 yards and cashed in on two KU fumbles and four interceptions as the home fans left disappointed following a 14-7 defeat.

The season rolled on, and so did the Hawks, losing only once more — at top-ranked Iowa, 21-7.

Well, the Jayhawks suffered another costly defeat in late October, but this one occurred off the field. The NCAA slapped Kansas with a one-year probation penalty resulting from the recruitment of Coan. The penalty resulted from a plane trip Coan made in August 1959 to Chicago with Bud Adams, a KU graduate and Houston resident, to see the College All-Star football game. The trip came prior to his enrollment at KU.

Other voices from The Hill • Don Fambrough

It was the most asinine thing I've ever heard of in my life. Bud didn't have any idea he was breaking the rules. Bert's father had worked for Bud Adams' father in Houston. Bud was taking some people up to Chicago to the All-Star game and happened to have an empty seat on his plane. As I remember he just happened to run into Bert on the street and asked him if he wanted to go to Chicago to see the All-Star game. Naturally, Bert said yes. They landed in Kansas City to refuel during the trip, and Bud got off the plane and called Coach Mitchell. I was sitting there in Jack's office when the phone rang. "Jack, this is Bud Adams," he said. "I'm on my way to the All-Star game, and guess who I've got with me in the plane? I've got Bert Coan with me." Jack almost went through the ceiling because he knew about that silly, asinine rule. But it was too late at that point.

Kansas concluded the season against rival Missouri in the annual Border War contest. No game was more important on the KU schedule than the annual game against Missouri. Historians trace the roots of this rivalry back to 1863, when William Quantrill and his gang crossed the Kansas border from Missouri and raided Lawrence, killing an estimated 150 residents.

Fambrough, in an effort to inspire KU, liked to insist that Quantrill was a Missouri alum. Adding a degree of spice to the emotionally charged atmosphere, Missouri entered the game ranked No. 1 in the country.

The game was in Columbia and, from the outset, the Jayhawk defense was dominant. The Tigers didn't manage a first down until midway through the third quarter. The Jayhawks upset the nation's top-ranked team, 23-7, and claimed their first undisputed league football crown since 1930.

Because KU was on probation, Missouri accepted the bid to the Orange Bowl. About a month later, the Big Eight ruled that the Jayhawks would have to forfeit the Missouri and Colorado wins because Coan had played in both games. In addition, Coan would have to sit out KU's first five games the following year. Thus, the Tigers ascended to the league throne, Colorado finished second, and Kansas' record dropped from 7-2-1 to 5-4-1 and third place in the final official standings.

There were compelling headlines throughout the off-season in 1961 concerning a new, unique contract for Mitchell, the switch of Hadl to quarterback, a season-ending injury to Coan, the recruitment of Gale Sayers and a ruling by the KUAC Board to allow women in the football press box.

It all started with Mitchell, who was being treated like the mayor of Lawrence.

General Jack's rebuilding efforts earned him job security at Kansas, something unique for KU football coaches. In March 1961, the Board of Regents announced that Mitchell would be given a lifetime contract at KU. It was reported to be the first of its kind in intercollegiate football. As I remember, Mitchell's salary was hiked to $17,600 a year.

With a new contract and modest raise in his pocket, Mitchell set about the business of preparing for another season.

He was in his Allen Fieldhouse office when Hadl and Doyle Schick stopped by just prior to spring drills to address the plethora of running-back talent in the KU backfield. With McClinton and Coan already available to carry the pigskin, the two players proposed that Hadl be switched to quarterback for his senior season. Mitchell, always eager to unleash the unexpected, bought the suggestion and took it to his coaching staff.

Hadl started the spring at quarterback but was not overly impressive as he fumbled his way through the off-season drills. He lacked confidence in the position and struggled. Once spring drills ended, John continued to sharpen his skills. He even practiced calling signals, standing all alone in the middle of the Lawrence High School field barking out orders. He also practiced passing with Lawrence High athletes willingly serving as targets. Hadl has often credited his old high school teammate, Larry Hatfield, with helping him to learn the mechanics of the position that summer.

John Hadl was a legend in Lawrence — a home-grown football hero. John always said he hadn't missed a football game at KU since the fifth grade, and he never had to buy a ticket.

Kansas absorbed a major setback at the end of spring drills in 1961 when Coan suffered a leg fracture that would force him to miss the upcoming season. Bert never played another down in a Kansas uniform. In those days, professional football could draft players who were redshirt seniors, and the San Diego Chargers selected Bert in 1962. He played one season with the Chargers and six years with the Kansas City Chiefs.

Another headline event that spring involved a ruling by the Kansas University Athletic Board pertaining to the issue of women in the press box. During the 1960 season, a *Hutchinson News* reporter, Barbara Caywood, had been assigned to cover a KU football game. Barbara, however, was denied credentials by sports information director Don Pierce, who was guided by a policy that prohibited women and children in the Memorial Stadium press box. The KUAC Board ruled, however, that any regularly employed sports reporter for a newspaper would be accorded full press-box privileges. The ruling eliminated the gender barrier and allowed equal access for all reporters.

Interestingly enough, Barbara's son, Kurt, was later hired by the *Lawrence Journal-World* and assigned to cover KU football for several years. He currently covers sports for the *Topeka Capital-Journal*.

As Mitchell and the Jayhawks found success on the gridiron, the program was able to attract more prized recruits. Mitchell, always the salesman, put his skills to good use after the 1960 season and found a coveted high school performer out of Omaha, Nebraska, by the name of Gale Sayers. Although Gale attended high school in Omaha, he had spent his early years in Wichita.

Other voices from The Hill • Don Fambrough

Everybody in the world was after Gale, and we just took it for granted that he was going to Nebraska. Like a lot of people, we had contacted him and got no response. We had a recruit, who later signed with KU, named Ron Marsh on campus.

Ron had visited Nebraska at the same time that Gale had been there. Ron visited our school a little later and asked during his visit if we were interested in Gale Sayers. We all just laughed. Ron told us that Gale was not all that happy about going to Nebraska. He said that Gale was looking for more than was available in Lincoln and wanted a social life or something outside of football. We had some black fraternities on campus, and when Gale visited, we made sure he saw the social opportunities available to him at Kansas.

With Hadl and McClinton available to shoulder the offensive burden, KU fans had visions of a national championship when autumn finally arrived in 1961. Dreams of a January visit to the Orange Bowl, however, quickly disappeared. Kansas found a boatload of disaster at the start of the season. A 36-yard field goal with just under five minutes left to play gave TCU a 17-16 victory in the first game. In Game Two against Wyoming, the Jayhawks were uninspired, managing a 6-6 tie against the underdog Cowboys.

In the third game, against Colorado, the Hawks blew a 19-point fourth-quarter lead and lost the game, 20-19. The game still ranks as the largest comeback by an opponent in school history.

After the bad start, things fell into place. First, the hungry Jayhawks whipped Iowa State, 21-7. KU then traveled to Norman, Oklahoma, and blanked the Sooners, 10-0. The win over OU was KU's first in 15 seasons and its first in Norman since 1937.

Momentum continued to swing the Jayhawks' way as they marched past Oklahoma State, 42-8; Nebraska, 28-6; Kansas State, 34-0; and California, 53-7.

The Jayhawks concluded the year with a 10-7 loss to rival Missouri. It was a bitter defeat for Kansas, which had envisioned victory and the reward of a January bowl trip. After the game, Dutch Lonborg informed Mitchell that the team had been invited to the Gotham Bowl, scheduled for December 9 in New York.

"It's cold as hell up there in December," Mitchell told his players when giving them the option of playing. "It doesn't make any difference to the coaching staff one way or the other." The players asked if they could delay a decision until the following Monday.

In the meantime, an invitation surfaced from the Bluebonnet Bowl, and the Jayhawks jumped at the opportunity to face Rice in the December 16 game in Houston.

The Owls were considered a major challenge for the Jayhawks. The game was played in Rice Stadium, and the Owls came into the contest as runner-up in the Southwest Conference with seven wins.

Hadl made KU history when he was he was named All-America for the second consecutive season. John became the Jayhawks' first two-time All-America selection, earning the honor his junior season as a halfback and his senior year as a quarterback.

A note of controversy surfaced a few days prior to the Bluebonnet Bowl when it was reported that Hadl had signed to play professionally with the San Diego Chargers, a move that would have made him ineligible for a bowl game. John had been drafted by the AFL's Chargers and the NFL's Detroit Lions. Hadl and Chargers General Manager Sid Gilman strongly denied the rumor and smothered the controversy instantly.

Hadl played flawlessly, saving his greatest game in a Kansas uniform for last.

Late in the first half, John was in punt formation on fourth down. Instead of punting, he raced 41 yards and set up a KU touchdown just before halftime. Kansas went on to an impressive 33-7 victory over the Owls; the school's first-ever bowl victory.

Hadl and McClinton, meanwhile, celebrated the victory by inking pro contracts immediately after the game.

Other voices from The Hill • John Hadl

We signed our contracts right after the game. Right there on the field. Curtis came up and said, "Let's sign right now." I signed with the Chargers, and he signed With the Texans. I think I got a $5,000 bonus and a car. My deal was a two-year contract for $17,500. I think Curtis got a $10,000 bonus. We got the checks as we were leaving the field. We were all in the locker room celebrating the victory. Curtis had that bonus check and he'd stuck it in his shirt pocket, hanging in the locker as he went to shower.

We thought we'd have some fun with Curtis and took his check and stuck it in another player's (Larry Allen's) pocket. So Curtis comes back, dripping wet, and sees his check is missing. He starts screaming and yelling about his check being gone. We all get down on the floor looking all over the place for his check. He's about to go nuts with worry that his check is lost. All of a sudden, Larry notices it in his pocket and tells Curtis. We had a great laugh.

With the help of Hadl, McClinton and a host of other Jayhawks, Jack Mitchell had put Jayhawk football back on the national map.

However, when the 1962 season unfolded, fans wondered if the Jayhawks had enough weaponry to match their past successes.

Those concerns were quickly put to rest with the arrival of the "Kansas Comet." When Gale Sayers came to Kansas, he was the most introverted individual I'd ever met during my years following the team. He would look at the floor and showed little confidence. He didn't do any interviews and was very uncomfortable when responding to questions. But you could see him gain confidence with his speaking ability as the years went by. By the time he was a senior, he had improved 100 percent.

In his first varsity game in 1962, Sayers set a school record by carrying the ball 27 times in a 6-3 loss to TCU. Sayers rushed for 114 yards in his debut and quickly established the fact that he was something special.

Other voices from The Hill • Don Fambrough

Gale was a tremendous athlete. One day we were out on the practice field fooling around. This is in the spring, and Gale is playing defensive safety. The quarterback throws a pass, and Gale starts to go over and cover his man and go for the ball when the belt broke on his trousers. The trousers fall down to his knees. Gale reaches down with one hand and pulls up those trousers and jumps up in the air and intercepts that pass with his other hand. A normal human being can't do that.

Sayers was not a typical college football player. He was something special to watch in the open field. He was so fluid in his motion. We were all amazed at his ability to change direction at high speed with very few steps. He had the ability to go east and west without having to chop his feet.

He had several 100-yard rushing days early in his sophomore season, but it was against Oklahoma State in Game Six that Sayers really cut loose. He set a new Big Eight and school single-game record against the 'Pokes when he rushed for 283 yards and led KU to a 36-17 victory. He tied a long-standing school mark with a 96-yard touchdown run in the fourth quarter. That followed a scamper of 69 yards in the first quarter.

The win over the Cowboys improved the Jayhawks' record to 4-2. KU added another victory the following week when Sayers rambled for 156 yards in a 38-0 win over rival Kansas State.

Sayers had an eventful sophomore season. He rushed for 1,125 yards, just four yards shy of Wade Stinson's school record. The Jayhawks finished with a respectable 6-3-1 record but failed to qualify for a bowl game.

The 1963 season would mark Dutch Lonborg's final year as athletics director at the University of Kansas, and Mitchell was considered a candidate for the job. He would have been perfect in that role.

The Jayhawks dipped to a 5-5 record in 1963 and finished in a fourth-place tie in the conference standings. Sayers' numbers were 917 yards and eight touchdowns.

His rushing totals ranked third nationally and first in the league. He became the first Big Eight back in history to gain more than 2,000 yards rushing over two consecutive seasons.

The off-season brought new leadership to the KU athletic department. Wade Stinson, who played under J.V. Sikes, was hired as athletics director to replace Lonborg. Dutch stayed on in the department with the title of "manager of events." Stinson was returning to his alma mater after 14 years as an insurance executive in Chicago.

For the 20th season, Kansas had its traditional opener with TCU in 1964. The game was played in Lawrence before the largest opening-day crowd in school history — 38,000 fans. Lorne Greene, star of the hit TV series *Bonanza*, attended the game as the guest of a friend. The Jayhawks won the opener, 7-3, for only the second time in a 12-year span. The win was not an artistic masterpiece, but it gave Mitchell a reason for optimism.

Kansas lost its next two games, against Syracuse and Wyoming, and things started getting ugly on campus. About 300 students hanged Mitchell in effigy and burned his likeness early Sunday morning after the Wyoming loss.

Mitchell took the hanging in stride. "Well, I'll tell you one thing, the way I felt after the loss, if they had called me I would have helped them."

With Steve Renko — who'd go on to a solid major-league pitching career, including time with the Kansas City Royals — off to a shaky start, Mitchell changed quarterbacks. He inserted sophomore Bobby Skahan into the lineup against Iowa State and got impressive results. Mitchell also found help in the form of Ron Oelschlaeger at fullback. Oelschlaeger rocketed 73 yards on the Jayhawks' first play of the day, and it set the stage for a 42-6 Kansas victory.

Oklahoma came to Lawrence the next weekend, and the Jayhawks scored one of the most memorable victories in school history. It was about time for good fortune to smile on the Jayhawks! Gale Sayers took the opening kickoff and raced 93 yards and put the Jayhawks in front. OU scored twice in the second period and dominated the game until the closing moments.

With eight seconds remaining, Dave Crandall passed in the flat to Skahan, who cut diagonally across the field and lunged into the end zone just as he was being driven across the out-of-bounds line. Now the score was 14-13, Oklahoma. The clock read 0:00 when the Jayhawks lined up for their conversion attempt.

Having already achieved a miracle by scoring, KU decided to try for another.

And Mike Johnson scored on a reverse, giving KU a 15-14 victory. The Jayhawks had gained a victory by scoring on the first play and the last play of the game.

After narrowly defeating OSU, 14-13, Mitchell used his own "Yogi-ism" (a dialect popularized by baseball's gnomish Yogi Berra) to explain his team's mental approach: "They were so scared of not being scared that they got scared."

With momentum in his corner, Mitchell started puffing his cigar and blowing rings of concern as his team prepared to face Kansas State. Mitchell knew psychology and put it to good use that week. The Wildcats were off to an unimpressive 1-4 start, but the way Mitchell was talking; most fans had trouble picking a favorite. Sayers entered the K-State game needing just 67 yards to break the Big Eight career rushing mark. Late in the third quarter, Sayers broke a 0-0 tie and spoiled the Wildcats' hopes for an upset with a 77-yard touchdown run. It would be the only score of the afternoon, and the Jayhawks improved to 4-0 in the league.

The win over the Wildcats set the stage for a showdown the following weekend between KU and Nebraska in Lawrence. The two teams entered the contest sharing the conference's top spot. The Jayhawks had two single-point conference wins and two others determined by the margin of a touchdown. But they ran out of miracles against Nebraska, as the Huskers prevailed, 14-7, in front of 45,000 hopeful Jayhawk fans. Sayers was held in check, rushing for a season-low 27 yards.

The Hawks split the last two games of the season — beating Colorado and losing to Missouri — and their bowl hopes went down the drain even though they posted a respectable 6-4 record.

Honors poured in for Sayers. He was named to everyone's All-America team and was picked in the first round of the NFL draft by the Chicago Bears. Broadcasting Gale Sayers' glory days at KU ranks as one of the highlights of my career.

Jack Mitchell coached two more disappointing seasons. KU lost its first five games in 1965 and ended with a 2-8 record. The Jayhawks got off to a 2-1 start in 1966, but went 0-6-1 the rest of the way.

On December 3, 1966 — his 43rd birthday — Mitchell and the University of Kansas parted company. AD Wade Stinson called it a "mutually satisfactory" ending to the nine-year association. It was obvious to all that Mitchell's "lifetime" contract had been bought out by the university.

Mitchell compiled a 44-42-5 record at Kansas. He and Stinson had been at odds from the beginning. It was obvious to me that Mitchell had wanted the athletic director's job, and he thought Stinson was not qualified for the post.

Mitchell left the coaching profession and moved to Wellington, Kansas, where he owned a daily newspaper. His departure marked the end of one of the greatest eras in Kansas football.

Once again, Kansas was in the market for a new football coach.

Chapter 8

A Dash of Pepper and Back to Orange Bowl

Like his teams, Pepper Rodgers was unpredictable and imaginative.

Opposing coaches had nightmares trying to guess what the Jayhawks might do in any given situation. Prognosticators were just as perplexed when trying to determine where Kansas might finish in the league race. He took Kansas fans on a fascinating and memorable roller-coaster ride during his four seasons (1967-70) as he rescued KU football from the grave and gave it meaningful life, only to see it revert to its original condition.

Whistling, singing Pepper Rodgers, the man with the impish grin and the calculating mind of a riverboat gambler, brought a unique personality and inspiring showmanship to Kansas football. College football was a stage for Pepper, and Lawrence was the perfect location for his performances.

He could add an element of adventure, suspense or humor in any given situation.

I hosted a weekly pre-game radio show with Pepper as a lead-in for my game broadcast. Pepper suggested we incorporate the Saturday atmosphere in an otherwise dull interview and make believe we were positioned at the 50-yard-line just minutes before kickoff. During a typical Thursday taping session in the quiet of his office, as I twiddled with the dials on my recorder and initiated a question, Pepper interrupted, shouting, "Watch it, watch out." I jumped back, somewhat shocked and asked what was wrong.

"You almost got hit by that football," said a smiling Pepper. Imaginativeness was never a weakness of Pepper Rodgers.

KU's athletic barons had abandoned Coach Jack Mitchell following the 1966 season and were looking for new inspiration to accelerate the football program and make it a civic showpiece. Director of athletics Wade Stinson pursued Rodgers, then a UCLA assistant coach, for the position.

On December 16, 1966, Stinson named 35-year-old Franklin Cullen

(Pepper) Rodgers as KU's head football coach. Rodgers arrived with an impressive football pedigree. He was a quarterback and place-kicker on Georgia Tech teams that won 32 consecutive games over three seasons (1951-53). His last minute field goal gave Georgia Tech a 17-14 victory over Baylor in the 1952 Orange Bowl.

But Pepper liked to downplay his playing career: "Probably, my most glorious moment came when I once went into a game and 60,000 fans stood up and cheered.

I found out later, they'd just announced the World Series score." During his formative coaching years, he tutored offensive backfields under some of the game's stellar coaches – Bobby Dodd at Georgia Tech, Ben Martin at the Air Force Academy, Ray Graves at Florida and Tommy Prothro at UCLA. He worked directly with two Heisman Trophy winners, quarterbacks Steve Spurrier of Florida and Gary Beban of UCLA.

Pepper was an unusual guy. He was as flaky as a $3 bill and a natural entertainer. But put him on a football field, and he became a coaching genius. He also was passionate about winning.

He had a simple approach to life: "I try to have fun every day like I'm going to die tomorrow and work every day like I'm going to live forever." Then he would always add: "I heard that from a preacher in a filling station." Pepper had an Andy Griffith-like approach to coaching. He wanted to make sure everyone — players, coaches, fans and even the media — had fun.

But his free-spiritedness could be as unnerving to an interviewer as it was contagious. No matter what the question or topic, that smile wouldn't leave his lips. You kept looking around to see if someone was making funny faces at him behind your back. Even his nickname — Pepper — ignited a grin on people's faces. His nickname was provided by a grandfather who was a great baseball fan and admirer of Pepper Martin, the St. Louis Cardinals' star and hero of the 1931 World Series the year of Rodgers' birth.

His methods were anything but orthodox. Once in the middle of a season, while the team was holding a strategy meeting, a disheveled hippie walked into the room clamoring to tryout. He was strumming a guitar and wearing a borrowed wig.

The "hippie" was Rodgers, and the players swear he carried out the ruse for a half-hour before anyone caught on.

Soon after Rodgers arrived at Kansas, he assembled his coaching staff

— probably the best in Kansas history — which included Dick Tomey, Don Fambrough, Floyd Temple, Dave McClain, John Cooper, Charlie McCullers and Larry Travis.

McClain would become head coach at Wisconsin. Cooper would be a successful coach at Ohio State. Travis was to serve as athletics director at Kansas State.

His final hire that first season was Doug Weaver, who had been deposed as head coach at Kansas State after a seven-year tenure and was enrolled at the KU School of Law. Weaver had decided to change careers and put football in the past. Yet Rodgers persuaded Weaver to be a part-time coach while attending law school.

(The Rodgers-Weaver relationship later took an odd turn. When Rodgers left for UCLA after the 1970 season, Weaver joined him. But Weaver grew impatient and left Rodgers' staff for Southern Illinois. A few years later, Rodgers returned to Georgia Tech, his alma mater. And a couple of years after that, the athletic directorship at Georgia Tech opened. Weaver got the job, no doubt with the help of a Rodgers' recommendation. In 1979, a little more than 12 years after their friendship had begun, Weaver fired the man who had once hired him.)

Fambrough hooked up with Rodgers to secure the Jayhawks' first recruit of the year — a future Super Bowl Most Valuable Player and member of the Pro Football Hall of Fame.

Other voices from The Hill • Don Fambrough

He went back to California and called me. He said, "I'm coming back to Kansas just for a day. I want you to pick out who you think is the No. 1 prospect in the state of Kansas, and we'll go see him." I told him that would not be any problem for me. I sure knew who the No. 1 prospect was in Kansas.

Pepper got in town that night, and we started off for Centralia, Kansas. We got on some of those roads that are little more than a cow trail. I was driving, and Pepper kept asking me, "Are you sure this is the best way?" We would drive a little more and it was dark. You couldn't see anything. Pepper said, "I can't believe this. Do you know where in the hell you are going?" Finally, we pull up in front of this house. We knock on the door, and here comes a young man opening the door. He is about 6-foot-3, 225 pounds and Pepper eyes him and goes to work.

The recruit's name was John Riggins, and he turned out to be Pepper's first catch.

From the first moment he put on his Kansas coaching hat, Rodgers preached the need for a mobile and effective throwing quarterback. The prototype for the position, according to Rodgers, would be a bold, reckless individual who could handle a major share of the team's running and passing in addition to directing the attack.

That ingredient, Rodgers promised, was essential for the imaginative Jayhawk offense. Rodgers reached into the KU quarterback cupboard and found a junior southpaw with no starting experience by the name of Bobby Douglass.

Douglass had an ambition in life. He wanted to be an All-American. He had all the All-American attributes — good body, well-chiseled features, blond hair, and, most importantly, a head coach who would build an offense around his skills.

Douglass had been born in Manhattan, Kansas, and had trouble as a youngster choosing between baseball and football. He played Little League and threw so hard the mothers in El Dorado thought seriously of a protest march. But he was the product of a family whose life centered on football, and it eventually became obvious that he would concentrate his efforts as a quarterback.

Douglass possessed a high-powered rifle for an arm. He left a trail of broken fingers and split hands around the Big Eight Conference. The Jayhawks had a wide receiver named Jim Hatcher who was often on the other end of a Douglass bullet pass.

During a game, Douglass forced Hatcher to dive low to try to dig a dart out of the dirt. The football struck his hand with such force that it split, and six stitches were needed to sew it up.

Pepper's first season in Lawrence was relatively average. With no real possibility of a bowl berth, the Hawks held a 4-5 record when Mizzou arrived in Lawrence for the season-finale with a sparkling 7-2 record and a share of second place in the conference. KU had not defeated the Tigers in the previous six encounters and had not won at home against Missouri since 1957. Most observers thought the string would continue.

Pepper knew it was be a meaningful game, and he demonstrated his enthusiasm when the team ran out on the field. A few minutes before kickoff, Pepper sprinted out of the locker room with his team in pursuit. As he dashed onto the field, he turned a somersault. It represents one of the most memorable exhibitions by a coach that I can remember.

Perhaps the somersault was symbolic. Pepper was in the process of turning Kansas football upside down as well.

The Tigers out rushed, out passed, and out-returned Kansas, but the Jayhawks made the big plays all afternoon. The season ended in impressive fashion with a 17-6 victory.

The win gave KU a remarkable 5-2 conference mark, compared with a 0-6-1 record the previous season. Douglass ended the year ranked No. 8 in the country in total offense and earned all-conference honors for his performance. Rodgers shared Big Eight Coach of the Year honors with Chuck Fairbanks of Oklahoma.

There was a great deal of excitement when the KU coaching staff and team gathered in late August. I feel safe in saying there has never been a more impressive collection of football coaches and players at KU than that assembled for the start of that 1968 season.

Adding to the already impressive cast of assistants, Pepper had hired 24-year-old Terry Donahue to coach the defensive line. Donahue would later become the winningest head coach in UCLA history.

The Jayhawk roster was loaded with players who would later earn paychecks for playing football on Sunday. KU returned 26 lettermen, including 17 of 22 starters from its Big Eight runner-up team of 1967.

An infusion of high-octane power was added to the roster that fall in the form of 225-pound sophomore John Riggins. In its preseason college football preview, *Sports Illustrated* tabbed Riggins as one of the top five sophomores in the country.

John had been one of the most highly sought prep stars in the country following a brilliant career at Centralia High. The middle son of Frank Riggins, a railroad agent, John was a high school All-American in football, all-state in basketball, and the state's Class B 100-yard dash champion as a junior and senior.

"He did everything but sell popcorn and programs," said Fambrough.

Pepper had created a winning environment, and KU had enough talent in 1968 to inspire talk of a postseason bowl. Most observers thought Kansas was a team on the rise but not quite ready for prime time. Kansas was picked third behind Oklahoma and Nebraska in the Big Eight. Among the national soothsayers, only *Sports Illustrated* had the foresight to rank KU in its Top 25, picking the Jayhawks 20th.

Pepper put a big emphasis that season on the Jayhawks' first encounter against Illinois on the road. Beating a Big Ten powerhouse on its home turf would provide instant confidence and credibility. Jayhawk football teams had established a reputation for playing poorly in their season openers. Kansas had lost three consecutive season openers and had won its initial game just twice in the previous 15 seasons.

A sign posted on a bulletin board near the team dressing room read: "It's time for a change." The sign's unknown author would be proven prophetic.

With Douglass at the controls, the Jayhawk offense struck quickly and often. After taking a 20-0 lead into halftime, KU routed Illinois, 47-7. Riggins, operating off the bench, made his varsity debut with 45 yards on seven carries.

The Hawks continued to roll through the season.

After winning their first three games, the Jayhawks went to Lincoln in an eagerly anticipated game against Nebraska. Kansas would risk its undefeated record and its No. 6 national ranking against ninth-ranked Nebraska in Lincoln. The Jayhawks entered the game leading the nation in scoring with a 51-point average. Fittingly, the Cornhuskers featured one of the nation's top defenses.

The largest crowd in Big Eight Conference history, 67,119, sat under cloudy skies on a warm, muggy afternoon to witness one of the finest, most fiercely waged struggles ever fought in the long series between the two schools.

The Huskers led 6-0 at halftime, but the Jayhawks took advantage of Nebraska mistakes and scored nine unanswered points in the third quarter. The home team had the stadium rocking when it took the lead, 13-9, with just under 10 minutes remaining. But the Jayhawks were not finished.

KU, behind Douglass, stormed back and captured its first win (23-13) in Lincoln since 1961.

The Jayhawks won their next three and took an undefeated 7-0 into the game with Oklahoma. The Sooners stunned KU with a 27-23 win. The Hawks moved up the polls throughout the year, reaching as high as No. 3 for three weeks — before dropping the OU game. The defeat also knocked KU out of the conference lead. Missouri, undefeated in five games, moved in front. KU would conclude its regular season schedule with road trips to Kansas State and Missouri.

"Purple Pride" had been Vince Gibson's battle cry from the day he set foot in Manhattan. KU fans countered with crimson –and blue buttons that simply read, P.O.P.P. — translated, "Piss On Purple Pride."

No one fueled the rivalry better than Pepper and Vince. The intensity of the Jayhawk-Wildcat rivalry had simmered down somewhat since the days of Phog Allen and Jack Gardner in basketball, but it was now heating back up, thanks to the verbal punches from Pepper and Vince.

Against the Wildcats, Riggins ripped the K-State defense apart, finishing the day with 189 yards — including an 83-yard scamper — as the Jayhawks won, 39-29.

The following Monday, KU's football future unfolded when the Jayhawks learned they would spend New Year's in Miami. Rodgers and Stinson officially accepted a bid to face Penn State in the Orange Bowl on New Year's night in Miami. A crowd of more than 4,500 smiling students, many armed with sacks of oranges in anticipation of the news, gathered outside Strong Hall and cheered loudly when the news of the bowl was announced.

The bowl bid was secure, but a prize that was just as meaningful was at stake for the winner of the Kansas-Missouri confrontation that Saturday. Beyond the coveted bragging rights, a share of the conference title would go to the winner. The 7-2 Tigers had accepted a bid to play Alabama in the Gator Bowl, and more than 62,000 of their fans were anxious to see the Jayhawks' glorious regular season end on a sour note.

But the Jayhawks were stubborn and spoiled the Tigers' hopes for a title with a 21-19 victory. With the exception of the 27-23 loss to Oklahoma, the only game Kansas didn't win by at least 10 points was the MU game.

Kansas finished with a 9-1 regular-season record and shared the conference championship with Oklahoma. Douglass and John Zook were rewarded with first-team All-America honors. The Jayhawks placed six players — Douglass, Zook, Emery Hicks, John Mosier, Keith Christensen and John Riggins — on the all-conference team. Pepper shared conference Coach of the Year honors with Missouri's Dan Devine.

KU athletics department officials rushed to reward their second-year coach with a hefty pay raise, signing him to a new five-year contract shortly after the season. "The football program is in the hands of the most capable and knowledgeable individual I know," said Stinson in announcing the agreement.

Meanwhile, the Jayhawks prepared for their Orange Bowl game against powerful Penn State. KU officials had no problems selling their allotment of 12,500 tickets.

The trip to Miami and the Orange Bowl rekindled special memories for Fambrough and me. Fam had been a player on the Jayhawks' 1948 Orange Bowl team, while I was a young announcer who had spent the year covering KU. I had traveled to Miami in 1947 with a fraternity buddy, Robert Docking. This time around, Docking arrived at the Orange Bowl as governor of Kansas, and I remained an announcer. Once again, due to the restrictions of the bowl contract, I was not allowed to broadcast the game. I spent the evening in the press box, spotting for NBC radio.

Fam and I were not the only members of the KU travel party with memories of the Orange Bowl. Pepper had been an Orange Bowl hero. His last-minute field goal provided the winning margin in the 1952 classic for Georgia Tech. Pepper, in fact, became the first individual to both play and serve as head coach of a team in the New Year's Day bowl.

The team was treated in grand fashion upon its arrival. The Orange Bowl queen and her court welcomed the coaches and players with sacks of oranges at the Miami airport. Among the girls in the court was Victoria Principal, who would later achieve fame in television and movies.

It was a balmy 65 degrees when the two teams opened play in the 35th Orange Bowl Classic. The stadium was packed with 77,719 excited fans.

Penn State dominated play early in the game, but mistakes kept the Nittany Lions out of the end zone. KU got on the board first, thanks in part to an interception by Pat Hutchins. The Jayhawks moved 45 yards in nine plays as fullback Mike Reeves bulled in from two yards out with his first touchdown of the season. Penn State scored a second-quarter touchdown, and the two teams entered the dressing room at intermission locked in a 7-7 tie.

Defense dominated the third quarter, and neither team could find the end zone.

Early in the fourth quarter, Donnie Shanklin, who would earn MVP honors for KU in the game, fielded a Penn State punt at the KU 47, got a timely block from Hicks and skirted down the south sidelines, reversed his field, spun off a would-be tackler, and finally was lassoed from behind on the 7. Riggins carried to the 1 and scored on the next play with 12:38 remaining.

The KU defense stopped Penn State once again and the Jayhawks, on their next possession, marched downfield to the PSU 5-yard line, where the Jayhawks faced a fourth-and-one. A field goal would have given KU a 17-7 lead, but Pepper Rodgers decided to try for a first down. Riggins was stacked up at the line of scrimmage, and Penn State took over.

With just 2:04 remaining in the game, KU forced a Penn State punt. The Jayhawks needed to run out the clock to earn a victory. Twice Douglass was thrown for losses, and KU was forced to punt. Bill Bell's kick was deflected and rolled dead at the 50 with just 1:16 left in the game. When the KU defense trotted onto the field there was confusion. The Jayhawks would have 12 men in the game for the final three plays of the Lions' scoring drive.

Penn State quarterback Chuck Burkhart lofted a ball high to halfback Bob Campbell, who caught it and was run out of bounds at the 3. Twice, Penn State tried dive plays up the middle that KU stopped. Finally, Burkhart kept the ball, sweeping around left end for the score to make it 14-13 with just 15 seconds left to play.

KU linebacker Rick Abernathy should have left the field after the score. The Kansas substitution system called for the replacement to twice bang a player's shoulder pads and shout his name. But that never happened.

Penn State elected to go for two points and the win. Burkhart tried a pass into the end zone that was knocked down, and the Jayhawks started to celebrate. It may have been the shortest victory celebration in Orange Bowl history. The Jayhawks were finally penalized for having too many players on the field. This time, the Nittany Lions ran a power sweep and found the end zone to win the game.

The game was a huge disappointment. Our room was in the players' section of the hotel. We didn't get much sleep. I have seldom heard a more frustrated group of players. They cursed, roamed the halls, and generally expressed their disappointment. The hubbub lasted all night.

Despite the heartbreaking defeat, it had been a great season. Besides the Orange Bowl berth, nine wins were the most by a Kansas team in 60 years.

Douglass and Zook would move on to professional football. And Pepper lost assistant coach Dave McClain, who took a job on Woody Hayes' staff at Ohio State.

The cover of the 1969 Kansas football media guide pictured serious-looking kicker Bill Bell and smiling KU pompon girl Jan Merrick. They posed with Merrick holding the football while Bell approached as if to kick. The only thing unusual about the cover was Bell's jersey number: 100.

I think this was another Pepper Rodgers original. The '69 season marked college football's centennial year, and Pepper decided to pose his kicker in jersey Number 100 to commemorate the anniversary.

Pepper had stirred excitement in Lawrence. The bandwagon was unbelievably crowded — season-ticket sales soared to a school-record 28,000. KU returned standouts such as Riggins, Mosier and Hicks. Senior Jim Ettinger, who had spent the first two years of his career as an understudy to Douglass, would earn the nod as the Jayhawk starting quarterback.

Kansas fans entered that season full of hope but quickly found catastrophe. Anticipation turned into shock. After a stunning opening night loss at Texas Tech, the Hawks came back the next week and beat Syracuse in Lawrence. That was the only win of the season. KU's nightmare 100th season of football ended with a 1-9 record.

At the tail end of the disastrous 1969 football season — a year in which the Jayhawks won just once in 10 outings — Pepper Rodgers launched his weekly television show by taking the form of an ersatz corpse.

Viewers who tuned in that cool November night were greeted with a solemn view of a lone coffin. Emerging from the wooden casket, a la Frankenstein, was a smiling Rodgers declaring, "We're not dead yet." Shortly afterwards, he switched from the funeral to the festive, singing the first chorus of "Rudolph the Red Nosed Reindeer." That was vintage Pepper Rodgers. Even in the worst of times, he could trigger a smile.

The season did give birth, however, to a legendary moment in the KU-Missouri rivalry. The game itself wasn't spectacular, a 69-21 drubbing by the Tigers. But, rather, something that happened on the sidelines.

Other voices from The Hill • Don Fambrough

Dan Devine is the coach at Missouri and they are laying it on KU pretty good.

Pepper says, "My God, they were just killing us. I flashed the peace sign over to Devine on the other side of the field, and he gave half of it back to me. "

Although we'd see a couple changes heading into the 1970 season, there was one in particular that didn't set well with me. The old Memorial Stadium grass field — which had held the spikes of Evans, Hadl, Sayers and Douglass — was plowed away and replaced with a $240,000 artificial green rug. I love a grass field. To me, it's fundamental to the game. I'm not a fan of the artificial surfaces. It seems to insult a stadium's integrity.

Rodgers did manage to pull off a significant recruiting coup when he beat out Paul "Bear" Bryant at Alabama and a host of other teams to sign David Jaynes, a quarterback from Bonner Springs, Kansas, who was regarded as the top high-school player in the state.

Pepper's fourth season on Mount Oread kicked off in successful fashion as the Jayhawks and Washington State showed little regard for one another's defenses. Kansas won the explosive game, 48-31, as Riggins was out of the gates with 125 yards and two touchdowns in front of 34,000 at Memorial Stadium.

The Jayhawks then reeled off wins in four of their next five outings, including a 21-15 victory over Kansas State in Manhattan. Kansas won just one more game the rest of the season. The Jayhawks finished the year with an unremarkable 5-6 record.

It was not an eventful season for Kansas but enjoyable from my point of view, as I watched the curly-haired John Riggins. John responded to the challenge of his senior year, rushing for 1,131 yards to set a school single-season record. He also finished his career with 2,706 yards to move past Gale Sayers as the Jayhawks' career-leading rusher.

The following January saw the migration of another Jayhawk coach. Pepper ended his magical four-year reign as the Jayhawks' boss when he resigned to become head coach at UCLA. Pepper broke a 23-year streak by becoming the first KU coach since George Sauer in 1947 to resign and not be fired from the job.

The Rodgers era at Kansas, so saturated with memories, was over.

Coaches with the wit, wisdom and charm of Pepper have become an endangered species. I treasure that brief, four-year episode of my broadcast career.

Stinson wasted no time in locating Pepper's replacement. He walked into Don Fambrough's office and told Fam he was going to be the next coach at KU. Fam was speechless.

Although I was saddened to see Pepper depart, no one was happier to see Don Fambrough finally achieve his lifelong ambition.

Fam's loyalty was finally being rewarded.

Chapter 9

Smiling Ted

Ted Owens developed a reputation as a skillful coach during his four years as an assistant to Dick Harp. The Jayhawk staff brought in talented freshmen, and Owens molded them into a winning team. Owens, in fact, was having more success with the freshmen than Harp was having with the varsity.

There was a notion among a few KU supporters that Dick wasn't able to develop Owens' good freshmen and that Harp didn't know how to use talent when he had it, but that Ted did. I bristled every time the issue bubbled up. It was a foolish conclusion regarding Harp — considering that he had guided two KU teams to the Final Four — but it certainly helped Owens' ascension into the head-coaching chair following Harp's decision to relinquish the position in the summer of 1964.

Ted was open and cheerful, always eager to display a bright smile. Plus he had demonstrated a degree of coaching wizardry. He understood the massive responsibility that went with the Kansas territory. The previous two coaches had guided Jayhawk teams to the Final Four.

Ted Owens had been a standout guard at Oklahoma from 1948 to 1950. He was a three-year letterman under Coach Bruce Drake. After graduation, Owens had tremendous success at Cameron State Junior College in Lawton, Oklahoma. He joined Harp's staff in 1960 after Jerry Waugh left to enter private business.

The 35-year-old Owens became the first non-KU grad to guide the Jayhawks since W.O. Hamilton, a William Jewell alumnus, coached his final season in 1919.

But Ted recognized the power of KU's basketball legacy and looked for opportunities to fan that tradition. He wanted a visible reminder of those glory days and ordered the team locker room painted with the names of KU greats. He also commissioned an artist to develop a mural depicting scenes of notable KU triumphs.

From the very beginning, Ted worked to restore pride in the program. He was anxious to shed the Jayhawks' non-threatening label.

Other voices from The Hill • Roger Morningstar

We had what we thought was a great coaching staff. As they talk about chemistry on a team, there also has to be chemistry on the coaching staff. We called Coach Owens "Smiling Ted," because he always had an arm around you, asking how you were doing. Always being very positive. Then we had Sam Miranda, the drill sergeant. You wouldn't dare look at him wrong, or you were dead. When Ted came out and was in his normal mood, everything was great. When he tried to get mean, it was kind of funny. We never laughed, because we always had respect. But there were times that you started wiping the sweat from your mouth to hide the smile.

KU was far from desperate when Owens took over in 1964-65. But the team's stock as a challenger for the conference title dipped when George Unseld, a 6-7 all-league center and the club's top scorer and rebounder during the previous two years, quit the day after Thanksgiving. Also, 6-4 Steve Renko — third on the team in scoring as a sophomore — gave up basketball to concentrate on baseball and football.

Kansas won three of its first six games in Owens' debut season and then won seven in a row. Meanwhile, Miranda was busy shopping for new and better talent.

He was spending most of his time in St. Louis on the doorstep of a basketball prodigy at McKinley High School by the name of Joseph White.

Other voices from The Hill • Sam Miranda

I'm very prejudiced, but I would have to say JoJo White was the best guard ever to play in the Big Eight. In fact, he was the best guard in the Big Eight the day we got him. JoJo was a mid-year graduate and I knew that. I called a good friend of mine who was coaching in St. Louis and I asked him who the best juniors in St. Louis were. He said, "The best player by far is JoJo White. ... You don't even have to come back and see him. If you can get him, take him." So I called JoJo and went back to visit with him and his parents. I sat down with the family and Jodie Bailey, his high school coach. Now, Jodie Bailey was the key reason we were able to get JoJo.

I went back a lot, and in those days, you could take kids out to dinner. There was one instance when we were at dinner and I went through my pitch about KU and the role JoJo would play with us. Afterwards, Jodie says, "JoJo, that sounds good to me." That's all it took. He decided to come right then and there. He came for a visit and was here the day Gale Sayers took the opening kickoff against Oklahoma 93 yards for a touchdown. The Jayhawks won the game, 15-14, and all the students stormed the field. JoJo was impressed with all that.

JoJo White enrolled at Kansas in the spring of 1965, giving KU a much-needed franchise player for the following season.

Kansas finished 1964-65 with a 17-8 mark and placed second in the Big Eight. With all five starters returning and the much-heralded JoJo White already in the hopper, high expectations were inevitable.

It was not a good year in the Falkenstien family. A lot more than basketball was on my mind that season. My father had been diagnosed with lung cancer during the Christmas holidays. Dad had been a regular smoker for most of his life, but he had quit 10 years earlier after reading "You Can Quit Smoking If You Want To" in *Readers' Digest*. However, a later eruption on his lip, where he had let the cigarette lie, was a precursor of things to come.

The cancer was inoperable. We took him daily to the KU Medical Center for radiation and chemotherapy treatments, but he passed away at age 68 on April 12, 1965.

Dad was a kind and gentle man, very short in stature but very much respected and loved by all the coaches and athletes who came in contact with him during his more than 32 years as business manager for the athletic department. He had been a close associate of Phog Allen, E.C. Quigley, Dutch Lonborg and all the head and assistant coaches.

In the years since his death, whenever I see anyone who knew him, they never fail to tell me how much they thought of him. In Dad's day, it was a lot different than today. He was not only the business manager but also the ticket manager. He knew by heart where everyone's season ticket was and personally handled all the money collected for ticket sales, disbursed the money for expense trips, and made all the travel arrangements for the teams. Dad did what three or four other people do today.

By the start of the second semester, the Jayhawks were 15-3, having dropped games against UCLA, Southern California and Nebraska.

Waiting his turn in the Jayhawk bullpen was White, who became eligible at the start of the second semester. Owens wrestled with the perplexing question of whether to play White and risk unraveling team chemistry.

Other voices from The Hill • Ted Owens

At midterm, we knew we had a good team. What we sensed was that this was a team that could win the national championship. I asked Jo what he wanted to do and he said, "I want to play right now." I talked to our captain, Riney Lochmann, and I said, "Riney, we're trying to make a decision about JoJo.

"JoJo wants to play. He feels we have a great chance, and I feel that we have a great chance to win the national championship. But one thing is important: If he plays, he will be a starter and that means that you may not start."

Riney said to me, "Coach, it doesn't matter whether I start or not. We think JoJo can help us to win the national championship, and we want him to play." That sealed it as far as I was concerned.

White's first game as a Jayhawk came against Oklahoma State in early February, before a packed house in Lawrence. JoJo was the last player to depart the dressing room for the court that afternoon. As he passed Owens, he paused and smiled. "I'm all right, coach," he said.

JoJo buried a long-range jumper moments after his first touch of the ball that day. With his dazzling acceleration, he brought a new and exciting dimension to the lineup. Kansas dominated the Cowboys, 59-38, and proceeded to collect three more lopsided victories.

Then came the all-important rematch with Nebraska at Allen Fieldhouse.

Both teams entered the game ranked in the Top 10. Nebraska, coached by the flamboyant Joe Cipriano, played an up-tempo game and liked to full-court press. Instead of having White bring the ball up against the press, Owens stationed him at midcourt. The Jayhawks lobbed over the press to JoJo, and he attacked the basket. It proved to be a complete mismatch as Kansas swarmed past Nebraska, 110-73.

Owens later called it one of the great games in Kansas basketball history.

The Jayhawks ended the year by reeling off wins against Kansas State and Colorado to collect their 32nd conference championship and earn a bid to the

NCAA Tournament. Kansas had been dominating since White was inserted into the lineup, winning games by an average of 26.4 points an outing.

Kansas, 22-3, was sent to Lubbock, Texas, to face Southern Methodist in first-round tournament action. After taking care of the Mustangs, 76-70, the Hawks were one win from the Final Four.

Kansas faced Texas Western in the regional finals, and it was a tight game from the start. For the first time in his short college career, White would feel the pressure of an all-the-marbles finish.

The two teams ended regulation even at 69-69. The tension mounted in the first overtime. The final seconds ticked down with the game tied — each team had managed to score just two points.

Other voices from The Hill • Sam Miranda

In my opinion, the 1965-66 team was the best that has ever played at Kansas. We had five or six guys that played professional basketball. You have to keep that in mind when you consider that JoJo wanted the last shot to win the game against Texas Western. Here he is, a college sophomore, just eight games or so into his career; and he kept saying, "Let me take it. Let me take it." We had total confidence in him, and we designed something to get him the shot. He takes the ball behind some screens, and takes about a 28-footer and it goes in. We thought we had won the game. But they said his heel had touched the out-of-bounds line. We would have won the national championship if we had won that game.

The Jayhawks were staring squarely at a victory and Final Four journey when referee Rudy Marich waved the basket off, pointing to the out-of-bounds line. The contest went into a second overtime, and the Miners took full advantage of the opportunity, outlasting the Jayhawks, 81-80. Texas Western later defeated Kentucky to win the NCAA Championship.

In just his second season as head coach, Owens had easily reestablished the Kansas basketball tradition. He had guided the Jayhawks to a conference championship and come within a single point of the Final Four.

That summer brought a memorable day in my broadcasting career, as well as my personal life. It was the afternoon of June 8 and, at the time I was manager of WREN Radio in Topeka. Isobel and I lived at 2003 Brooklyn, between Burnett's Mound and Washburn University.

That afternoon, we had a men's golf stag at Topeka Country Club. Invited to be special guests and provide the evening program were KU assistant coach Don Fambrough and John Hadl. It had been cloudy all day, but we finished the golf match. By about 6:30 p.m., the skies in the west had darkened considerably, developing an ugly greenish hue.

I decided to get down to the radio studios at 10th and Fillmore, because it looked like we were in for a big storm, and WREN prided itself on its weather coverage. Our WRENMOBILE was routinely dispatched to a weather-watching position, and on this night Rick Douglass, one of our disc jockeys, was in the mobile unit, serving as a weather spotter. He was on his way to Burnett's Mound, a high position where he could look to the southwest. (Indian legend had it that the land occupied by the city of Topeka would never be hit by a tornado because Burnett's Mound would blunt it and cause it to veer away. How wrong the legend was.)

Meanwhile, the Weather Bureau had reports of a tornado over Auburn, heading right for Burnett's Mound and the center of Topeka. Shortly after 7 p.m., the Weather Bureau issued a take-cover, and we interrupted all programming to report it. We switched to Douglass. He confirmed that a huge storm was heading our way and told everyone to take immediate cover.

He never made it to the top of the mound. As the tornado hit, he jumped out of the car and dove under a culvert. He was seriously injured. The *Topeka Capital-Journal* ran a picture of him in the emergency room, covered in mud with a broken Coke bottle imbedded in the back of his head. Fortunately, he recovered.

The WRENMOBILE was later found several blocks away. Unquestionably we saved dozens, if not hundreds, of lives with our warning.

It was, however, Bill Kurtis of WIBW-TV who achieved national fame for his warning: "For God's sake, take immediate cover." Our coverage was equally effective, but because our station wasn't owned by the local newspaper, we didn't receive as much credit. I was at the studio microphone, broadcasting every report I could get. When it became obvious the storm was headed directly for us, the engineer and I ran to the basement. During our 10 minutes under cover, we could hear the tornado roar by about two blocks south of us. (Miraculously, it skipped over the Falkenstien house.) Someone came by later and said that Washburn University had been destroyed, and it nearly had been. It was a terrible night that I will never forget.

In the end, the storm was responsible for 16 deaths with over 500 injured and more than $100 million in damage.

As KU went through the 1966-67 season, winning its first six games by an average of 22 points, Miranda searched for future Jayhawks.

His efforts fueled KU's budding dynasty. During the spring of 1967, Kansas signed 6-10 Roger Brown and 6-9 Dave Robisch. The Jayhawks also landed 6-4 Pierre Russell from Kansas City.

Kansas was a dominating team in the second half of the 1966-67 season. Aside from a 62-59 loss at Colorado (the Buffaloes scored three points in the final five seconds for the victory), the closest league game in a 13-1 conference season was a 60-55 win at Kansas State.

The Jayhawks claimed another conference title and finished the regular season 22-3. KU served as an NCAA regional host with Houston as its first opponent.

Louisville and SMU were paired on the opposite side of the bracket.

The fairy-tale season came to an end, though, as Houston won the game, 66-53. The Jayhawks returned the following night to down Louisville, 70-68, in the third-place game. KU finished the year 23-4, matching its record of the previous season.

During the year, I made a career switch, moving from WREN to WIBW-TV as manager of news and sports. Leaving WREN was a difficult decision. I had spent my entire adult career at the station, eventually becoming general manager. My staff and I had labored hard, and WREN was well regarded in Topeka. In the early 1950s, I had negotiated the purchase of WREN by Alf M. Landon from the Jackman family in Lawrence. Landon already owned KSCB in Liberal, and he was interested in acquiring additional properties.

The governor was not an easy man to work for. It was a frustrating existence but a satisfying one as the station progressed. One day, Wayne Duke, the commissioner of the Big Eight Conference, called and asked me to do the television play-by-play on the league's Saturday afternoon game of the week. This was "the plum" of sportscasting in the area at that time. TV stations in seven states carried the games. I approached Mr. Landon and told him of this opportunity. I said that although we were in radio, the exposure I would obtain from this assignment would make me an even more salable product for all the other games I would be doing on WREN. Landon refused to allow my work in TV, saying: "We are not going to promote TV when we are in the radio business."

That night I called Thad Sandstrom, the vice president of WIBW-AM-

FM-TV in Topeka and asked if I could talk to him.

We met, and the next day he offered me the position of manager of news and sports at the Stauffer stations. Although I hated to leave, I took the job.

I did the Big Eight TV series for four years and enjoyed it immensely. When Wayne left to go to the Big Ten, Chuck Neinas came in and made a change. Norm Stewart, Joe Cipriano, Glen Anderson at Iowa State, and others had never liked the concept of a KU announcer doing the Big Eight series. Where Wayne had stood firm, Chuck did not.

After losing two of its first three encounters to start the 1967-68 season, Kansas won 10 of its next 11 games. Owens and Company were sending the message that they would contend for a third consecutive conference title.

But midway through the conference race, KU dropped a pair of games to Missouri and Kansas State. There would be no trip to the NCAA Tournament.

KU accepted a bid to the National Invitation Tournament at Madison Square Garden. After beating Temple, Villanova and St. Peter's, KU lost in the championship game to Dayton, 61-48. In that game, the Flyers held a 25-2 advantage from the charity stripe.

White led the Jayhawks in scoring, averaging just over 15 points, and was named to nearly every All-America team. The Jayhawks had won 22 games with only one senior — Rodger Bohnenstiehl — on the roster.

The Jayhawk coaching staff was once again having impressive results luring new talent. Kansas signed Aubrey Nash, a 6-2 guard from Hyattsville, Maryland, and Bob Kivisto, a 6-1 guard from Aurora, Illinois.

But it was the recruitment of another player — Bud Stallworth, a 6-5 trumpet-playing forward from Hartselle, Alabama — that became legend in KU basketball annals. He was "discovered" while attending a music camp at KU.

Other voices from The Hill • Bud Stallworth

I was staying in Templin Hall on the Hill, and there was an intramural program for the campers, and we got the opportunity to play a little basketball in our off-time.

I had made friends with another camper, and he told me I was wasting my time playing with the kids in the camp. He told me, "There are a bunch of guys who play at Robinson Gym, and they play real good basketball." I didn't have a lot of free time, but I found out there was a game every day around noon, which was perfect for my schedule.

So I started going down to Robinson and playing pick-up ball with these guys.

I got back one afternoon from one of my rehearsals and a counselor came up to me and said, "Bud, do you know who Ted Owens is? He's been calling up here to find you. He's the head basketball coach at KU." I had never heard of Coach Owens, but I decided I'd better call. So I called him and he told me that some of the guys who play for KU had told him I was a pretty good player. He also said that he had never heard of me. I explained that I played on a team from a small high school in Hartselle, Alabama. I told him that Alabama was a football state and that basketball was not a real big thing in my town. I also mentioned that I shouldn't be playing basketball at the camp because my father didn't want me to get hit in the mouth.

We talked for awhile, and Coach Owens indicated that based on what the players had told him, Kansas would be recruiting me. I had been playing against JoJo White, Vernon Vanoy, Rich Bradshaw and Bob Wilson.

Kansas was on the cusp of a great athletic year in 1968-69. The Jayhawk football team was Orange Bowl-bound when basketball season opened in late November. White had certified himself as a college basketball star by helping lead the USA to the gold medal in the 1968 Olympic Games in Mexico City.

Because JoJo had enrolled at KU at mid-semester and played those nine games as a sophomore, he had just one semester of eligibility remaining his senior year.

The Jayhawks played 18 games during the first semester, so Owens opted to use JoJo at the start.

Kansas played well early in the year, winning 13 of its first 14 games, including the conference holiday tournament. The year was full of basketball drama with an abundance of story lines to follow. Owens approached the 100-career-victory plateau at Kansas, and the Jayhawks had an opportunity to become the first school to win 1,000 basketball games.

Other voices from The Hill • Ted Owens

We were in a battle with Kentucky to see who was going to be the first team there. We thought we were going to be No. 1. In fact, we won a couple of games at Stanford and Utah State. I told the guys that if you win these two, we are going to beat Kentucky.

Then just before we were getting ready to win that 1,000th game, we picked up the paper and Adolph (Rupp) and all them together down at Kentucky, they had a cake and they said they had won their 1,000th game. They figured out that in 1902 or whatever it was, they had beaten the Lexington YMCA twice. We had really built up as a big thing to be No. 1 and be the first to win 1,000 games. We didn't think there was any doubt we were going to be the first. Then they found those records.

During his 19 years as KU's head coach, Ted Owens (right) won 348 games.

JoJo White's final appearance in Jayhawk silks came February 1 against Colorado in Allen Fieldhouse. The backcourt wizard had become the highest-scoring guard in Kansas history and averaged a team-high 18.1 points in his final season.

White gave a virtuoso performance against the Buffs. He scored a career-high 30 points as the Jayhawks took an 80-70 victory. After the game, Owens presented White with the game ball in recognition of his brilliant career. It was also a milestone victory for Owens, the 100th in his KU career.

Two nights later, the Jayhawks hosted Oklahoma State and recorded the coveted 1,000th victory in school history. The game produced one of the lasting images in my broadcast career. Midway through the second half, Owens ripped out the seat of his plaid trousers and was forced to cover his posterior with a white towel.

Needless to say, it was an unusual sight to see a towel covering Owens' backside as he handed Chancellor W. Clarke Wescoe the game ball in a courtside ceremony following the win.

White was an indispensable part of the team. The Jayhawks won five of the six games after his departure but dropped a 75-67 decision to Colorado that secured the title for the Buffs. Kansas again accepted an invitation to play in the NIT but was quickly ousted, 78-62, by Boston College.

The Jayhawks were in a building phase as they entered a new decade. The 1969-70 team had plenty of firepower, but they finished the year with a 17-9 record and placed second in the Big Eight for the third consecutive year. For the first time in five years they wouldn't be seeing postseason play.

The Jayhawks appeared big, deep and talented when they opened practice for the 1970-71 season. Back in the fold were Robisch and the always-hustling Russell. Roger Brown returned at center with backup support available in 6-10 sophomore Randy Canfield. Kivisto, Nash and Stallworth gave the Jayhawks three high-voltage guards.

Kansas opened the season by hosting Long Beach and its towel-chewing coach Jerry Tarkanian. The game started with a bomb threat in Allen Fieldhouse, but the Jayhawks provided the only explosion during the evening. Displaying superior firepower and an unyielding defense, KU built a 42-8 half-time advantage in the contest. It was torture for Tarkanian.

Beginning with a 33-point win over Missouri the day after Christmas, the 6-1 Jayhawks overcame an assortment of challenges and never lost another regular season game. They ran off a string of 21 consecutive wins and compiled a perfect 14-0 mark in the Big Eight. At that point, only the 1959 Kansas State team had achieved an unbeaten conference season.

A conference title brought KU an invitation to be in the NCAA Tournament.

KU went to Wichita for regional play and got 29 points from Robisch and 25 from Stallworth for a 78-77 victory over Houston. Robisch had 27 two nights later in a 73-71 win over Drake. The charmed Jayhawks had earned a trip to the Final Four at the Astrodome in Houston.

Kansas entered the Tournament with a sparkling 27-1 record and was matched against UCLA, which featured Sidney Wicks, Curtis Rowe, Steve Patterson and Henry Bibby. The Bruins had won the previous six NCAA Tournaments.

Other voices from The Hill • Bud Stallworth

The mystique of UCLA didn't bother us. The thing that bothered us was the first game going into overtime. We were ready to go, but there was a delay. I think it hurt us emotionally. Henry Bibby had the game of his life. Patterson hit some big shots. It was just one of those games we didn't win.

Kansas dropped the third-place game, 77-75, to Western Kentucky. Disregarding their Final Four meltdown, Kansas had enjoyed a remarkable season. and a 27-3 record.

That summer, I left WIBW and moved to Lawrence to serve as general manager of the new cable television franchise. Dolph Simons, who owned the *Lawrence Journal-World* and Sunflower Cable, made me an attractive offer to get the station up and running. I had grown tired of doing the 10:15 p.m. sports on television and this opportunity would get me back to regular hours.

After about a year at Sunflower, I approached Odd Williams, who was president of Douglas County Bank in Lawrence, about a position in public relations with the bank. Odd liked the concept and hired me as a bank vice-president in June 1972.

The euphoria of a Final Four season quickly faded as the 1971-72 Jayhawks crumbled in the face of a difficult schedule. It was an abysmal performance as the Jayhawks won only three of their first nine games and never showed signs of life.

Stallworth, however, left his mark as a senior. Kansas hosted Missouri in the final home game that season and the 1952 national championship team was back in Allen Fieldhouse for a reunion.

Other voices from The Hill • Bud Stallworth

Missouri had a player named John Brown, and there had been a quote from Norm Stewart in the paper saying that Brown was the best player in the league and he should be the Player of the Year. Norm said I had nice statistics, but Brown deserved the award. I guess that bothered me.

I was sitting in my apartment that morning, not really feeling well. My mom had come to Lawrence, and it would be the first time she had seen me play in Allen Fieldhouse. She called me, and I told her I wasn't feeling well. She said, "Just go out and do your best." My roommate was Aubrey Nash and I told him this was an important day. He said, "Bud, you just get open, and I'll get you the ball." Norm started out with a small, quick guard on me. Then he went to a bigger, heavier player. It helped starting out with a smaller player. I was taller than he was and just as quick. I loved shooting the basketball, and once I got in the zone, it didn't matter who was on me. All I had to do was run to a spot, and Aubrey got me the ball. I hit a few jump shots and felt the flow of the game. I couldn't have written a better script for myself. When they introduced me, I ran on the floor and threw a Frisbee into the crowd that had been signed by all the players. I later learned that the Frisbee became part of a property settlement in a divorce.

A sign unfurled before the game left a clear message: "When you say Bud Stallworth, you've said it all." And the KU band followed with the jingle from the popular beer commercial. Stallworth poured in 50 points that day, connecting on 19 of 38 shots. His point total was a record for a Big Eight Conference game and the second-highest point total in Kansas history. Only Wilt Chamberlain's 52-point game against Northwestern in 1957 was bigger.

Kansas defeated Missouri, 93-80, but lost its final two games to finish with an 11-15 record.

Stallworth led the team with a 25.3 average and earned all-conference and All-America honors. Stallworth, the only Jayhawk to average in double figures, was also named Player of the Year in the conference.

By the time the 1973-74 season arrived, Kansas was a team anxious to showcase its talents. Tom Kivisto was a senior and emerging as a leader. He had averaged only 8.6 points his junior season but earned Most Valuable Player honors for his overall play. Rick Suttle gave the Jayhawks a player with the potential to dominate games. The veteran trio of Dale Greenlee, Kivisto and Danny Knight were all versatile players.

Miranda had spotted a 6-6, 210-pound forward by the name of Roger Morningstar during a trip to the National Junior College Tournament in Hutchinson, Kansas. Morningstar had averaged 18 points in leading Olney (Ill.) Junior College to a third-place finish in the tournament. Roger joined KU and gave the Jayhawks another outside scoring threat.

Perhaps the final ingredient that turned the 1973-74 Jayhawk squad from a good team into an outstanding one was 6-8 freshman Norm Cook, a high-school All-American from Lincoln, Illinois. From the moment he hit the practice floor, it was obvious that Norm had star potential. To secure

Cook's services, Owens hired his high school coach — Duncan Reid — as an assistant coach.

It was a compelling blend of veterans and brassy, young talent that inspired a wave of optimism among KU fans who longed for an opportunity for postseason tournament play. But KU was out of sync early, posting a 5-3 record after back-to-back losses to Vanderbilt and Colorado.

Other voices from The Hill • Roger Morningstar

There were two turning points in that season. We played Vanderbilt early in the year, and they had a pretty good team that season. They kicked our butt real good. We played real ugly. We flew home and rode back to Allen Fieldhouse from the airport. About five minutes before we arrived, Coach Owens stood up in the bus and told us we had 10 minutes to get our ankles taped and be out on the practice floor. They worked us about three or four hours. I think he wanted someone to quit. We all hung in there. It really got our attention.

The other time was after we lost to Colorado in the holiday tournament. We had a team meeting, and all the players were sitting around trying to figure out what's wrong. Finally, Kivisto raised his hand and said, "Coach, I'll tell you what the problem is. We don't like this offense." We were all shocked that Tom would come out and say that in front of coach. But Coach Owens reacted in a positive way. He asked what we didn't like about it, and we talked through the problems.

From that point on, we had an entirely different team. It was amazing.

The Jayhawks won 10 of their next 11 games — their only loss coming at South Bend, Indiana, against a Notre Dame team ranked No. 1 in the country.

Owens settled on a lineup with Knight at center, Morningstar and Cook on the wings, Greenlee at the off-guard and Kivisto as the point guard. He brought Suttle and Smith as the top reserves off the bench.

It was obvious early in January that Kansas would be one of college basketball's elite teams.

Once again, the Jayhawks won the close games. Six of their 14 conference games that season were decided by four points or fewer. KU trailed Oklahoma by five with 1:25 to play but rallied for a four-point victory. Against Colorado,

Cook drilled a 22-footer with 25 seconds left for a two-point win. The Jayhawks celebrated another conference championship on March 6 with a 60-55 win over Kansas State.

Kansas was dispatched to Tulsa for the NCAA Midwest Regional. After a first-round bye, the Jayhawks faced Creighton, coached by Eddie Sutton. KU trailed by five with just over seven minutes remaining, but three Morningstar jumpers helped secure a 55-54 win.

In the regional finals, Oral Roberts University played a dizzying, rapid-fire game with an assortment of skilled athletes and potent outside shooters. It was a racehorse tempo, and the Jayhawks pulled out a narrow 93-90 victory to earn Ted's second trip to the Final Four. It was a wild weekend. Ken Trickey, the ORU coach, had been arrested Friday night and charged with drunken driving. The ORU School President was going to suspend him for the KU game but had second thoughts and forgave him at the last moment, and he did coach in the game.

Owens had regained lost dignity with the 1973-74 Jayhawk team. Overcoming challenges, he had weathered the experience of two consecutive losing seasons and rebuilt KU into an exciting Final Four team.

KU arrived at the Big Dance in Greensboro, North Carolina, as a long shot. The Jayhawks probably had the fourth-best talent among the four teams. Kansas was paired against Al McGuire's Marquette team, which featured Maurice Lucas and Bo Ellis. UCLA, with Bill Walton, Keith Wilkes and Marques Johnson, faced the David Thompson-led North Carolina State Wolfpack.

Marquette employed a pesky full-court trapping defense, and the Jayhawks had trouble adjusting to the pressure. The game was tied at halftime, but the Warriors won the contest, 64-51. Kansas then lost to UCLA, 78-61, in the consolation game. It appeared for a time that there might not even be a game. Bill Walton said he would not play in a third-place contest, and Coach Wooden said if he didn't want to, he didn't have to. There was some thought the Bruins wouldn't play at all, but Walton changed his mind, did play, and the Bruins won the meaningless third place game. Soon, the NCAA eliminated third-place games. KU ended the year with a satisfying 23-7 record.

After the season, I was asked by the NCAA to interview Phog Allen on film for a special project. Phog's health had been failing him for several years, and he could no longer walk. I arrived at his home with the film crew and found Phog in that familiar KU warm-up with the ever-present towel wrapped around his neck.

We spent about an hour talking basketball with the camera rolling, and it was very enjoyable experience for me. Phog's mind was still sharp.
It would be the last time I would see Doc. Several months later — on September 16 — Phog Allen died at the age of 88. He is buried in Lawrence's Oak Hill Cemetery.

KU was once again projected as a powerhouse in 1974-75. Six lettermen, including the top five scorers, returned, making KU the preseason conference favorite.

Kansas faced an ambitious non-conference schedule with Notre Dame, Kentucky and Indiana on the menu. The Hawks lost all three of those contests.

Once KU got into conference play, however, it found success.

It boiled down to a dramatic race between Kansas State and the Jayhawks late in the season. The Wildcats held a one-game lead when they visited Allen Fieldhouse for a showdown in late February. Suttle scored 26 points, and Cook had 13 rebounds as the Jayhawks mashed K-State, 91-53, to pull even in the conference race.

Kansas found itself needing a win over Nebraska to keep its conference title hopes alive. KU had had many interesting battles with the Huskers during the Joe Cipriano years, and this proved to be one of the greatest. KU battled back from a 19-point deficit to pull within five points with 40 seconds to go in the game. The Jayhawks tied the game at the buzzer and went on to win, 79-77, in double overtime.

Other voices from The Hill • Roger Morningstar

Joe was the Billy Tubbs of that time. Everyone loved to hate him. I remember that Nebraska had a real good guard by the name of Jerry Fort. Jerry went for a driving lay-up, and Norm Cook knocked him about four rows into the stands. Norm blocked the shot, and Jerry went flying. The ball stayed in play. There could have been a foul but nothing was called. I was the wing man, and Norm grabbed the ball and I'm screaming, "Outlet, outlet ... let's go." I have my back to the basket yelling for the ball as Norm throws me the ball. I get the ball, turn, take two dribbles, and Cipriano is right there in front of me on the floor. He's spread out and says, "Roger you're not going anywhere." I had to take the ball and

just stop. That was an immediate technical. In my two years at Kansas, Joe never finished a game on the bench.
He got tossed out of both games.

Joe Cipriano developed cancer while still actively coaching, but it moved fast and was spreading all over his body. He let his assistants do most of the coaching, but he did his best to hang in there. I remember the last time we saw him — he was so gaunt and thin. Jim Valvano's death reminded me of Joe Cipriano's.

Kansas won the title outright with a 74-63 win over Oklahoma in the final game of the season, and the Jayhawks returned to Tulsa to face Notre Dame in an NCAA first-round game. The Jayhawks had lost to the Fighting Irish by 16 earlier in the season, and, once again, Notre Dame proved it was the superior team. KU made an early exit from the tournament, dropping a 77-71 decision.

KU had five players average in double figures during the 1975-76 season, but crumbled to a 13-13 record. The Jayhawks finished the conference race a disappointing fourth with a 6-8 record.

The Jayhawks showed progress in 1976-77 and finished the year with an 18-10 record.

But fans were growing restless for another conference championship, and there was a faction of KU supporters who thought it was time for a coaching change. With his job on the line, Ted shook up his staff. Sensing he was going to be fired, Sam Miranda resigned, shocking all of us.

In addition to Miranda, Duncan Reid also resigned. Owens had no problem in filling the void. In an obvious package deal, he hired Lafayette Norwood, who had guided Wichita Heights High School to an undefeated season the previous year.

Norwood brought along his star player — Darnell Valentine.

It proved to be a great stroke for Owens. Lafayette and Darnell were inseparable during their years at KU. In fact, it was a strange coach-player relationship.

They were always together. In airports, hotels, they were generally in tandem, separated from the rest of the team. I always questioned whether this was a good situation for team unity, but we never talked much about it. Owens also hired Bob Hill as his other assistant coach that season. Bob became a close friend and has had great success as an NBA coach.

Although he was just one year removed from high school, Valentine was an instant hero. He arrived at Kansas and played an extraordinary role from the start.

He was a tremendous athlete and was impressive in all phases of the game. He could dominate not only on offense but also on defense. Darnell moved immediately into the lineup, combining with Douglas, Koenigs, 7-1 center Paul Mokeski, and senior guard Clint Johnson.

The Jayhawks opened the 1977-78 season with a 121-65 win over Central Missouri. Kansas, in fact, surpassed the century mark in three of its first four outings.

Kentucky made a visit to Lawrence for an evening game on December 10. Earlier that day, news came that Adolph Rupp had died. It seemed fitting that Rupp would die on the same day that Kentucky and Kansas played. The top-ranked Wildcats won the game, 73-66.

KU played with renewed enthusiasm that year, winning 15 of its first 17 games.

Kansas State, with Rolando Blackman, Mike Evans, and Curtis Redding, was a heavy favorite to win the conference that season. When the Wildcats and Coach Jack Hartman visited Lawrence, both teams were unbeaten in Big Eight play. The students showered the floor with hot dogs at the introduction of Redding, who played with a cocky flare. The Jayhawks were the superior team that day, winning 56-52.

K-State students, not to be overshadowed when it came to insulting behavior, were ready when Kansas visited Manhattan later in the year. Several students, masquerading in monkey suits, tossed bananas and chickens — painted blue — onto the court during the KU introductions. The game was delayed more than 20 minutes to clean up the mess.

The pre-game insults provided inspiration, and Kansas continued the cleanup by sweeping the Wildcats, 75-63, as Douglas and reserve Wilmore Fowler pitched in 18 points apiece.

Kansas was back, having captured its 35th conference title with a 13-1 mark.

The Jayhawks were seeded first in the first postseason conference tournament and paired against Kansas State in first-round action. But this time, K-State won, 87-76.

KU was sent to the NCAA West Regional to face UCLA in Eugene, Oregon. The Bruins subdued the Jayhawks, 83-76.

Despite losing six lettermen and three starters from the Big Eight championship team, Kansas launched the 1978-79 season as the conference favorite and ranked in everyone's Top 10. KU, however, emerged in uninspiring fashion.

Valentine and Mokeski had solid years, but KU didn't live up to its championship expectations. The Hawks finished with a respectable 18-11 mark, tied with Kansas State and Missouri for second in the conference. The non-conference schedule left a lasting scar on Owens, who had a reputation for failing to win the big game. The Jayhawks endured a bitter defeat, blowing a six-point lead with just 40 seconds left against Kentucky. I think that defeat hurt Ted more than any other I can recall. He usually was one to bounce back quickly after a loss, but I remember the next morning at the airport everyone was still in a deep funk. We had done everything wrong in that 40-second span — calling a time-out when none was available, throwing the ball away on an inbound pass, and so on.

Kansas slid a little farther as the '70s came to a close, as they dropped to 15-14 in 1979-80.

Valentine was a senior as the Jayhawks entered the 1980-81 season. Once again, Ted's job appeared to be on the line. And just as before, Ted found a way to pull his program out of a valley. The Jayhawks started strong, winning 15 of their first 17 encounters. They finished the regular season with a 19-7 record.

The Jayhawks tied Kansas State for the Big Eight championship, and then overwhelmed the Wildcats, 80-68, in the finals of the league tournament.

The Jayhawks were seeded seventh and were matched with Mississippi in the NCAA sub-regional at Wichita. KU struggled against Mississippi but managed a 69-66 victory. KU followed two nights later with an impressive 88-71 win over Arizona State behind a career-high 36 points for Tony Guy.

Those two wins set the stage for a game against Wichita State in the NCAA Regional in New Orleans. The two teams had not faced one another in 25 years, and the Shockers were poised to make history. Wichita State had a talented team, including Cliff Levingston and Antoine Carr, a teammate of Valentine's in high school.

In dramatic fashion, Wichita State won the game, 66-65. The game ended with a no-call as Valentine was clobbered on the game's final play. It was a monumental victory for Wichita State. Billboards went up throughout Wichita with just the score. The Jayhawks returned to

Lawrence with a 24-8 record, and Owens earned a two-year contract extension. Valentine ended his career with 1,821 points, becoming the first Kansas player to hand out more than 600 career assists. Darnell was a fabulous player for KU, but I felt that often he tried to do too much at the expense of the team.

Once again the Owens roller-coaster ride hit bottom. Kansas won just 13 games in 1981-82 and fell to 13-16 the following year. Attendance sagged as KU averaged fewer than 10,000 fans for the first time in several years. Clearly, the proud program was in trouble.

Owens, following the up-and-down pattern that characterized his career, brought in a recruiting class that gave promise for the future. He returned players such as Kelly Knight, Brian Martin and guard Tad Boyle. The 1982-83 recruiting class featured Calvin Thompson, Ron Kellogg, Jeff Guiot and Kerry Boagni. The Jayhawks also added Carl Henry, a scorer who had transferred from Oklahoma City. In addition, 7-1 giant Greg Dreiling had enrolled at KU after moving from Wichita State. It appeared that the resilient head man was once again ready to mimic a phoenix.

But he had flirted with disaster once too often.

Monte Johnson, who had played at Kansas and served as an assistant athletic director for several years before moving into the banking business in Wichita, assumed the job as athletic director in 1983. Monte made a difficult decision and dismissed Owens that spring.

I understood Monte's desire to make a move — although unpopular among some fans — and though he was acting in the best interest of the program. Ted's many coaching lows had left him vulnerable. The news stung Ted, and he wasn't shy in saying how he felt. There was no smile on his face as he walked away after 19 seasons.

The departure of Owens left a talented team with an unsettled future. It was an intriguing moment in the long history of Kansas basketball.

Monte needed to find a special kind of coach to heal a wounded program.

Chapter 10

Don Fambrough: The Most Loyal Jayhawk

I may be the only radio announcer in broadcast captivity for whom a silverback gorilla has been named.

Back in the late 1960s, I served as president of the Topeka Rotary Club. One of the members was Gary Clarke, who was director of the Topeka Zoo. At the time, there were no gorillas in the state of Kansas, and Gary proposed that the Rotary Club fund the acquisition of the first gorilla in the state.

He sold us on the concept of spending $5,000 to purchase a baby gorilla that was being housed at the Dallas Zoo and bring him to Topeka. Gary and I — along with Dr. Mark Morris, the pilot of our airplane, and Lauren Nash, the Topeka park commissioner — flew to Dallas to pick up this gorilla.

We received the little fellow at the Dallas Zoo, and he was cute as he could be.

He wore a diaper for the plane ride (fortunate for me because he spent much of the trip in my lap). Just like any little baby, he investigated my shirt pocket and pulled out the comb and pen I was carrying. Eventually, he wore down and used my lap as a nest for an afternoon nap.

We arrived at the Topeka Airport and were greeted by a horde of area newspaper and television photographers. The gorilla immediately retreated to the security of my arms. The next morning's paper carried a picture of me and the gorilla with the caption: "Topeka Rotary Club president Max Falkenstien, right, and the new baby gorilla arrive in Topeka." I never understood why they thought it necessary to note that I was on the right.

The members of the Rotary Club wrestled with the question of giving the zoo's newest attraction an appropriate name. King Kong had already been taken, and the little guy, at that point in his life, didn't look the part. They considered all sorts of possibilities, and finally Gary Clarke suggested

Max. Gary told the club that the name was short and easy for the gorilla to comprehend. Everyone agreed and adopted it as the name. I'm sure my parents would have been proud knowing their son's name had also been deemed appropriate for a gorilla.

Suffice it to say, having a gorilla named for me is one of the high spots of my life. I was like a proud father during those first years and visited my namesake often. I carried pictures in my wallet and shared them with friends. The junior Max was extremely strong. When he would put his arms around me, it was impossible to disengage his grip.

I was invited to participate at his first birthday party. We took him out in the yard at the zoo, and he held tightly to my pant leg. The wind was blowing that morning, which was a new sensation for him, and he kept biting at the breeze. I was just happy that he was able to distinguish the wind from my leg.

Like all baby gorillas, Max quickly emerged from diapers and blossomed into a beautiful 450-pound adult gorilla. Needless to say, he became a little bit too large for me to play with anymore. Max eventually showed signs of loneliness, and the zoo decided he needed gorilla companionship. Money was raised to purchase a female gorilla named Tiffany — approximately the same age as Max — from a zoo in Kansas City.

The hope was that Max and Tiffany would become a couple, fall in gorilla love, and make a family of gorillas. But as they matured, Max and Tiffany grew up more as brother and sister and they never showed an interest in mating. The zoo decided that Max and Tiffany needed professional help with their mating instincts, so they shipped Max to Denver and Tiffany to Buffalo, N.Y., to be paired with other gorillas. Unfortunately, none of those mating expeditions was successful in producing offspring. So in 1996, the Topeka Zoo shipped Max to the zoo in Santa Barbara, California. I felt very sad when he left Kansas.

Don Fambrough once took his grandchildren to the Topeka Zoo just to see Max. Don told me he could always distinguish between Max and Tiffany: "Max was the one in the corner playing with himself."

I'm sure Fambrough would have loved to have a football player with the size and strength of Max when Don became head football coach at Kansas in 1971. But he succeeded Pepper Rodgers, a coach who absolutely hated recruiting, and the program was short of talented players.

Fambrough lived by the motto: "Don't let the truth get in the way of a good story." Chronicling Fambrough's coaching career at Kansas results in a story that doesn't need embellishment.

Fambrough is in an exclusive club at KU, having received more pink slips than any coach in Jayhawk history. Three times during his KU coaching career, including twice as an assistant, Fam was issued his walking papers. And a fourth time, he was forced to resign. Although he never enjoyed job security in Lawrence, he remained unbending in his love for the University of Kansas football program. With the exception of three years when he coached in Texas, Fam has spent his entire career with a Jayhawk embroidered on his shirt.

He has easily earned the title of The Most Loyal Jayhawk.

"All I ever wanted to do was coach football at the University of Kansas," Fambrough has often said. He was passed over more than once. And, yet, when the day finally came — January 7, 1971 — Fam found himself speechless.

"I can't tell you what I felt, exactly," said Fambrough. "Wade Stinson walked in the day after Pepper left and said, 'Don, you're our head coach.' I don't think I said a word. I just got up, got my coat and walked out." Fam's annual salary was a modest $21,000 when he was tapped by Stinson to pull KU football from its downward slide.

Fambrough took over a program that was not on stable ground. His debut as a 48-year-old rookie head football coach at Kansas also marked the beginning of David Jaynes' career as the Jayhawks' starting quarterback. Jaynes was a highly sought-after prep standout from nearby Bonner Springs with impressive size (6-2, 210) and Hollywood good looks. He was intelligent, friendly, and an outstanding leader. It didn't take long for Fam to put the football and the fate of his offense in Jaynes' hands.

Fambrough had another talented sophomore in the backfield that season in speedy Delvin Williams, who led the Jayhawks in rushing despite missing two games and all but two plays of another.

Fam showed patience and built his team from the ground floor, understanding the autumn football harvest would not reap many wins. He was a motivator who framed his philosophy around confidence and enthusiasm.

Fambrough walked off the field feeling a degree of satisfaction in his inaugural game as head coach. The Jayhawks were impressive in a 34-0 win over Washington State in Lawrence. Baylor came to town the following weekend, and once again the Jayhawks provided the home fans with a reason to be excited. KU prevailed, 22-0, and the Jayhawks entered Week Three of the season undefeated and unscored upon.

Fam had warned the Jayhawk faithful that it would take two years to restock the KU roster with the necessary Big Eight-caliber players to compete with the big boys. The rest of the season brought home the truth in those words.

I suspect that the KU staff knew what was coming. Fam suffered through the longest hour of his brief head coaching career the following weekend at Florida State. Despite getting a hard-earned 101 rushing yards from Williams, the Seminoles dominated KU, 30-7.

The humbling defeat hung on the Jayhawks by Florida State opened the floodgates. KU lost seven of eight games during the stretch, but it proved to be a year in which KU fans could measure their team's success in wins over both rivals, Kansas State and Missouri. In the 39-13 victory over the Wildcats, Jaynes showed what the recruiting fuss two years earlier had been about. He connected on 12-of-18 passing attempts for 163 yards and three touchdowns.

KU finished the year 4-7 after a defense-dominated 7-2 win over Missouri in the final game of 1971. The Hawks finished the '72 campaign in similar 4-7 fashion.

Fam was a specialist on the recruiting trail and particularly effective in luring talent from the Sunflower State. His ability to spin yarns in that trademark Texas drawl often gave him the upper hand when he talked to young Kansans who lived off the beaten path. Certainly one of the biggest was after the 1972 season when he was rewarded for his countless trips to Ransom, Kansas, when he secured the signature of an exciting young prospect named Nolan Cromwell.

Other voices from The Hill • Don Fambrough

If I had to sit down and pick out the greatest athletes that I've ever been around, I would list Ray Evans, John Hadl, Nolan Cromwell, and a few others. Nolan was from a tiny town — Ransom — and the recruiting battles for him were hot and heavy. Everybody in the world was after him. When he finally announced that he was staying in his home state, I felt real good because it took care of about 150 schools.

It boiled down between KU and K-State. I knew Vince Gibson would battle hard for this one. As signing day got closer, I was in Ransom about every day. Nolan lived in the country at the top of a hill. After a visit to Nolan's home, I would drive off and see Vince parked at the bottom of the hill near the home. I would pass his car and see him take off for the house. Then I would get worried and waited my turn to go back.

We would trade our visits, going back and forth.

One night I got out there about 6 p.m., and the Cromwell family was at the barn milking. I thought to myself, this will be to my advantage. I needed something to get over the hump, and this old Texas boy knows how to milk. I was all dressed up in a coat and tie. I just took off my coat and sat down and started milking a cow. They couldn't believe the head football coach at the University of Kansas could milk a cow. So when I finished, I was convinced that I had won their hearts. I thought to myself, "I've got him." I grabbed my pail of milk and headed back to the house.

As I got to the house, I looked up on the porch and sitting there was old Vince, churning butter.

Cromwell's decision to attend Kansas left Fambrough and his staff optimistic about the future. In addition, the Jayhawks inked another exciting prospect that winter in Wichita running back Laverne Smith. That feeling of comfort, however, was tempered when Stinson resigned as athletics director. In July 1973, KU replaced Stinson with Clyde Walker, who had served in the athletic department at North Carolina.

Another high-profile newcomer to the KU administrative staff was two-time All-American Gale Sayers. Sayers had retired from professional football in September and returned to his alma mater as assistant to the athletics director in February 1973.

I've been through some KU football seasons that tested my creative skills as a broadcaster to keep the audience involved in one-sided games. I didn't have that problem with the 1973 team. Outside of the first three outings, this Jayhawk team kept the radio audience captive the entire game. KU opened with an impressive 29-8 win over 20th-ranked Washington State.

The Jayhawks were equally impressive in one-sided wins over Florida State and Minnesota. The unbeaten Jayhawks, still unranked in the football polls, traveled to Knoxville in the final non-conference encounter to face ninth-ranked Tennessee.

Fam decided to bank his team's offensive success on the arm of Jaynes. The senior quarterback set school records for most passes attempted (58) and completed (35) as he threw for 394 yards.

The Jayhawks scored late in the contest, pulling within a single point of the Vols, 28-27. Fam opted for a two-point conversion, and Jaynes was stacked up at the 2-yard line giving Tennessee the victory. Despite the loss, KU entered the Associated Press poll at No. 18.

Jaynes was a hero the following weekend as KU came from behind in miracle fashion to defeat Kansas State. Trailing 18-17 with less than two minutes remaining, Jaynes guided KU down the field and scored on a one-yard run with 1:04 remaining. Once again, the Jayhawks had cheated defeat.

Kansas found itself involved in its third consecutive close finish the following Saturday at Lincoln. This time, however, the 11th-ranked Huskers came out on top, 10-9.

The following weekend against Iowa State, Kansas once again found itself staring at defeat. But the Jayhawks staged a game-saving 67-yard scoring drive in the final minutes to edge the Cyclones, 22-20, and improve their record to 5-2.

It was a cardiac finish again in Week Eight. Oklahoma State missed a 19-yard field goal with just five seconds remaining, and KU and the Cowboys settled for a 10-10 tie.

Colorado visited Lawrence as the Jayhawks entered the home stretch of the season. The Jayhawks' success — and fetish for last-second finishes — had captured the attention of ABC, and the game was televised nationally. Following a familiar script, KU played this one down to the wire. KU was clinging to a 17-15 advantage and the Buffs were on the move. CU running back Billy Waddy broke loose with less than a minute remaining but had the ball jarred lose on a hit by KU cornerback James Bowman. Safety Rick Mudge fell on it with just 21 seconds on the clock, and KU walked off the field a winner.

The regular season ended with a loss to Oklahoma, 48-20, and a 14-13 win over Missouri.

The 1973 Jayhawks won six games decided by two points or fewer, an enduring NCAA record.

Kansas earned a bid to play North Carolina State in the Liberty Bowl in Memphis, and the Jayhawks entered the game as a slight favorite.

Jaynes completed 24 of 38 attempts for 218 yards, but the Wolfpack took advantage of a controversial fumbled punt by Bruce Adams in the third quarter to break a 10-10 tie. Adams signaled for a fair catch on the play and was hit by a Wolfpack defender just prior to making the catch. No penalty was called, and N.C. State scored in short order. The play opened the floodgates, and N.C. State won the game, 31-18.

Jaynes ended his KU career as the most prolific passer in school history, passing for 5,132 yards and a school-record 35 touchdowns. David spent some time in the broadcast booth following his football career and remains a loyal Jayhawk fan.

When the dust had settled on a painful 4-7 season the next year, Fambrough met with Clyde Walker and requested an extension of his contract. Fam had just one year remaining on his original agreement and thought he needed a firm commitment to be successful on the recruiting trail. He wanted a show of administrative support.

Walker turned him down, and Fam shocked all KU fans by announcing his resignation as head football coach at a December 2 news conference. Fam told reporters that without a contract extension, he would be a considered a lame duck coach in recruiting circles. It was a sad day for many of us who admired Fambrough and understood his passion for KU.

Fam agreed to stay in the athletic department and became an assistant in the Williams Fund office. For the first time in his long career, Fambrough retreated from the sidelines and accepted a dull desk job.

Walker was a Southerner, and it figured he would look in that direction for a new football coach. Fambrough assistant Jim Dickey, who later became head coach at Kansas State, and Arkansas assistant Merv Johnson were among the finalists for the job, but Walker was more impressed by a young assistant coach on Paul "Bear" Bryant's staff at Alabama by the name of Bud Moore.

Clyde concluded that anyone who coached with Bryant (in addition to playing for him) had the stuff to build a winner in Lawrence. But recruiting for Kansas wasn't quite the same as recruiting for Alabama. Moore was not used to battling for players.

Moore, who grew up near the tiny Alabama town of Bug Tussle, officially accepted the job December 17. He signed a four-year contract for $30,000. To no one's surprise, Moore's coaching tendencies were similar to his mentor's, right down (or up) to the huge tower constructed on the KU practice field.

It would be his observation point, allowing him to survey the entire practice field each day. Bryant had made the practice tower famous at Alabama.

Moore also scrapped the Veer-T offense in favor of a Wishbone attack. KU's uniforms soon mirrored those worn at Alabama. He even had the Jayhawks in white helmets at one time during time at KU.

Moore quickly established that toughness would be a trademark of his team.

He instituted three-a-day practice sessions during the preseason and pushed his players hard in those drills, putting an emphasis on hitting, and testing the heart of those players he had inherited. He came from the old school of coaches and even denied players water on the practice field. His grueling practice sessions often ran in excess of three hours. As a result, there were several departures from the ranks.

Other voices from The Hill • David Lawrence

One day we all noticed a big thunderstorm brewing in the west. We were all watching it out of the corner of our eye. It started getting close, and it was obvious it was going to be bad. All of a sudden, there was the massive bolt of lightning. It didn't hit the tower, but it came close. Bud Moore, who was always slow reacting to things, came out of that tower like his pants were on fire. It was almost like he slid down a pole.

Moore made a significant position move that spring, sending Nolan Cromwell to quarterback, where he would compete with Scott McMichael for the starting job. But Nolan came to Kansas with the understanding he could also run track, a sport that conflicted with spring drills. Moore wanted Cromwell full-time that spring and thought it was particularly important because the offenses were changing. But track was important to him, so a compromise was reached. Nolan would participate in most of the football drills, then put on his track gear and finish the day with Bob Timmons.

McMichael concluded the spring as the clear number-one quarterback and held the job as the Jayhawks opened the 1975 season. Washington State served as KU's first opponent, and McMichael trotted out under center. Cromwell watched most of the action from the sidelines. The Jayhawks stretched their losing streak to seven games with a four-point loss to Washington State.

Bud Moore tasted his first victory the following Saturday as the Jayhawks downed Kentucky, 14-10. Moore was alternating his quarterbacks, splitting time between McMichael and Cromwell. He decided to start Cromwell the third week of the season as the Jayhawks hosted Oregon State.

Cromwell was magnificent in his debut as a starter. The Ransom Rambler was the perfect triggerman for a Wishbone attack, with his ability to quickly curl around the corners. Cromwell set an NCAA record for quarterbacks that day as he rushed for an amazing 294 yards, including a 79-yard touchdown gallop. His yardage total is even more impressive considering that Moore stuck with his plan that afternoon to alternate the quarterbacks. McMichael started the second and fourth quarters in a 20-0 Jayhawk victory. The Wishbone offense was still somewhat of a novelty in those days, and opposing defenses didn't have an answer for the rolling Jayhawk offense, which featured Cromwell, Laverne Smith and Norris Banks. The Jayhawks ranked seventh in the nation that year with an average of 317 rushing yards a game. KU rarely put the ball in the air. Cromwell led the team in passing, completing just 20-of-49 attempts for 333 yards — the entire season!

During the season, the Jayhawks achieved one of the milestone wins in the program's history.

On November 8, KU traveled to Norman to face the Sooners. Barry Switzer had a tremendous team that was undefeated and ranked second nationally. The Jayhawk defense was stubborn that afternoon and keyed a memorable 23-3 upset over Oklahoma. The win ended a 28-game Sooner winning streak and 37-game unbeaten string. The Jayhawks also became the first team to hold OU without a touchdown in 99 quarters.

Other voices from The Hill • Jim Fender

I had a lot of respect for our coaches because they knew we had a good chance to win the game. At halftime, Lance Van Zandt, our defensive coordinator, came over to the offensive side in our meetings and said, "Fellows, we just won the game." We didn't understand what he meant. "We're ahead 7-3 at halftime, and my defense guys have already said they're not giving up another point today, so if you guys don't do anything, we still win, 7-3. You guys can do more if you want to, but we've won the game." I remember Bud Moore later saying it was the greatest game in NCAA history.

When the OU game was over, I made my way down from the high Oklahoma press box and caught a ride with KU assistant coach Jim Webster. Anyone who has ever attempted to escape the traffic after an Oklahoma football game in Norman understands it's one of the toughest traffic jams in college football.

Jim had a rented car and he pulled in behind the KU team buses. We were all escorted from Norman to the Oklahoma City Airport. The police escort steered us down the shoulder of the bumper-to-bumper interstate highway at about 75 mph. We were rolling down that road at breakneck speed on the shoulder behind three chartered Greyhound buses. Jim was floating with excitement, pumped up, screaming and hollering, and I wasn't sure if we would survive the 40-minute drive. We were slipping and sliding on that gravel shoulder, and I was absolutely scared pea green. That's what I remember the most about that great win.

Oklahoma won every other game it played that season and also captured the national championship.

With a 42-24 victory over Missouri, the Jayhawks finished with a 7-4 regular season record and earned KU a bid to face Pittsburgh in the Sun Bowl at El Paso.

I was looking forward to the El Paso trip, figuring we would be nestled in a nice warm part of the world for a week. Of course my dreams were shattered when we arrived to find the ground covered with snow and frigid temperatures. About 4,000 Kansas fans made the excursion to El Paso for the Christmas week activities.

Pittsburgh's offense was built around the talents of running back Tony Dorsett, and he showed everyone his greatness that afternoon. Dorsett rushed for 142 yards, and the Panthers had 372 yards on the ground against the KU defense in a 33-19 win.

Bud Moore's first year, however, had been a great success. Moore was selected conference Coach of the Year after turning a 4-7 program into a 7-5 bowl team.

Cromwell returned in 1976, and the Jayhawks quickly emerged as one of college football's elite teams. The Jayhawks rushed for 331 yards and overpowered Oregon State, 28-16, in the season opener. Laverne Smith busted lose for 142 yards on just 15 carries, and KU amassed 467 yards on the ground in a 35-16 win over Washington State in Game Two. Wins the following two weeks, over Kentucky and Wisconsin, gave KU a 4-0 record and propelled the Jayhawks to a No. 8 national ranking.

Everything seemed in place for Kansas to make a strong run at a conference title and a major bowl. KU was guilty of overlooking Oklahoma State the following weekend, and the Cowboys pulled a 21-14 upset.

The following Saturday against Oklahoma, disaster struck. Leading 10-3 at halftime and seemingly with the game under control, Kansas turned the ball over four times in the second half, all leading to Sooner scores. As a result, OU left with a 28-10 victory. Not only did KU lose the game, but it also lost Cromwell, who suffered a knee injury in the third quarter. The injury required surgery, thus ending his brilliant career.

With Cromwell out, McMichael took control. Kansas bounced back from the two defeats with a 24-14 win over Kansas State. But the Jayhawks were vulnerable without Cromwell. The season concluded with losses to Nebraska, Iowa State, and Colorado, and a win over Missouri. Moore's second Kansas team finished 6-5.

After finishing the 1977 season with a 3-7-1 record and heading into the '78 season finale with only one win, a coaching change was obvious.

Other voices from The Hill • David Lawrence

Bud brought in Don Fambrough to speak to the team before the Missouri game in 1977. He thought Don would get us fired up. I was aware of him, but I had never heard him speak.

He started talking about Missouri, and that vein popped out in his neck. Don looked at us and said, "I don't know when I started hating those bastards. I think it was when Quantrill came over and burned down Lawrence. You know he was an MU alumnus." A lot of guys believed him. That whole episode worked against Bud, because we got to see a real motivator; and it planted in our minds there was something better out there.

On the Thursday before the finale against Kansas State, Bud Moore was fired.

KU showed up for the Kansas State game, but it was obvious that the players didn't have their hearts in it. The Wildcats, coached by former KU assistant Jim Dickey, won the game 36-20. Moore left the locker room after the game without talking to the media.

Bud Moore finished his coaching career with a 17-27-1 record over four seasons. He had made intelligent moves in switching Cromwell to quarterback and installing the Wishbone offense. But Moore was also living off the profits of Fambrough recruits, and the well was running dry. After his coaching stint at Kansas, Bud went into the beer distributorship business in Florida and made a lot of money.

A search committee headed by Fambrough was assembled by athletics director Bob Marcum to find Moore's successor. Among the names that surfaced were John Hadl, John Cooper, Emory Bellard and Bo Rein. Rein might have been the leading candidate, but he withdrew his name from consideration. He later took the head coaching position at LSU and shortly after being hired, died in a plane accident.

Marcum made a curious, but popular, decision that surprised everyone. After looking at the candidates around the country, he turned the program back over to the 56-year-old Fambrough.

Professor Fambrough was back in his classroom, pacing the sidelines on Saturday and coaching at the school he loved. I remember his first game as head coach in 1979. The Jayhawks opened at Pittsburgh, and Fam knew he didn't have the greatest talent in the world. I ran into him while walking through the hotel lobby the morning of the game and invited him to take a walk. He was a bundle of nervous energy. About halfway through our journey, Fam turned to me and snorted, "I don't know why I got back into this. Here my stomach is turning end over end. I've been enjoying these Saturday mornings the last four years. Now I'm in it again and I feel terrible." I knew better. Fam was the happiest man on the face of the earth. But he had an uphill battle in 1979.

The Jayhawks won just three times in 1979, defeating North Texas, Iowa State and Kansas State. But it was impressive progress, considering that KU had finished with a 1-10 mark the previous year.

But the off-season helped brighten the prospects for 1980. Among a recruiting class that included four Kansas kids, Fam's top recruits that season came from Huntington Beach, California.

Quarterback Frank Seurer and running back Kerwin Bell would have an immediate impact on the Jayhawk football program.

Seurer and Bell moved right into the lineup as the Jayhawks opened the 1980 season on the road at Oregon. Seurer demonstrated poise in his debut. Trailing 7-0 in the final minutes of the game, Seurer connected with David Verser on a 14-yard pass with just 16 seconds left. Bruce Kallmeyer, also in his first collegiate game, hit the extra point, and the Jayhawks left Eugene 0-0-1.

The Jayhawks finished with a 4-5-2 record in 1980, but the story of the season was the running of Bell.

Against Kansas State in Manhattan, Bell erupted for 216 yards on 38 carries. He carried for 157 yards in a 42-3 win over Colorado. He established a school and Big Eight freshman rushing record with 1,114 yards and earned all-conference and Newcomer of the Year honors.

Hall of Fame trainer Dean Nesmith was one of my all-time favorite Jayhawks. "Deaner" started with KU in 1938.

Fambrough's third year at the helm offered promise. In his first stint as head coach at KU, it had been the third season that produced a bowl team. Many observers wondered if history would repeat itself.

In a nutshell, the 1981 season was pure storybook. KU won its first four games of the season, with three of those wins by five points or fewer.

Kansas reeled off consecutive wins against Iowa State, Colorado and

Missouri to finish the regular season with a sparkling 8-3 record, its best mark since 1968.

The Missouri game was full of drama as more than 47,000 poured into Memorial Stadium for the final game. Third place in the league and bragging rights in the oldest rivalry west of the Mississippi were just two of the things at stake.

Bowl scouts from the Hall of Fame, Tangerine, and other bowls were in the press box. Everyone knew a win over the Tigers would send the Jayhawks to a nice holiday bowl. Marcum was not unmindful of the possibilities and, ever the showman, he knew that if the students tore down the goal posts, it would make a good impression on the bowl scouts. Consequently, he loosened the screws on the south goal post so it could be easily dismantled. Late in the game, with the Jayhawks leading 19-3 and victory assured, the students stormed the field and began tearing the posts down.

Quickly, the south posts fell. But the north ones hadn't been loosened, and they were only bending. But the game wasn't over. Missouri scored late, and there was no way it could kick an extra point because there weren't any uprights to kick the ball through. So the Tigers successfully went for two, making the score 19-11.

The students paraded the uprights up the hill and dumped them in Potter's Lake. Marcum rescued them and cut them into souvenirs upon which he painted the final score. He gave them to a certain few loyal followers.

Other voices from The Hill • David Lawrence

We thought if we beat Missouri, we would be going to the Tangerine Bowl. We went out there and physically whipped a really good Missouri team that day. But the Missouri game was costly, as we lost Seurer to an injury.

Kansas accepted an invitation to play Mississippi State in the Hall of Fame Bowl in Birmingham, Alabama. Bumper stickers soon appeared with the slogan, "Going With Fam To Birmingham." Fambrough was named Big Eight Coach of the Year and Lawrence punter Bucky Scribner, linebacker Kyle McNorton, and wide receiver Wayne Capers earned all-conference honors.

The Hall of Fame Bowl required each participating school to sell 10,000 tickets, and the KU athletic staff was hard at work securing buyers.

Marcum asked the KU Endowment Association for help. "Sure we will take some tickets," he was told. "Put us down for two."

Bob had been a close friend of mine who often stepped in as my color announcer in basketball. For the KU Endowment Association to take just two tickets was insulting to Marcum and demonstrated a lack of support. He decided it was time to look for a school that could do better than that.

On the trip to Birmingham, Marcum interviewed with South Carolina. He accepted the job as athletics director shortly after the game.

The Hall of Fame Bowl was played on a cold and rainy afternoon. (Among the assistant coaches on the Mississippi State sideline that day was Bob Valesente. Four years later, Valesente would be the head coach at Kansas.)

Without Seurer — who would finish with a KU career-record 6,410 passing yards the next season — playing in the bowl, the Jayhawk offense lacked its leader. Steve Smith, an outstanding young man, subbed and did the best he could. But Mississippi State had an impressive team and won the game, 10-0.

With Marcum gone from the athletics director's office, KU Chancellor Gene Budig appointed faculty representative Del Shankel to serve on an interim basis. In early 1982, Budig announced the hiring of Monte Johnson as athletics director.

Monte had played basketball at KU and served in the department with my dad for several years. He had been loyal to my father in the last months of his life, and I respected Monte's business skills in running the department.

The Jayhawks entered the 1982 season full of hope but quickly found catastrophe. An unheralded Wichita State team, which would drop football in the mid 1980s, came to Lawrence in the season opener and administered a 13-10 embarrassment on the Jayhawks. It was a damaging defeat that caused many to quickly forget about the success of 1981. The Hawks won only two games that year, beating TCU and Iowa State. They finished the season 2-7-2.

The long ride for Fambrough finally came to an unhappy ending when Johnson decided the football team needed a change. It was a highly emotional and controversial decision. Fambrough had been down this road before, but in this instance, he felt bitterness toward the athletic department's leadership.

Fambrough's loyalty to the school he loved was tested. I know he harbored a lot of bitterness toward Johnson and Chancellor Budig, but his love for KU never changed. For several years following his firing, Fam kept his distance from Memorial Stadium and the football program. The wounds finally showed signs of healing late in the decade when new football coach Glen Mason solicited his friendship.

In 1995, David Lawrence, Scott McMichael, David Jaynes and several other of Fambrough's former players organized a reunion for him. I was asked to serve as master of ceremonies. It was a tremendous event.

The next day, at halftime of the game, Fam was ushered onto the Memorial Stadium turf and surrounded by hundreds of players and former teammates. A portrait of Fambrough was unveiled, and he received a standing ovation from the crowd.

He had earned it.

Chapter 11

Changing Times

I'm not sure who first came up with the adage, "Coaches are hired to be fired." But it was never more apparent than at Kansas in the early 1980s.

The 1982-83 Jayhawk basketball team finished with a 13-16 record and placed seventh in the Big Eight Conference standings. The 1982 KU football team slumped to 2-7-2 and wound up sixth in the league race. Attendance was sagging in both programs.

Together, Ted Owens and Don Fambrough represented almost 50 years of coaching at the University of Kansas. They were fixtures on the Jayhawk athletic landscape, as familiar as waving the wheat or the Rock Chalk chant.

Monte Johnson arrived at Kansas in December 1982 as a bottom-line athletics director, and he didn't like the direction either program was headed.

It was a homecoming of sorts for Monte, who had played basketball at KU (1957-59). He had also spent nine years (1961-70) working as an assistant in the athletic department, where he had learned the business end of the college athletics business from my dad. When my father became ill, Monte visited him about every day. Dad always thought that Monte was a tremendously talented young man with a bright future.

Monte walked into his office as the AD, rolled up his sleeves, and went to work.

He swept the football and basketball house clean in a matter of months as a pair of Kansas icons — Ted Owens and Don Fambrough — were asked to turn in their office keys. These were changing times in the athletic department as Monte brought a strict and sound business approach to its management.

He was in his office early, around 6 a.m. He would tour the facilities regularly and make his maintenance staff aware of the slightest deficiency in up-keep. He kept a close eye on the budget, solicited outside, professional assistance in promotions, and was closely involved in all fund-raising activity. He cracked the whip in the department and asked his staff to be at their desks by 8 a.m. and observe a proper dress code.

After making the decision to change coaches, Monte then faced the challenge of finding new ones. His first order of business was in football. There were a multitude of candidates for the position, but Johnson was most impressed with Mike Gottfried. He had been highly recommended by Dallas Cowboys General Manager Gil Brandt, and his record of healing troubled teams seemed to make him a natural choice to cure the ailing KU football program. Gottfried arrived at Kansas on December 27, 1982, with the label of fix-it man. In his five seasons at Murray State and Cincinnati, Gottfried had taken football programs that were at rock bottom and turned them into winners.

Monte then tackled the vacancy in basketball. He had lined up 10 interviews at the 1983 Final Four in Albuquerque, New Mexico. Before Monte left, though, he received a call from two people, including CBS Sports' Billy Packer, saying that Larry Brown might be interested in the KU job. At the time, Brown was coaching the NBA's New Jersey Nets.

Other voices from The Hill • Monte Johnson

I had Lonnie Rose, chairman of the selection committee, pick Larry Brown up at the (Kansas City) airport and bring him to my hotel room. They knocked on the door, and when I opened it and met Larry, I thought maybe they had sent a substitute. This was the most mild-mannered, low-key individual I had ever met in my life. He shuffled in, shook my hand, and looked down at the floor. But we had the most delightful conversation you could imagine, and he never asked about salary or benefits. I told him if he was sincerely interested in the job, he would have every consideration.

A little later I was in my office and Larry called. I was on the phone with another candidate — Eddie Sutton — and Lonnie Rose was holding with Larry. I could tell that Eddie was not that sincere in his interest and wished him good luck. I got on with Larry, and he told me he had a problem. His owner had found out about his interest in the KU job and had issued an ultimatum: Either

take the Kansas job, or get on the plane to Detroit and coach the Nets. He said,
"Monte, either you tell me I'm going to be the coach at Kansas, or I'm going to
have to get on this plane to Detroit." I said, "If you want the job, it's yours." He
said he'd take it, and that was the way he was hired.

We didn't even talk about money.

I began my career as a color announcer when Bob Davis was hired as the "Voice
of the Jayhawks."

Gottfried's first season, 1983, wasn't the turnaround that KU fans had
hoped to see as the Jayhawks finished 4-6-1 (2-5 in the Big Eight). Maybe
the next season would produce better results. The 1984 season certainly
brought a significant change in my broadcasting career.

During the summer, Monte had made a decision to sell the radio
rights for KU football and basketball to an outside vendor. Learfield
Communications of Jefferson City, Missouri, was awarded the exclusive
rights to KU sports, which meant my radio network was out of business.

Prior to that season, the KU athletics department had always allowed
my broadcast network to do the games. Tom Hedrick and Kevin Harlan
were the broadcast team on the Jayhawk Network, which was considered the
official radio network. By awarding rights to Learfield, Monte had decided
to clean the slate and create a new broadcast team for the new network.

I assumed it was the sunset of my Jayhawk broadcast days.

Bob Davis, who had spent many years as the broadcast voice at Fort
Hays State University, was the athletic department's choice to serve as play-
by-play announcer. But Doug Vance called me one summer afternoon and

asked if I would be interested in working with Bob as the color announcer. I was very apprehensive, because I had never been in that role. But I talked with Bob and decided to give it a try. After 38 years of broadcasting games, I felt like a rookie announcer.

It was a tough adjustment for me. I never pretended to be an analyst, because I didn't have the background to understand the technical part of the game. I just wanted to convey the excitement of the event and talk about the athletes, the coaches, the rivalries and the emotions.

It was typical late October weather — cool and rainy — when No. 2-ranked Oklahoma came to Memorial Stadium in 1984. The Jayhawks were dedicating Anschutz Sports Pavilion that Saturday, and Gottfried told equipment manager Mike Hill that the team would not participate in pregame drills at the stadium. Instead, the team warmed up in Anschutz.

It was curious picture: one team warming up on the Memorial Stadium field and the other side vacant. Finally, the Jayhawks arrived with about five minutes remaining until kickoff. KU shocked the Sooners from the beginning. On the Jayhawks' first possession, quarterback Mike Norseth connected with wide receiver Tommy Quick on a long pass play. Two plays later, tailback Lynn Williams scored the first rushing touchdown that OU had yielded all year. Offensively, OU couldn't get much going with freshman quarterback Troy Aikman, who was making his college starting debut.

The Hawks went on to win 28-11 in what represents one of the biggest upsets in school history. The Jayhawks, who ended the year with wins over Colorado and Missouri, finished with a 5-6 record in Gottfried's second year, including a 4-3 conference mark.

For his efforts, Gottfried was named conference Coach of the Year. That was as good as it got for Gottfried and the Jayhawks. Although the team finished 1985 with a 6-6 record (2-5 in the conference) and appeared to be headed upward, Gottfried resigned on December 12 to accept the head coaching job at Pittsburgh.

Monte Johnson wasted no time in naming Gottfried's successor. One day later, he announced the appointment of Bob Valesente. Those of us close to the program applauded the decision. The 45-year-old Valesente was one of the warmest coaches I've ever been around. He was always upbeat, even in the worst of times, and had a constant smile on his face. In fact, Val was always concerned about his nice-guy image. He would always say, "I can be a tough guy. I'm not always nice on the field."

But Val wasn't really mean. At the height of anger, he might scream, "Cheese and crackers." There couldn't have been a nicer guy in the world who had no chance for success.

Val inherited a fairly depleted roster. KU won three of its first four games in Valesente's first season. But those wins came against three cream puffs — Utah State, Indiana State and Southern Illinois. It also happened to be 75 percent of his wins as KU's head coach. Valesente followed his 3-8 debut season with a 1-9-1 mark.

I will say that one of the closest disasters during my 60 years with KU happened in Val's second season, 1987. We were set to open the season at Auburn. Three buses were on hand to take the team from the airport apron to the practice field after arriving early Friday afternoon. The lead bus, fully loaded with players, started to ease away from its location near the airplane. The driver apparently didn't notice the massive wing of the airplane, and as he pulled forward it came crashing through the front window. Fortunately, he hit the brakes just in time to avoid a serious accident, and no one was injured. The results on the field the next night weren't much better, as the Tigers won 49-0.

The day after the Jayhawks lost to Missouri in the 1987 finale, new athletics director Bob Frederick — a former KU basketball player and assistant coach who replaced Johnson as the AD before the '87 season — informed Val he was making a change. Val was the wrong guy, at the wrong place, at the wrong time. He was a good and honorable man and probably an effective coach. Kansas fans really never had the opportunity to find out.

Larry Brown would enjoy slightly more success than Valesente as he took over the Jayhawk basketball program in 1983. Brown was nothing like I expected. He was somewhat shy, soft-spoken and often embarrassed by all the attention he received. Fans would approach him for autographs or just to wish him good luck, and Larry would tuck his head into his shoulders and softly make the appropriate acknowledgment.

Larry fought to change his transient image, which overshadowed what he should be known for — winning.

Other voices from The Hill • Monte Johnson

We could only pay (Brown) $53,000 in salary and a $57,000 guarantee in radio and television money. That's all I could guarantee him (that first year). But

I set up a final severance package with him, which was a deferred compensation plan. By the time he left KU, his gross income — not net income — including camps, television and radio salary, shoe contract, and speaking was between $700,000 and $800,000. It was set to be paid over three years. And since he left early, he didn't really get the entire amount. There wasn't another coach in the country, except Jim Valvano, who was close to that. And it didn't cost the University hardly anything. The shoe and camp money came from outside sources. We had the salary and radio/television package, which all added up to $160,000. Larry never knew how much money he got. At his request, we sent his checks to his manager.

Off the floor, Brown managed to stir up plenty of controversy within a short period of time. Midway through the spring, it became apparent that Larry and assistant coach JoJo White were having conflicts. As a result, JoJo was asked to say good-bye.

Then Larry made an interesting move. He hired one of his former players — Ed Manning — who didn't have much coaching experience. But Ed had a 6-10 son named Danny, a senior in high school that year, who happened to be the most coveted prep player in the land.

Ed, who had worked as a truck driver, turned out to be a great addition to the coaching staff, and we developed a good friendship during his years in Lawrence. He related well to the team, and I think he made a real contribution to the program. It isn't any secret that Larry hired Ed to get Danny. Ed always handled that with a smile on his face. So, to no one's surprise, Ed's son soon announced that he would sign with the University of Kansas.

Brown may have been the most superstitious coach I've ever met. Every morning before arriving at work, Larry would stop by the Carol Lee Doughnut Shop and buy six glazed doughnuts for the office. It was always Carol Lee. His other rituals ranged from bowling on game days to tossing away neckties that he had worn during losses. Larry thought it was bad luck for his players to get haircuts on game days, and he had the Jayhawks leave the floor after pre-game warm-ups before the 10-minute mark on the clock. Coaches always shook hands in the locker room, never outside, before a game. Just before tip-off, the Jayhawk staff also had to wish each other good luck with a touch of some fashion.

Perhaps the strangest superstition came on the bench. In close, down-to-the-wire games, Brown would call for his staff to "go to the power," which meant each would reach down and squeeze his left testicle.

Larry even had an "official" good-luck charm in Ryan Gray, a youngster with a slow-growing, malignant brain tumor who loved the Jayhawks. Ryan would attend every home game in a wheelchair, and Larry always made a point of visiting with him before a game. They developed a special relationship, and after the Jayhawks won the 1988 national championship, Ryan rode in the car with Larry during the victory celebration parade.

The Jayhawks had an abundance of talent for Brown in his first season. The roster included gifted long-range shooters Ron Kellogg and Calvin Thompson. Guard Carl Henry was an all-Big Eight performer, and 6-8 forward Kelly Knight was an impressive force inside. Brown also had 7-1 sophomore Greg Dreiling, who became eligible that season after moving from Wichita State.

Brown got the Jayhawks on track quickly in his first season. KU went 8-3 during the non-conference portion of its schedule. In conference play, Kansas finished second and then defeated Wayman Tisdale and the Billy Tubbs-coached Oklahoma Sooners to win the Big Eight Conference Tournament. It was a sweet victory for Brown and the Jayhawks.

Earlier in the season, the Sooners had been overly cocky in a 92-82 conference championship-clinching victory at Allen Fieldhouse. The players taunted the KU crowd from their bench, pointing at their ring fingers (referring to a conference championship). They also cut down the nets. Afterwards, Brown told reporters, "The world is round. What goes around, comes around."

After a two-season layoff, KU was back in the NCAA Tournament. The Jayhawks squeaked past Alcorn State before being dismissed by Mugsy Bogues-led Wake Forest. But Kansas basketball was back, as the Jayhawks finished with a 22-10 record.

The next season, 1984-85, Danny Manning and nine other newcomers made their KU debuts. We quickly learned Manning was an unselfish player with tremendous talent. He didn't have to be a big scorer his freshman season with players such as Thompson, Kellogg, Dreiling and Cedric Hunter in the lineup.

Kellogg and Thompson rank as two of my favorite all-time players. Kellogg, with his rainbow jumpers, and Thompson, with his thunderous slams, were exciting to watch on the floor.

But they were equally fun to be around during the trips. Calvin was the practical joker and unbeknownst to me once slipped a couple of ice cubes in my pocket during an airplane trip. Of course the ice proceeded to melt and made it look like I peed my pants. Calvin got so tickled over that that to this day, every time I see him, he'll bring up something about the ice cubes and then he'll start laughing.

One of my all-time favorite KU basketball stories involves Kellogg, who sometimes was completely detached from games. During one game, Larry became really frustrated with Ronnie because he was too offensive and not passing enough. He jerked him out of the game and got right in his face on the bench and told him to "pass the damn ball." He then shouted, "Any questions?" Kellogg said, "Yeah, coach, I got a question. When are we going to fix the whirlpool in the training room?" Larry then ran down the bench and screamed to the trainer, Dave Lucy, to get the whirlpool fixed.

The Jayhawks won 13 of their first 15 games in 1984-85, and Kansas was back on the national college basketball map. Kellogg picked up the nickname "Mr. Saturday" for his string of five consecutive Saturdays of 30-point games during the heart of the conference schedule.

The excitement of the impressive start of 1984-85 faded in the last half of the season. KU reached the NCAA Tournament again, only to see the trip cut short with a second-round loss to Auburn, 66-64. Kansas finished with a glossy 26-8 record, but the season had ended on a sour note.

It's difficult and probably meaningless to make comparisons. But the 1985-86 Jayhawk basketball team may have been the best in school history. It was one of the most well meshed groups I've ever watched on the court. With Manning, Thompson, Kellogg, Hunter and Dreiling as starters — and players like Archie Marshall and Mark Turgeon coming off the bench — KU had offensive firepower from all angles. They were a joy to watch.

KU rolled through the non-conference portion of its schedule, losing only to Duke in the preseason NIT by six points and on the road in overtime to Memphis State. Manning stepped forward as a consistent scorer. Kellogg and Thompson were in double figures in nearly every outing, and Dreiling took care of the inside game. Hunter, the catalyst, evolved into one of the game's top playmakers and set school records in nearly every assist category.

KU made its annual visit to Manhattan to face rival Kansas State on February 1, but this Jayhawk-Wildcat encounter carried more than the usual drama. Just a few days prior to the game, long-time K-State coach Jack Hartman announced he would retire after the season. Led by a quartet of KU players in double figures, the Hawks overcame the inspired Wildcats, though, in a 64-50 win.

Three weeks and six straight wins later, Kansas hosted K-State for Hartman's final game in Allen Fieldhouse. The fans treated Jack with great respect, and the KU athletic department presented him with a golf bag and clubs in a pre-game ceremony. A banner in the crowd proclaimed, "We'll Miss You, Jack."

KU was not as cordial on the floor, as Kellogg poured in 30, and the Jayhawks clinched the conference title with an 84-69 victory.

Two nights later, KU slipped down to Norman and beat the Sooners, 87-80. The win snapped a 48-game home winning streak by Oklahoma at Lloyd Noble Arena.

The Jayhawks avenged their only conference loss of the season and sent their senior class out in style in a highly emotional 90-70 victory over Iowa State. It marked the season finale in Allen Fieldhouse.

After winning the league title, the Jayhawk then disposed of K-State, Oklahoma and Iowa State for the tournament championship.

The Jayhawks were dispatched to Dayton for NCAA first-round action. After marching past North Carolina A&T in the first game, KU was impressive in a 22-point win over Temple.

Kansas returned from Dayton just two wins away from the Final Four. Its next venue was friendly Kemper Arena in Kansas City. The Jayhawks faced Michigan State in the opening round while North Carolina State went against Iowa State in the other match up. The KU-Michigan State encounter ranks as one of the most entertaining college basketball games I've ever witnessed.

The game was close throughout and came down to the wire. The final minutes of regulation were marked with controversy as MSU coach Jud Heathcote protested a clock malfunction, and Brown was slapped with a technical when he accidentally hit referee Bob Dibler's whistle with his program. Spartan guard Scott Skiles canned both technical foul shots to move Michigan State up 78-74. The Spartans increased the lead to six at the 1:39 mark of the game, and yet, somehow, the Jayhawks came back. Then, with Kemper shaking with noise, Kansas super-sub Archie Marshall proved to be a hero as he rebounded an errant Calvin Thompson shot and tied the game 80-80 in the final seconds.

The Jayhawks took control in overtime as Thompson, who was plagued with leg cramps in the extra period, scored nine of KU's 16 points, making the final score 96-86.

Manning was magnificent in the Midwest Regional final, scoring 22 and earning tournament MVP honors, as the Jayhawks grabbed a 75-67 win over North Carolina State. For the first time since 1974, we were headed to the Final Four.

The Jayhawks took a remarkable 35-3 record and a No. 2 national ranking to Reunion Arena in Dallas. Their opponent was Duke, ranked No. 1 in the country. Everyone was optimistic that KU would be playing in the national championship game.

The Jayhawks had a set of red uniforms they had worn a few times during the season, and Brown decided KU would wear red in the Final Four. The 1952 KU team was dressed in red when it won the national championship, and Brown thought it might be appropriate to win another with the same look.

The Blue Devils had already achieved a victory over KU back in early December. As the semifinal game unfolded, it was obvious that the Jayhawks were in trouble. Manning got in early foul trouble and was not much of a factor. The usually reliable Hunter was having a bad game, and Brown sent Mark Turgeon in to run the team.

But the big blow came midway through the second half, when Marshall suffered a serious leg injury and had to be carried off the floor. He was done for the game. The Jayhawks hung close, but Duke ended their ride with a 71-67 victory.

The NCAA title was won by Louisville that year, a team KU had beaten twice during the regular season.

After KU lost in the Sweet 16 to Georgetown in 1987, Brown had high hopes for Manning's senior year. Chris Piper was back, and Marshall, after rehabilitating his knee, would also return. In addition, the Jayhawks had Kevin Pritchard, Mark Randall, Milt Newton, Keith Harris, Sean Alvarado, Jeff Gueldner and Scooter Barry on the roster. But Brown was excited about his recruiting class also, which included junior-college transfers, Marvin Branch, Lincoln Minor and Otis Livingston. Brown recruited Mike

Maddox, the Oklahoma high school Player of the Year and highly regarded freshman Mike Masucci.

Manning was asked to pose for the cover of *Basketball Times'* preseason edition and was stationed next to the sign at the city limits of Kansas City, directing drivers to the NCAA Final Four in 1988. The magazine was the only national publication to pick the Jayhawks as their preseason No. 1.

There had been speculation during the spring that Manning might skip his senior season and enter the NBA draft. But Manning decided to stay in school.

It was a season of great expectations that quickly found heartbreak and adversity. Players were sidelined with medical problems and academic deficiencies. A couple were just sent packing. The 1987-88 team picture, shot in early October, barely resembled the group of players that found itself still playing basketball in March.

Piper missed the first four games of the season after undergoing arthroscopic knee surgery and played with pain throughout the year as a result of a summer groin injury.

Randall decided to redshirt after determining that he needed surgery to correct a breathing problem. Branch was ruled ineligible on January 13 for the remainder of the season. Perhaps the most painful loss was Marshall, who suffered a career-ending knee injury on December 30 against St. John's. Larry cried on the bench in New York as Marshall was carried off the floor.

Two other performers who played a key role at times during the season — Livingston and Masucci — were suspended from the team in March. Brown had to seek help from the football roster just to field a team, adding Clint Normore and Marvin Maddox. Earlier, Brown learned that Mark Pellock, who had started 26 games the previous season, was leaving the team to "resolve personal problems." As it turned out, Pellock left school and went to work for a Lawrence T-shirt firm. In early April, he was making Jayhawk championship shirts.

Brown used 12 different starting combinations that season. He tried about everything to pull this team together. In early December, the Jayhawks hit the road to face Western Carolina.

Shocking a lot of the Jayhawk faithful, KU ran onto the floor in yellow uniforms. Kansas won the game, but looked terrible in the process, and we never saw those uniforms again.

The low point in the year came in the games following the Jayhawks' league opening victory over Missouri — they lost five of their next six, leaving them with an unimpressive 12-8 record. KU athletics officials discussed printing NIT tickets, figuring the team would never qualify for the NCAA Tournament.

But eventually the adversity melted away, and Brown took what was remaining and weaved together something special. It was a combination of a sticky defense and the sometimes brilliant play of Manning that made the difference. KU picked up the pace in February and March. The Jayhawks' only losses were at Oklahoma, at home in overtime against Duke, and at Kemper against Kansas State in the Big Eight Tournament semifinals.

The final home game that season concluded with one of the most emotional moments I experienced in my 60 years of broadcasting. The Jayhawks hosted Oklahoma State, and late in the contest it was obvious that KU would win the game. As the final seconds ticked away, Brown stood up and called for Archie Marshall to enter the game.

Marshall was a crowd favorite, but a player who never had the opportunity to excel after suffering two major knee injuries. He was probably the most beloved player on the roster.

Brown had told Archie to suit up for the game, even though his knee would not allow him to play. So with those final few seconds remaining, Brown gave Archie one final moment of glory.

Archie entered the contest — wearing that awkward leg brace — and there was not a dry eye in the house. Larry was crying; the players were a combination of tears and excitement. Archie positioned himself safely near the bench. Oklahoma State Coach Leonard Hamilton had his players back away from Marshall. A KU player threw him a pass and Archie took a 40-foot shot. It was an air ball, but nobody cared. The Jayhawk bench signaled time-out and brought Archie out of the game. He was greeted with hugs and hand slaps. My eyes water just recalling the moment.

The Jayhawks received an at-large bid as a sixth seed to the NCAA Tournament and were assigned to a familiar court — the Devaney Center in Lincoln — for first-round action. KU drew 17th-ranked Xavier in the first game, and the Musketeers made a couple of turnovers before they even hit the court. First of all, Xavier center Tyrone Hill suggested in a published story that KU was overrated and he thought he could stop Manning. Later in the week, the Xavier players ripped Lincoln and the state of Nebraska. When the Musketeers ran onto the floor that night, the local Cornhusker fans returned the insult.

Manning then outscored Hill, 24-4, and the Jayhawks cruised to an 85-72 victory.

Up next for KU was Murray State, which had upset North Carolina State in the first round. It looked like another NCAA meltdown for KU as the Racers held a three-point advantage late in the game.

But the Jayhawks survived and advanced with a 61-58 victory. Next up for Kansas, a trip to the Pontiac Silverdome to face Vanderbilt. The NCAA selection committee had lined up an interesting possibility in Michigan as both KU and Kansas State were assigned to the same regional.

A pair of Sweet 16 wins by the Sunflower State schools would set up the fourth meeting of the season between the two teams. For probably one of the few times ever, KU fans were pulling for the Wildcats and Kansas State supporters were cheering for the Jayhawks.

Manning scored 38 points, and the Jayhawks eliminated Vandy by a 77-64 count in front of more than 30,000 in the Silverdome. In the second game, Kansas State upset Purdue.

It set up a storybook matchup between two in-state rivals for a trip to the Final Four in Kansas City.

Other voices from The Hill • Bob Davis

It ranks as the most memorable KU-Kansas State game of all time. It's the only one ever played outside Lawrence, Manhattan or Kansas City, and was played in front of the largest crowd to ever see the two teams play. It was probably one of the three or four greatest K-State teams of all time, with Mitch Richmond. KU trailed at the half, but Scooter Barry hit a big three-point basket. And after we got control of the game late, Max broke into a chorus of "Goin' To Kansas City."

Other voices from The Hill • Mark Turgeon

When we found out that Kansas State had beaten Purdue, we went to bed saying to ourselves that we're going to the Final Four because we knew we could beat K-State the way we were playing. K-State was a tired team when we played them.

They'd put so much into the Purdue game. Milt played a heck of a game and everybody came together and played a great game. All of a sudden we're in the Final Four, and you're thinking destiny at that point.

Returning from Detroit after the victory over Kansas State, the Jayhawks were welcomed by about 2,000 fans at Topeka's Forbes Field and more than 7,000 at Allen Fieldhouse. The 1986 trip had been expected, but not many gamblers would have wagered money on the Jayhawks' qualifying in '88.

Right away, the KU team earned the nickname, "Danny and the Miracles." Everyone was thrilled that KU would be playing just 40 miles down the road from Lawrence, with the possible exception of Frederick. He faced the burden of figuring out a proper method of distributing the 1,625 Kemper Arena tickets the NCAA made available to each school. Needless to say, he was going to make a few people happy and a lot more mad.

The 1988 Final Four was an anniversary celebration. It marked the 50th Final Four, and the NCAA brought back some of the great coaches and players from past tournaments. It was also a proud moment for the Big Eight Conference as the league represented half of the field: Oklahoma and the Jayhawks.

Meanwhile, the ever-superstitious Brown imported a good luck charm he found during the regional tournament in Detroit. The Jayhawks had been driven to and from the Silverdome in a Greyhound bus by a driver named Jimmy Dunlap, and Larry thought he had brought the team luck.

So Brown had Jimmy flown in from Detroit. In Kansas City, it was Dunlap who ferried the team from its headquarters at the Marriott Plaza to Kemper Arena.

As it had in 1986, KU found itself in the Final Four against Duke. Manning and Newton provided the offensive fireworks in 1988, out dueling the Blue Devils' standout, Danny Ferry, and defensive whiz Billy King. KU jumped out to a 14-0 lead and pushed it to 24-6 at the halfway point of the first stanza. The Jayhawks withstood a late rally and earned a spot in the finals with a 66-59 win.

Not only was it shocking for KU to be in the national championship game, but it was also against all odds that the Jayhawks would be paired with Oklahoma, which had beaten Arizona. It was only the third time that two teams from the same conference had met in the title game. KU's last three losses prior to the NCAA Tournament had been against Kansas State, Duke and Oklahoma. To win a national championship, the Jayhawks had to beat Kansas State, Duke and Oklahoma.

In the first half, the two teams set a title-game record for total points in a half, going to the locker rooms tied, 50-50. It was somehow fitting, considering the NCAA was marking the 50th anniversary of the event.

KU shot 71 percent in the first half, and OU countered with seven-of-11 shooting from three-point range.

Brown slowed the tempo in the second half, and Manning took control. In the end, Manning's totals were 31 points, 18 rebounds, five steals and two blocks. He clinched the contest with four free throws in the final seconds to secure the 83-79 win. The Kemper Arena floor turned into a massive celebration, and I ventured out on the court and interviewed some of the happiest players you could imagine. Milt Newton's voice broke into shrillness as he told me of his excitement.

Kansas became the first team in the 50-year history of the tournament to win the title with more than 10 losses. Manning joined Clyde Lovellette, B.H. Born and Wilt Chamberlain as NCAA Tournament Most Outstanding Players. It was a great thrill for me to see another national championship banner in KU's possession.

The next day, Kansas returned home, and more than 20,000 people greeted the Jayhawks in a wild celebration at Memorial Stadium. The euphoria, however, was tempered the next morning as news spread that Brown would be headed back to UCLA. Sportscaster Jim Lampley broke the story on his morning broadcast, and the news rocked Lawrence.

Other voices from The Hill • Bob Frederick

I got up the next morning after the championship game and drove back from Kansas City straight to my office. I walked in the door; and my secretary informed me that the UCLA athletics director was on the phone. I remember telling my secretary, "We just won the national championship. Don't you think he would give us one day to enjoy it?" I talked to him, and he asked permission to talk with Larry.

That weekend, I think it was Friday night or Saturday morning, Larry called my house at 2:30 in the morning. He wanted to talk about his situation, so I got dressed and headed for his house. He was still interested in UCLA and needed advice. I stayed there the rest of the night talking about his options. He was real confused about what he wanted to do. I suggested Larry take some time and not talk to anybody.

Tuesday afternoon, Larry Brown waltzed into Allen Fieldhouse and in front of fans and reporters — with the saddest look of any human being I've ever seen

— announced he would return to Kansas. But the haggard Brown did a curious thing in making the announcement. He covered his mouth quickly after saying these words: "I came back and after thinking about it, I've decided to stay at the University of Kansas." Those closest to Larry have told me he was planning to head back to UCLA but just couldn't bring himself to say the words.

Larry fought back the temptation of a return coaching engagement at UCLA.

The champion Jayhawks visited the White House, shook hands with President Ronald Reagan and presented him with a Kansas letterman's jacket. The team returned from Washington, and emotions continued to soar. A victory parade in downtown Lawrence brought a crowd that police estimated at more than 60,000-equivalent to the city's entire population.

Later that night, the team banquet attracted more than 1,500 fans at the Lawrence Holidome. A young lady from Disney World — dressed as Cinderella attended and presented Brown with a glass slipper. Manning got the largest ovation when he did his own impersonation of Brown, complete with horned-rim glasses, a rolled-up program and a limp.

Several weeks after the season, a group of supporters pooled their resources, purchased a cherry red BMW, and presented it to Brown as a gift.

About a month later, on June 13, Larry was gone. The San Antonio Spurs offered him a contract he couldn't refuse. Larry got in his brand-new BMW and headed to Texas, back to professional basketball, still in search of Camelot.

The Larry Brown era at Kansas was suddenly over. In his five years at KU, Brown had returned excitement and tradition to the proud program. Shortly after Brown's departure, Frederick received disturbing news. An ongoing NCAA investigation of the basketball program was apparently going to result in more serious penalties than expected. Frederick would be faced with the challenge of filling Brown's job and dealing with the prospect of severe NCAA sanctions. It was amazing how quickly things had turned from triumph to turmoil.

Chapter 12

Glen Mason: Lead, Follow, or Get Out of The Way

Glen Mason was eager to accept the overwhelming challenge of rescuing a struggling KU football program that had suffered through 15 consecutive conference games without a victory. But he didn't have much with which to work.

When the Jayhawks assembled for the start of fall drills in 1988, Mason counted just 63 scholarship players on his roster. Of that number, 33 were from the freshman class. Five of those 63 had come to Kansas as walk-ons.

"We've got more coaches than players around here," he told the media during press day.

Mason was relentless in breaking down the Jayhawks' fragile exterior in preseason camp. As a product of a tough New Jersey neighborhood who had learned his football skills from no-nonsense coaches like Woody Hayes and Earle Bruce, Mason could accept the fact that his team lacked size, speed, depth, experience and overall talent. The one thing he would not tolerate, however, was a team short on toughness.

Other voices from The • Hill Matt Nolen

Coach Mason stayed in the dorm with us during preseason camp. Guys wanted to quit, but they were so scared of Coach Mason that they would sneak out of the dorm and go home in the middle of the night. We called it going AWOL. They didn't want to face Mason, so they would just slip out of the dorm — leaving about half of their stuff in their rooms — and you would hear a car squealing out of the parking garage. A lot of guys left that first year, but I don't think we could have won with them anyway. Mason just did what was necessary to turn the program around.

Those of us who have observed Mase at work or shared close quarters after a challenging question has been hurled in his direction would never debate the issue. In fact, numerous times during the course of a football season, he would be compelled to remind those who are listening where they can find his patience, his thought processes, his anger, or his motivation.

"I wear my emotions on my sleeve." It's a signature Mason quote.
In my first postgame interview experience with Mason, I found out that he also sometimes wears them on his knuckles. And in the color of bloody red. It sent a ripe message my way. This was a coach with ambition and drive. The heat index was at a boiling point in Memorial Stadium when Mason and his young and rather undersized Jayhawk football team first sprinted out on the turf in 1988 to face Baylor.

The first game was payday for Mason, his staff, and those surviving players who had endured nine torturous months' preparation. No college football team had worked harder or paid a more exhausting price than Mason's Jayhawks.

The green-clad Bears arrived in Lawrence that humid afternoon as a prohibitive favorite. It was a classic David versus Goliath episode — Kansas was probably the youngest and smallest college football team in the country. About 30 freshmen were on the field for the Jayhawks during the game. There were just seven players on the roster over 250 pounds.

Buoyed by their hopes but burdened by those of others, the Jayhawks broke out of the gates in inspired fashion. KU defensive back Peda Samuel got the Jayhawks rolling in the second quarter as he picked off a Bear pass. Quarterback Kelly Donohoe, a player short on size but massive in heart, then found Quintin Smith in the end zone for KU's first touchdown of the season. A few minutes later, Donohoe hooked up with Willie Vaughn for a 58-yard strike, and the Jayhawks had the KU faithful on their feet with a 14-3 halftime advantage.

With Kansas leading 14-6 midway through the third quarter, the Bears found an alley in the Jayhawk interior and blocked a field-goal attempt. Robert Blackmon returned it for a 64-yard momentum-shifting touchdown. The play shattered KU's fragile confidence, and the Hawks never recovered. Final score: Baylor 27, Kansas 14. The opportunity for a meaningful payday had slipped away.

After the game, I hustled from the broadcast booth into the Jayhawk interview room. Mason bolted through the door, his face full of anguish, and with a couple of long strides found his way to my interview perch as the rest of the media waited with notebooks in hand.

His emotions were highly visible. On his face, his sleeve and beyond. I looked down at Mason's knuckles. They were stained with blood. I found out later that KU was minus one locker-room chalkboard. The head coach vowed there would be no more blocked field goals.

After the 1987 season, when athletics director Bob Frederick faced the most challenging task of his tenure — locating a successor to Bob Valesente — Mason was one of the first coaches he called. But, Mase wasn't Frederick's first choice.

Frederick thought he had found his man in deposed Ohio State coach Earle Bruce. He had also talked to Mason, former USC coach Ted Tollner and Appalachian State coach Sparky Woods.

Considered one of the icons of college coaching, Bruce had been axed by the Buckeyes in a surprise move. He had fallen out of favor with the leadership in Columbus and appeared an attractive, big-name candidate for Frederick and his selection committee.

Frederick reached a verbal understanding with Bruce before Christmas to become the next football coach at Kansas. They just had to iron out the numbers before attending the mid-morning press conference.

Other voices from The Hill • Bob Frederick

(Bruce's attorney) told us that Earle had been "really screwed" by Ohio State and asked that we pay him $1 a year for the first 18 months he was head coach at Kansas. Under that arrangement, Ohio State would then be forced to continue to pay him under the terms of his firing. I told him we couldn't do that. I said we're a university, and we were not going to be a party to that type of arrangement. I said that was between you and Ohio State. They were adamant about the deal. We refused to compromise and left.

The next morning, I called Glen and told him I wanted to talk with him. He said he was still interested in the Ohio State job.

Christmas arrives, and we still don't have a football coach. I knew that John Cooper was the No. 1 candidate at Ohio State, so I called him. John and I had been friends for awhile. He said, "Bob, I've got a contract from Ohio State in hand. My attorney is working on the details, and I expect to be named head coach." Glen didn't know that, and John told me I couldn't tell anybody.

So, here I am knowing that John Cooper is going to be named head coach at Ohio State, and Glen still believes he's a candidate for the job. So I called Chancellor Budig and asked if he would call the Ohio State president and get this deal moving. Several days later, Jim Jones, the Ohio State athletics director, called Glen and told him of his plans to hire Cooper.

We then got on the phone and worked it out to hire Glen Mason.

In 1987, Kansas traveled to Auburn for a big athletic department payday. The contract called for a return engagement in Lawrence the following season. But Auburn made Frederick an offer he couldn't refuse. Instead of coming to Kansas, Auburn negotiated to serve as host again in Year Two in exchange for a king's ransom.

So, in '88, KU packed its bags for 85,000-seat Jordan-Hare Stadium while the athletics department cashed a much-needed $400,000 check. Mason knew right away his team didn't belong on the same field with the War Eagles. Auburn scored on its first four possessions and took a 56-7 victory. Several months later, the *Atlanta Constitution* ran a story that revealed that the game clock had been kept ticking during dead-ball situations. The newspaper implied that a deal had been worked out at halftime among the officials, Mason, and Auburn coach Pat Dye to allow the clock to run and speed a mercy killing. Mason, however, played no part in the alleged clock maneuvering.

Other voices from The Hill • Glen Mason

I guess they ran the clock, but I was not aware of it. I got a bad rap on that game, and I still resent that the Big Eight Conference didn't come to my defense. To me, it was no big deal. Auburn is playing Kansas, and it's not an even match up. Pat Dye did one of the great humanitarian things when he played his first-team defense just seven plays. It was a joke.

Was I mad they ran the clock? No, I wasn't. I resent that they said I asked to have the clock run. I never thought about it. If I had, I would have done it!

After losing tough games during their first eight weeks of the season, payday finally arrived for the 1988 Jayhawks in Week Nine. Tony Sands had a career-best rushing day against rival Kansas State with 122 yards, and Arnold Snell ran for 94 yards and two touchdowns in leading the Jayhawks to a 30-12 victory over the Wildcats.

Live post-game interviews with Coach Glen Mason were fun after a Jayhawk victory. But I never looked forward to interviewing the head man after a loss.

Mason flashed a bright smile after the game. For the first time, I was able to conduct a happy post-game interview with the head coach. That was about the only smile of the year. That season of massive bumps and bruises — including KU yielding an NCAA record 536 yards per game — harvested a 1-10 record. Mason promised there would be better days ahead.

Kansas football turned 100 years old in 1989. KU opened the season impressively, winning two of its first three games. In Game Six, Donohoe passed for a career-high 411 yards, but KU lost to Iowa State, 24-20. It was the third of four straight losses.

Two weeks later, KU traveled to Manhattan and altered its offense to a ground attack. Sophomore Tony Sands, with touchdown runs of 59 and 62 yards, finished the day with a career-high 217 yards, and the Jayhawks earned a 21-16 victory. The Governor's Cup would remain in Lawrence another year.

The Hawks finished the season three weeks later in Columbia against Missouri. It was a classic confrontation between the two programs. KU won the battle of offenses, defeating Missouri, 46-44, to conclude the year with a respectable 4-7 record.

Chip Hilleary moved up from reserve to starting quarterback as the Jayhawks opened a new decade of football. Dana Stubblefield also made his debut as a regular in the defensive line. Slowly, Mason was building a good football team and bringing in more quality players each season. The Jayhawks were young in 1990, with just three seniors in the starting lineup.

It was obvious that Kansas was a much-improved football team that year, but its record would not reflect it. KU won just once in its first seven games. The Jayhawks visited Miami midway through the season and before kickoff, one of the more bizarre episodes of Kansas football occurred.

Other voices from The Hill • Glen Mason

We didn't have the caliber of players that Miami had, but we had tough kids. I knew they wouldn't back down. They were kids that would fight. Kids that had a lot of pride. Miami came out of the locker room for pre-game warm-ups and thought they could run right through us and bully us around. It didn't happen that way.

I don't condone fighting on the field, but my guys did the right thing. Miami was used to pushing people around and there is only one way to deal with a bully... and that's to hit him right in the nose. There wasn't another incident the whole game.

The Hurricanes whipped Kansas, 34-0, and we boarded the plane for a long return flight. As always, Bob Newton, who serves as producer/ engineer for our radio network, was along. Bob is a pilot, and he often visits the cockpit during long charter flights.

About midway through the flight, Newton emerged from a visit with the flight crew and revealed alarming news for the few of us sitting near. We had lost an engine, and an emergency landing would be necessary. The pilot came on the public-address system and issued the report to the rest of the travel party. I was seated next to the Reverend Vince

Krische, a priest from the St. Lawrence Catholic Center, who traveled with the team. Needless to say, I took a little comfort in the fact I was in the company of a man with good connections in high places.

The captain instructed us to prepare for touchdown. I overhead someone close by say, "That will be the Jayhawks' first touchdown of the day." It brought a good laugh and broke the tension. The plane made a safe and secure landing. We were moved to a new plane and made it back to Kansas without further problems.

The highlight of the season came late in the schedule when Kansas State paid a visit to Memorial Stadium in front of 45,000 fans. They weren't disappointed as KU racked up more than 300 yards of total offense. Freshman kicker Dan Eichloff was the hero as he connected on two field goals, including a school record 58-yarder, in KU's 27-24 victory. The Jayhawks finished the 1990 season with a 3-7-1 record.

"It's no faint praise to call the Jayhawks the best three-victory team in the nation," wrote *The Sporting News* as the season concluded.

From my point of view, Kansas turned a significant corner in 1991. The Jayhawks opened the year with three consecutive wins and then took conference victories at Iowa State, Oklahoma State and Missouri to finish with a 6-5 season record.

It marked the first winning season at Kansas since the 1981 Hall of Fame Bowl team and spoke volumes about the direction Mason was taking the program.

The winning season was a tribute to the play of Tony Sands. Pound-for-pound, inch-for-inch, there may not have been a tougher, more productive running back in Kansas history. Just a shade over 5-foot-6, the 175-pound Sands represented the classic Mason football player. He was small and overlooked by most major colleges. But he had a tremendous heart and great courage.

It was hard not to like Tony. He almost always had a smile on his face. They called him "Tuxedo Tony," because he always wore a tuxedo to and from the stadium.

Sands put on one of the most remarkable performances I witnessed in my broadcasting career in the final game of the season versus Missouri, setting two NCAA records with 58 carries and 396 yards.

Other voices from The Hill Golden Pat Ruel

(Tony) was having a great game and had a shot at the school career rushing record. After he passed that mark, we were about ready to pull him out of the game. But Missouri kept scoring. So we decided to keep feeding him the ball. I started calling plays just for Tony. After he broke the school record, we found out on the sidelines that he was close to the Big Eight career standard, so Mase says, "Let's get him the Big Eight record." We kept giving the ball to Tony. We'd run him inside a couple of plays and then outside.

I asked Tony how he was doing and he said, "I'm doing great coach. I want to play all day." He was so excited that he was playing well in his last game. After he gets the conference record, someone says he can get the NCAA record next. I remember that when he finally broke the NCAA record we took him out of the game and he was just four yards away from 400 and we were just four yards from a touchdown.

On that last drive, (quarterbacks coach) Dave Warner called down from the coaches' booth and suggested that we just throw the ball one time. All we were doing is handing it to Tony, going inside and outside. We were thinking that we needed first downs so we could maintain more possessions for Tony. So we threw a little pass that was incomplete. After the pass, Mason walks over to me and he says, "You call a pass one more time, or you give the ball to anyone else but Tony Sands, and you're fired."

KU blasted the Tigers, 53-29, and Tony was carried off the field by his teammates. The post-game radio show with Mason was about the most emotional that I can remember. The valiant effort brought overdue recognition to Tony. There was a huge crowd of reporters waiting when Mason charged through the door with Tony — still dressed in full pads — to share the post-game interview.

I asked Tony a few questions and he responded in the same fashion he carried the ball that afternoon: nonstop. He had tears in his eyes but was giddy with excitement, and Mason was about the same way.

Everything seemed in place for the 1992 season. Hilleary returned at quarterback and, despite the loss of Sands, the Jayhawks had Monte Cozzens and Maurice Douglas returning as ball carriers. On defense, the Jayhawks featured Stubblefield, Gilbert Brown and Chris Maumalanga. In the secondary, transfer Kwamie Lassiter would add an exciting dimension.

The Jayhawks got off to a fast start, beating Oregon State (49-7), Ball State (62-10), and Tulsa (40-7).

For the first time since October of the 1976 season, Kansas appeared in The Associated Press poll, breaking in at 24. That week, ESPN came to town for the final non-conference game against California. The Jayhawks had impressive moments but lost the game, 27-23.

Mason had his team fully focused the following Saturday when Kansas State arrived in Lawrence. In front of a sell-out crowd, the Jayhawks hammered the Wildcats. The Jayhawk defense was suffocating as it held K-State to a school-record minus-56 yards rushing in a 31-7 victory. K-State didn't get a first down until the third quarter.

KU played one of the strangest football games I've ever witnessed the following Saturday in Ames against Iowa State. It was a game straight from a Hollywood script.

The Jayhawks bounced out to a 21-7 lead in the first quarter, and I figured it would be one of those one-sided encounters during which I would be reading a lot of material from the media guide. The Cyclones then proceeded to outscore KU 40-8 in the second and third quarters and at one point held a 26-point advantage (47-21) late in the third quarter. It was a nightmare game and a real challenge to keep a positive tone in the broadcast booth. The Cyclones were just completely dominating the Hawks.

And then momentum changed uniforms. Hilleary engineered a comeback in what might have been one of his finest games as a Jayhawk. First, he scored on a 17-yard scamper at the close of the third quarter. He then connected with Dwayne Chandler for 30 yards and a touchdown early in the fourth quarter. Later in the final period, Hilleary found Matt Gay on a 12-yard pass to bring the Jayhawks to within five points, 47-42.

On the next possession, KU linebacker Larry Thiel scooped up an Iowa State fumble and raced 37 yards for a score. Douglas added the two-point conversion, and the Jayhawks recorded an unbelievable return-from-the-dead triumph. The 26-point comeback represents the largest in school history.

KU next returned home to face Oklahoma, a team the Jayhawks had not defeated since 1984. Cozzens and Douglas each rushed for 100-plus yards and Kansas shocked the Sooners, 27-10. Cozzens scored the Jayhawks' final touchdown on an amazing 15-yard blockbuster gallop in which he ran through and around a host of Sooner defenders.

The Jayhawks took an uninspiring 26-18 win over Oklahoma State to improve their record to 7-1. For the first time in many years, KU was talking about first in the Big Eight with Nebraska, Colorado and Missouri left on the schedule. KU proceeded to lose each of those games, leaving its bowl hopes in doubt.

But on Thanksgiving Day, Nebraska beat Oklahoma. The Jayhawks had finished third in the conference, which positioned them as the league representative in the Aloha Bowl on Christmas Day. It would mark KU's first bowl game in 11 years.

Because of the basketball schedule, the radio crew didn't fly with the football team. We arrived in Paradise a little later, but we were scheduled for a long stay because the basketball team would start play in the Rainbow Classic a few days after Christmas.

On a blazing hot day in Honolulu, Brigham Young provided the opposition and struck like lightning in the game's opening moments. Hema Heimuli returned the Jayhawks' opening kickoff 94 yards for a TD.

Two plays after Heimuli's touchdown for BYU, Gay took a lateral from Hilleary and tossed a 74-yard touchdown pass to Rodney Harris, and the Jayhawks were even.

The game stayed close throughout and boiled down to the closing moments.

Hilleary marched the Jayhawks down the field while one of college football's best field goal kickers, Dan Eichloff, waited on the sideline. There was only one problem. Eichloff had to, well, go.

Other voices from The Hill • Glen Mason

We kept moving and I'm thinking, "We're going to kick a field goal to win it." Dan Eichloff comes up to me and says, "Coach, I've got to go to the bathroom." At first I said OK, thinking that if he didn't make it back I would have Pat Ruel fake a heart attack to stop the action. But truthfully, I told Dan there was no way he was leaving the field. Just hold it! Finally, I told him to get in there and kick the field goal.

Eichloff held on and kicked a 48-yard field goal in the final minutes to give KU a 23-20 win and its first bowl victory in 31 years. Stubblefield was a dominating force on defense and earned the Player of the Game award for KU.

Mason was honored as conference Coach of the Year and was also a finalist for national Coach of the Year.

The 1992-93 athletic year at Kansas was one of remarkable progress by all the Jayhawk teams. KU became the first school in NCAA history to win a bowl game, send its men's basketball team to the Final Four, and have its baseball team in the College World Series.

Success spurs ambition, and the Jayhawks displayed no fear in accepting an invitation to face top-ranked Florida State in the 1993 Kickoff Classic at Giants Stadium. In my years of being around and observing Mason in action, I've never seen him back down from a challenge.

Other voices from The Hill • Richard Konzem

I remember the pre-game press conference at Giants Stadium. It seems like it's, 130 degrees on the turf and everyone is just covered with perspiration. Bob Davis and I were walking in a tunnel area under the stadium, near our locker room in the bowels of the stadium. We're all just dripping with sweat.

Davis finds a nice shady spot where he can sit down on this wooden box that's painted blue. We are waiting for Florida State to make their appearance on the turf. Bob is wearing a brand new pair of denim Docker shorts. When it comes time to head back out on the field, Bob puts both hands down to lift his rear off the box and discovers that he has wet paint on both palms of his hands. At this point, he realizes he has a bigger problem. He gets up and discovers a wider patch of blue paint across the back of his brand-new shorts.

Poor Bob has to spend another hour getting interviews with this blue stripe across his posterior and deal with the constant reminder "Hey, Bob. Did you know you've got blue paint all over your shorts?" The next day we made a sign, "This space reserved for Bob Davis." We taped it to the box where you could still see the imprint of his rear end.

The 1993 season got off to a bad start. Then it got much worse. After Florida State dominated the Jayhawks, 42-0, KU suffered through season-ending injuries and nagging injuries that hampered consistency. At one point in the season, 11 starters were on the sidelines. Considering everything the team had endured throughout the year, the Jayhawks' 5-7 record in 1993 was a miracle.

In spite of opening the '94 season with wins over Houston and Michigan State, and crushing UAB 72-0, the Hawks finished with a 6-5 record. Still, Mason never lost faith in himself.

I had mixed feelings heading into the 1995-96 year.

The Big Eight Conference was closing operations at the end of the season, and a new, expanded league — the Big 12 — was taking shape. Longtime Big Eight Commissioner Carl James was handed his pink slip. The league office was moved to Dallas.

Bob Frederick took a run at the commissioner's job, but the league CEOs selected Southwest Conference Commissioner Steve Hatchell for the post. Like many Kansas fans, I detected a disturbing Texas influence in the movement of the Big 12.

As fall rolled around to start the 1995 football season, I didn't feel much excitement. Like a lot of the fans and media, I was apprehensive about the Jayhawks' talent level. Mark Williams was untested at quarterback, and the Jayhawks would have a completely rebuilt defensive line.

Things got worse before the season even started. Linebacker Ronnie Ward, the team's top defender, reinjured a shoulder playing pickup basketball in the spring and was knocked out for the year. Defensive back Tony Blevins had not fully recovered from a knee injury the previous year and decided to redshirt.

Mason had made wholesale changes on his staff before the season. He fired defensive coordinator Bob Fello, a truly unique coach whom I had learned to appreciate, and secondary coach Mark Dantonio. Mike Hankwitz arrived from Colorado to be the Jayhawks' defensive coordinator, and David Gibbs, also a CU assistant, was hired to coach the KU secondary.

No one gave KU much hope for being anything more than a second-division Big Eight team. The Jayhawks were picked to finish fifth in the preseason writers' poll.

But Mason was quietly building a team.

The first couple of games didn't change anyone's feelings. The young Jayhawks, with 15 new starters in the lineup, were unimpressive in a 23-18 victory over Cincinnati in the season opener. KU moved its record to 2-0 with a 27-10 win over North Texas in Week Two.

People started believing a little the next week when the Jayhawks played inspired from the start in a nationally televised game at Memorial Stadium against TCU. KU raced to a 21-0 lead and held off a late rally for a 38-20 victory. June Henley and L.T. Levine combined for 300 yards on the ground to set the pace.

KU escaped with a 20-13 win over Houston the following Saturday, giving the Jayhawks a sparkling 4-0 record. But they had only played consistently against TCU. With Colorado on the horizon, Week Five would be the real test.

On paper, the game figured to be no contest. The Jayhawks had 14 players from the freshman and sophomore classes on their two-deep defensive depth chart. The Buffs entered the game ranked fourth nationally, with impressive wins over Wisconsin, Texas A&M, and Oklahoma. The game had special meaning for Hankwitz and Gibbs, who had been part of the success story at Colorado.

No one could argue, though, that on that October day in Boulder, KU was clearly the superior team. The Jayhawks upset Colorado, 40-24, marking their first win over a Top 10 team since 1984. The victory moved the Jayhawks into ninth in the coaches' poll and 10th in The Associated Press rankings.

All of a sudden, Kansas football was the talk of the country. The Jayhawks, unranked in preseason polls, bolted into the national spotlight. KU didn't stop with Colorado. It reeled off an impressive win against Iowa State and then downed Oklahoma in Norman for the first time since 1975.

However, the unbeaten string came to an abrupt end against Kansas State the next weekend as the Wildcats spoiled the victory parade with a 41-3 win.

Kansas rebounded with three wins in its final four outings to finish the regular season with an 8-2 record and a tie for second in the Big Eight Conference. Once again, the Jayhawks' finish put them in the Aloha Bowl, this time against UCLA.

The Jayhawks' success ignited rumors of Mason's departure as head coach.

UCLA, the Jayhawks' Aloha Bowl opponent, had an opening, as did Rutgers and Georgia. The day prior to KU's planned departure for Honolulu, Georgia director of athletics Vince Dooley announced the hiring of Mason as the Bulldogs' head coach.

I didn't travel with the football team to Hawaii. With the Jayhawk basketball team busy during the holiday season, the broadcast crew split. I stayed with the basketball Jayhawks while Bob Davis took the bowl trip.

Other voices from The Hill • Bob Davis

Mason was in a horse-crap mood all week. The night before the game, we had a Christmas Eve party. I was hoping to talk with Mase and at least set a time to tape our pre-game interview because the kickoff was set for 10 a.m. Hawaii time. When I asked him about that, he said loudly, "I haven't got time to talk about that tonight." I said, "Well, we start real early tomorrow, coach."

He said, "By God, you can't get up earlier than I am."

"You know, Coach, I do go to work at 3:30 every morning."

He kind of laughed and said, "Listen, Davis, you are never going to forget Christmas Day, 1995. Just remember that."

The next day, he was a totally different guy. Obviously he was going through a lot that night.

So, like a lot of KU fans, I was sitting in front of my television on Christmas morning ready to watch Mason coach his final game.

What most people didn't know was that Mase had a change of heart. The day after KU arrived in Hawaii, Mason went to Chancellor Bob Hemenway and said that he was considering not taking the Georgia job — which he'd already accepted. The Chancellor was in a pickle. He had been the school's chancellor for about six months. On top of that, athletics director Bob Frederick didn't make the trip to Hawaii, deciding to stay in Lawrence to start his exhaustive search for Mason's replacement.

Other voices from The Hill • Robert Hemenway

The thought pattern I had was that Glen is just as good of a football coach the day after he's announced he's not going to Georgia as he was the day he was going to Georgia. We couldn't really say, "Sorry, but because you thought that maybe Georgia would be a better place, that would exclude you from ever coaching in Kansas again if you wanted to." It didn't seem right for me to say that.

Shortly before the game, the news broke that Mase had changed his mind about Georgia. He announced officially after the bowl game that he would coach a ninth season at KU, saying Georgia just wasn't the right fit.

Other voices from The Hill • Bob Frederick

We were opening Christmas presents when the phone rang. It was the Chancellor. I thought, it's five o'clock in the morning in Hawaii. Why is he calling me now and calling me on Christmas morning? He said, "Bob, I just wanted to let you know that I made a decision last night to let Glen Mason come back to the football team." And I said okay. What else was there to say?

The rest of that day was one of the most surreal situations I've ever been in because all these cars started pulling up in front of the house, and guys were getting out with their video cameras and microphones on Christmas Day, wanting interviews about what just happened. At one point, while we were eating, there was a knock at the door. A reporter was there and he asked if he could interview me briefly. When I told him we were having dinner right then, he said, "Well, my dad is waiting for me out in the car and he's cold."

The news of Mason's decision might have helped the team that day. The Hawks proceeded to play inspired football. Mark Williams looked like an all-American as KU thrashed the Bruins, 51-20.

Although one might assume that the 1996 season would be full of optimism and excitement — coming off a bowl win, having your head coach say he's turning down football-tradition rich Georgia to stay at Kansas and the start of a new conference, the Big 12 — that wasn't the case. In fact, just the opposite was true. There was this feeling that Mase didn't really want to be at Kansas. Plus, who knew what was going to happen in the new conference with the Texas schools coming aboard.

As it turned out, we won our first Big 12 game in history down in Oklahoma, by a lopsided score of 52-24. John Blake was the coach at Oklahoma, and they weren't worth a darn then. (How quickly things changed for them.)

But, after winning that game, Mason and the Hawks lost six out of the last seven games on the schedule. Kansas State was rolling, ranked 13th in the nation when we played them. They beat us badly, 38-12. The next week, unranked Texas came to Lawrence and won big, 38-17. Then, in the season finale at Columbia, Missouri won 42-25. KU finished the season with a 4-7 record (2-6 in the Big 12). So it wasn't a great year. Subsequently, Mase resigned and went to Minnesota. Mason finished his career at KU with a 47-54-1 record.

(In an interesting twist for Mason, KU's first football coach in the Big 12 era, he stayed at Minnesota until the end of the 2006 season. His Gophers were on the short end of the biggest comeback in bowl history, when — and here's the interesting part — the Big 12's Texas Tech erased a 31-point second-half deficit and won the Insight Bowl. Mase was fired two days later.)

Chapter 13

Roy Williams: From Unknown to America's Winningest coach of the 90s

It was probably pure happenstance, but Kansas was looking for a basketball coach about the same time 37-year-old Roy Williams was looking for his first collegiate head coaching job. He didn't have a marquee name or impressive resume, but his work ethic inspired recommendations from a couple of influential coaches.

Even before Larry Brown left, Bob Frederick had heard about Roy Williams, from former KU coach Dick Harp. He was about to hear more about the Carolina assistant.

Other voices from The Hill • Bob Frederick

When Larry left, the first call I made was to Dean Smith. He laughed when I asked if he would be interested in the job and said, "I don't think it would be appropriate for me to leave after they named the building after me." We then talked about some of the candidates, and he asked me to consider Roy Williams for the job.

Shortly after, I talked with Gary Williams and he withdrew from consideration, I called Roy. He had just gone to Bermuda for a short vacation. He flew back to the Atlanta airport and we met in the Delta Room. There were two things that I distinctly remember from that first conversation. First was his sense of organizational skills. Secondly, he had a real appreciation for the tradition of Kansas basketball.

That ended up being a significant factor in my own mind. We had gone so long with so few coaches. Then Larry stayed five years, and I didn't want to get into a situation where we were hiring a new coach every three to five years.

I'm not sure Roy realized how many friends he made that early July morning when he was introduced by Bob as head basketball coach at KU. Jayhawk fans never appreciated the constant rumors that had swirled around Brown during his five seasons in Lawrence. Roy may not have been a household name in basketball circles, but everyone quickly found out that he wasn't a butterfly.

"My hope is that you don't have to go through another press conference to hire a basketball coach for about 30 years," said Williams, prompting a loud ovation from well-wishers attending his first press conference. "I coached at the same high school for five years. I coached at North Carolina for 10 years. I've had the same wife for 15 years. The same set of golf clubs for 17 years. I'm a guy that if I find something I like, I'll stick with it."

With that one lasting comment, Williams quickly disarmed many of the doubters.

Roy's first order of business was to hire a coaching staff. His first choice for an assistant coach was Jerry Green, a longtime friend who had spent nine seasons as head coach at North Carolina-Asheville. Jerry was an excellent on-the-floor coach and one of the funniest individuals I've ever met. When he opened his mouth and let loose with that slow motion, deep-South accent, he evoked a smile without really trying. In the tension-packed moments of that first season, I think Jerry more than anyone else helped lift spirits on the team and among the staff.

Jerry always called people "Big Frog." I really can't explain why, but it became his trademark. Greener and I had many fun battles on the golf course.

Kevin Stallings, who had spent six seasons on Gene Keady's staff at Purdue, and Steve Robinson, an aide for two years at Cornell, were the next to come on board. Williams then completed the staff picture by rehiring Mark Turgeon, a former player and assistant under Brown.

Roy Williams knew he was following a tough act. He also fully understood that the Jayhawks were about to be sanctioned by the NCAA. Frederick had revealed the NCAA probe to Williams during that meeting in Atlanta. Frederick told Williams that he didn't anticipate major penalties.

The news finally arrived, appropriately, on Halloween night. Frederick called Williams into his office and stunned him with the NCAA's decision. The team was banned from the 1989 NCAA Tournament — the first team barred from a title defense — and hammered with rigid recruiting restrictions that Williams thought would handicap the program for several seasons. The Jayhawks lost scholarships and could have no paid recruiting visits to campus for a full year.

Roy later said that if he'd known the punishment was going to be that severe, he wouldn't have taken the job.

What a coaching staff! After serving on Roy's staff (seen here in 1989-90), each one has coached at the Division I level. (From l to r) Kevin Stallings, Steve Robinson, me, Roy Williams, Mark Turgeon and Jerry Green.

There may not have been any Danny Mannings on the roster in 1988-89, but Roy had players who were passionate about winning. That Jayhawk team went through the season on a mission. They used the probation as fuel to ignite the full force of their emotions in every game. Without the reward of postseason play, the Jayhawks sought satisfaction in each win.

Any questions about Williams' ability to coach were erased in those first months of the season. A 115-45 win over Brown set the record for largest victory margin. The Jayhawks won 13 of their first 14 games and went over the century mark six times during that stretch. KU opened conference play by registering a school-record 127 points in a 45-point win over Iowa State.

Although not found in any preseason rankings, KU moved up to 16th in the January 10 Associated Press poll. It was all happening for a team with just nine scholarship players.

Kansas stood 16-3 following a 20-point win over Wichita State in late January. After that, everything seemed to go wrong.

The Jayhawks faded to 16-11 overall and just 3-8 in conference competition. The drought finally ended, and KU captured its final three regular season games.

Other voices from The Hill • Roy Williams

That first year — when we hit the slump — we tried so many things to keep everyone positive. We would go back to the fieldhouse on Friday and watch Rocky III — because it dealt with getting hungry again and finding the eye of the tiger. We took them back the next Friday night and watched Hoosiers. We'd pop popcorn in the office and take it down to them. I was trying anything just to get the kids to stick together.

It all finally came to an end in the first round of the conference tournament as Kansas State eliminated the Jayhawks, 73-65. Roy paced outside his team's locker room for a few moments, tears in his eyes, before entering to say good-bye to his first team.

Other voices from The Hill • Roy Williams

To me, that first bunch is the one that "made Roy Williams." I really believe that.

When I came to Kansas, I inherited a group of guys that had just won a national championship, and they gave me a chance. Everything I asked them to do, they tried to do. I was big on positive thinking and confidence, and that was something guys like Mark Randall, Scooter Barry and Kevin Pritchard needed. That team didn't have the tough Danny Manning-type guy who could stand being beat down. They accepted me and accepted what we were trying to do.

A touching editorial in *USA Today* shortly after the season summed up the 1988-89 Jayhawks in proper fashion.

Ex-Champps Are All Heart

The kids who couldn't win anything at least won more than a few hearts.

Kansas — college basketball's first non-defending national champion — played this season as if they hadn't read the headlines.

Because a coach who is no longer there broke some rules to recruit a player who never came, Kansas was put on NCAA probation last fall.

"They're calling us outlaws," said senior guard Scooter Barry. "That isn't right, just isn't right. We're not outlaws." The Jayhawks' season ended when they lost to Kansas State in Friday's quarterfinals of the Big Eight Tournament. But, from beginning to that end, basketball's unlikeliest outlaws did something for the dignity of competition.

New Coach Roy Williams marveled "that they haven't had their heads down more than two days." There is no prize for that gumption as sweet as the one the Jayhawks won last April in Kansas City.

You did yourself proud. And thanks.

The probation shackled Williams' efforts in recruiting. In the months leading up to the announcement of penalties, he had secured word from three prized prep standouts that they would attend KU. In addition, he had others ready for visits.

When the bombshell hit, however, a couple of fish got away.

Other voices from The Hill • Roy Williams

We had verbal commitments from Thomas Hill, who would play at Duke, and Harold Minor, who became a standout at USC. They changed their minds. Thomas did it quickly, but Harold held on for a week. We had some other good ones who canceled their visits.

Adonis Jordan was the only player who stuck with his promise to attend KU. I believe Adonis won a permanent place in Roy Williams' heart with his decision to saddle up with the Jayhawks through the bad times.

Other voices from The Hill   •   Roy Williams

*I had gotten to know Adonis while I was still at North Carolina. I had
seen him that summer. We needed a point guard at Kansas, because Kevin was
going to be a senior and we needed someone to back him up and step into the
job the following year. I thought we were leading with Adonis from the first
day. I went into the home and Rick Barnes of Providence was going into the
home the same night after me. He got really mad, because he came in and we
were having a party with cake and ice cream. He felt like it was a ridiculous
situation, because the mom liked me. Rick told me later it was the most wasted
night of his life because it was a done deal.*

*But, when the probation hit, Seton Hall called Adonis back. The
assistants from Seton Hall hit him six straight nights hard on the phone.
But he stuck with us.*

*I remember getting a phone call from Bob Braswell, his high school coach.
He said, "Adonis wants to talk with you. He said you have 30 minutes with
him and you have to do a good job." I told him, "Adonis, some time in your
life you have to have faith in somebody. And that's what I'm asking you to
do. Have faith in me."*

*That's when he told me he was still coming, and I went back and wrote
"hooray" on the blackboard in the office.*

The Jayhawks had plenty of inspiration to open the 1989-90 season.
With the doors to the NCAA Tournament now open, KU rode on a no-
respect theme all year. Jayhawk players found little mention of their team
in preseason rankings, and they considered it an insult. A highly respected
national publication even predicted KU would place last in the Big Eight
Conference.

One reporter wrote that the Jayhawks were a team of short, skinny
players who could not jump over a telephone directory.

But the 1989-90 Jayhawk team was one of the most well meshed
gatherings of players I've ever watched on the court. Kevin Pritchard
was an intense leader who could drive hard down the lane or hit the
open three-point basket. Jeff Gueldner was a deceptive performer who
could drain the long-range shot and play solid defense at the other end.
Indiana transfer Rick Calloway brought a degree of mental toughness
on both ends of the court.

Mark Randall emerged as one of the best passing big men in college basketball. Pekka Markkanen, the 6-10 import from Finland, was a textbook post defender. Off the bench, Williams could call on instant offense from Terry Brown and find an offensive spark in Freeman West and Mike Maddox. Jordan and Sean Tunstall were also solid in reserve.

In addition, the Jayhawks got a bonus the second semester in Alonzo Jamison, who had become eligible in December. Jamison was a rugged 235-pounder with the ability to shut down a high-scoring opponent.

The Jayhawks opened in the preseason NIT, hosting Alabama-Birmingham and blazing the Blazers in the opener, 109-83. In those days, the NIT waited for scores and then paired teams in accordance with their hopes for a high profile, final-four gathering at Madison Square Garden in New York. Obviously, KU was not on the NIT's preferred invitation list.

As a result, Kansas was next dispatched to Baton Rouge to face an LSU team that featured Chris Jackson, Stanley Roberts and Shaquille O'Neal.

Other voices from The Hill • Roy Williams

I told the players, the next morning after we beat UAB, to think about how much fun it was going to be to beat LSU in Baton Rouge. I said, "By God, we're going to do it." They left and Jerry Green said, "What in the world are you doing telling them that? We couldn't beat those guys in a 100 years." I laughed and told him to shut up.

We got to the airport and found out the plane was 30 minutes late. I got the players together and said, "All right, we have 30 minutes to wait. I want you to sit here and think about how much fun it's going to be to beat LSU." We got to Baton Rouge and headed over for a workout. We arrived and I saw Dick Vitale. Dick tells me something I already know. "They want LSU in the Garden," said Vitale. I told him that we planned on spoiling the party. He said, "You can't beat these guys." I immediately blew my whistle and called the players over. I said, "I just told this guy we're going to spoil the party and we're beating this bunch tomorrow night." They walked away and Vitale says to me, "You got balls."

The next morning, in the paper, I read a quote from (LSU coach) Dale Brown, which said that he hadn't worked much on defense, "because the offense takes so much time." At our pre-game meal I told our guys, "We're going to set screens and move the ball." I said, "We'll have them spinning like a top that may bore a hole in the floor." They left and Jerry Green looked over at me and said, "You're crazy." I said, "Now our team believes we can do it. Wait and see."

I told them before the game that this one was going to be a "hugger." "Everyone is going to want to hug each other after this one, no matter how sweaty you are."

I was talking with Loren Mathews, one of the big executives with ESPN, a few years later, and the preseason NIT pairings came up in the conversation. He told me that the NIT went to a more structured pairings because they never got what they wanted when they attempted to choreograph the situation.

He said, "One year we sent some dog down to LSU when they had Shaquille O'Neal, Stanley Roberts and Chris Jackson. And they beat them." I said, "You (blankety blank). That dog was Kansas."

After beating LSU and earning a trip to New York, the upstart Jayhawks were matched with top-ranked UNLV in the first game. The team and coaches were guests of the tournament at a banquet at Tavern On The Green shortly after arriving in New York. Each coach was asked to stand up and say a few words about his team.

When the moment arrived for the Kansas head coach to stand up, the master of ceremonies introduced Ron Williams. Williams used the blunder to help motivate his team. By the end of the tournament, everyone in New York and throughout the country knew Roy Williams.

KU bounced UNLV by 15 points and then upended St. John's, 66-57, to claim the championship trophy. Suddenly, the Jayhawks were the talk of college basketball. The Jayhawks made one of the biggest poll leaps in history, going from no votes to second place in the next rankings.

The NIT ignited an amazing 19-game winning streak that featured a 150-95 pounding of Rick Pitino's first Kentucky team. Terry Brown played 19 minutes and scored 31 points, and Allen Fieldhouse was as loud as I've ever heard it.

The Jayhawks traveled to Miami in early January and Coach Williams invited the radio crew along with the team for a tour of the Miami Sea Aquarium. We were enjoying the sights, and I happened to be at Roy's side when he was observing a dolphin gliding through the water. I got the head man in trouble that day, and he's never let me forget it.

Other voices from The Hill • Roy Williams

I was standing at the dolphin tank, munching on some popcorn. I asked Max if he thought dolphins liked popcorn. He said, "Sure they do. Toss some down there." So, I threw a few corns into the water and the attendant comes out and starts ranting and raving at me. I point my finger in the direction of Max and tell the guy, "He said it would be OK." When I look around, Max is already over with the whales! He's nowhere in sight.

How was I supposed to know that popcorn was bad for dolphins?
KU moved to No. 1 in the national rankings twice during the season and both times, Missouri shot the Jayhawks out of the top spot. Still, KU took a sparkling 29-4 record into the NCAA Tournament.

But by then, the Jayhawks were carrying a heavy burden of expectations. KU beat Robert Morris, 79-71, and then faltered at the end in a heartbreaking 71-70 setback against UCLA.

Aside from the NCAA meltdown, Kansas had roared back into the limelight. In just his second season, Williams had guided the Jayhawks to a 30-5 record and earned national Coach of the Year honors. All the doubters disappeared.

Despite heavy personnel losses, Kansas was picked second in the conference poll as the 1990-91 season unfolded. Jordan replaced Pritchard at point guard. Brown, with his arching jump shot, was the obvious choice for shooting guard. Randall, Maddox and Jamison formed the interior. Off the bench, Williams counted on a trio of freshmen — Richard Scott, Steve Woodberry and Patrick Richey.

After dropping three of its last six contests, KU entered NCAA play looking like a team destined for an early exit.

The Jayhawks survived a first-round slow-down contest with New Orleans, 54-49, and then played impressively in a 77-66 victory over Pittsburgh in subregional action in Louisville. KU advanced to the regional in Charlotte, North Carolina.

Other voices from The Hill • Roy Williams

The NCAA Tournament was a great run. After we beat New Orleans and Pittsburgh, the next three teams ended up being the teams ranked two, three and four.

First we played Indiana and we got up 25-6. They stopped the game because of a problem with the floor. The referee was standing there looking at it, and Coach Knight walked out on the floor and asked if they could start the sucker over again.

The next game, we face Arkansas. It was another one of those games when Kevin Stallings says, "They're better than we are at the top eight spots." After the first 17 minutes of the game, the score is tied. They outscore us 14-2 and have a 12-point lead. At half I tell the kids, "Just do what I tell you to do. It will work. We're going to be back here smiling at the end of the game." I looked in the back of the room and all of my assistants have their heads down.

Spurred by a dose of locker-room confidence, KU scored the first six points to start the second half and suddenly, Jayhawks fans were going "hog" wild.

Confidence, maturity, and a bit of coaching wizardry made the difference as the Jayhawks were a dominating team in the second half. The excitement was riveting at the end as KU sent Arkansas packing in a 93-81 victory.

Other voices from The Hill • Roy Williams

The Arkansas game will always stand out in my mind. We won the game in my home state, and my whole family was there.

When I got home, the people in the neighborhood had put a sign up in my yard which had "40 Minutes of Hell" marked out and replaced with, "20 Minutes of Heaven." That was a game and a time when I said to myself, "This is pretty good."

The triumphant Jayhawks returned to Lawrence and Allen Fieldhouse for a wild celebration following the game. The victory earned Kansas a trip to Indianapolis and the Final Four, and it put Williams on a collision course with his mentor, Dean Smith, and North Carolina.

The media seized on the angle of The Coach vs. The Student. There was nothing that Dean or Roy could do or say to get the reporters to take a different tack.

The pairing of Kansas and North Carolina in a Final Four game brought back memories of 1956-57, when the Tar Heels beat the Jayhawks in three overtimes to win the national championship. Seeing Dean Smith also reminded me of the days when I had broadcast Topeka High School games and he was a hustling guard. I was both nervous and excited as I strolled into the massive Hoosier Dome that day, with a record crowd of 47,000 in the building. More than 1,200 games over 45 years had not dulled my enthusiasm for a game like this one.

In the early going, North Carolina was in control of the game. The Tar Heels built a 24-15 advantage, and Williams was forced to use a time-out.

Momentum switched uniforms and the Jayhawks went on a 17-1 run to take a 43-34 halftime advantage. Richard Scott came off the bench to spark at late run and KU hung on for a 79-73 victory. The final minutes, however, were bittersweet when Smith was slapped with a technical and ejected. His exit took him past Williams, and he paused to shake his pupil's hand as well as the respectful players on the KU bench before disappearing from the arena.

Other voices from The Hill • Roy Williams

I was concerned because all of the media attention on me and Coach Smith took away from the kids. And then the end of the game, something else took away from the kids. When Coach Smith got thrown out, my first reaction was that he didn't deserve it. My second reaction, almost immediately afterwards, was that this was not right because they were not going to give our players credit for a great victory. Coach had not even reached our bench, and I've already thought about that. He got in front of me stopped, shook hands, and said, "You know I didn't plan this." I told him I understood. He said, "I'm sorry."

The second game featured Duke and top-ranked UNLV, an overwhelming favorite in the contest. When Roy finally escaped the post-game interviews, he found an empty seat on press row next to me to watch the action. He surprised me by expressing the hope that Jerry Tarkanian's team, the dominant unit in college basketball throughout the year, would win the game. Roy feared Duke the most, feeling his team could handle the intense UNLV pressure. He became "ticked off" that KU fans were cheering for the Blue Devils.

Duke surprised everyone, except maybe Roy, and upset the Rebels. During Monday's championship, the Jayhawks had a bad shooting night, hitting just 41.5 percent and Duke won the title, 72-65 in front of 47,100 fans.

Mark Randall led KU with 18 points and connected on a three-pointer, the first and only one of his career.

After the season, Williams' friend and assistant coach, Jerry Green, resigned to accept the head coaching position at Oregon. Williams found an impressive replacement when he hired Matt Doherty, a member of the 1982 national championship team at North Carolina, to join the staff.

Soon after the Jayhawks played in the national championship basketball game of 1991, my mother, Edith, passed away. Because of my father's association with KU athletics and mine, she had been an avid fan. She went to all of the home games, and after my father's death, my wife, Isobel, took her to all the games.

Even after her eyesight failed, she followed every contest from start to finish.

After a shocking loss to UTEP, 66-60, in the second round of the 1992 NCAA Tournament, Kansas got back in the Williams groove.

The 1993 version of the Jayhawks won 16 of their first 17 games and solidified themselves among the elite teams in college basketball. The senior guard duo of Rex Walters and Adonis Jordan played in perfect harmony, keying the Jayhawks' performance.

Other voices from The Hill Roy Williams

I still say the three best competitors I've ever been around were Michael Jordan, a girl who played on the basketball team when I coached in high school, and Rex Walters.

KU won its third consecutive conference title but was upset by Kansas State in the second round of the Big Eight Tournament. The loss left a slight chink in the Jayhawk armor but also allowed KU an extra day of rest prior to starting play in the NCAA Tournament.

Kansas was dispatched to Chicago for first-round tournament action and played two great games, beating Ball State and Brigham Young. Walters put on a shooting clinic in the Windy City, lighting up BYU for 28 points.

The Jayhawks' NCAA trail carried them to St. Louis for second-round action and the start of the famous spitting episode. When Roy had been an assistant at North Carolina, the Tar Heels were playing for the national championship in New Orleans.

He had been told it was good luck to spit in the Mississippi River. So he did. Coincidence or not, his team won.

Williams decided to revive the superstition, and he took the entire team to the river in St. Louis where they unloaded.

With a fresh means of inspiration, KU carved up California and highly regarded Jason Kidd as Walters exploded for 24 points. (The game was also significant because KU attracted the attention of California freshman guard Jerod Haase, who became a Jayhawk a few months later.) The win set up another duel with Bob Knight and his Indiana Hoosiers. The Jayhawks hit nearly 60 percent of their shots and I sang a few verses of "Way Down Yonder in New Orleans" in the final moments of an 83-77 victory. After the game, I watched with great pride as each player took his turn at cutting down the nets.

When Roy finally made his way up the ladder in the end, he clipped a strand and I noticed tears in his eyes. I later learned that Roy was thinking about his mom, who had passed away the previous summer. It was on to New Orleans and the Superdome for another game against North Carolina.

In a rematch of the 1991 Final Four semifinals, history did not repeat itself.

Carolina, led by center Eric Montross, was much too strong inside and the Jayhawks' ride finally came to an end in a 78-68 loss in front of 64,000 fans.

Over the next two seasons, Roy Williams and the Jayhawks continued their destructive swath in college basketball. In 1993-94, KU won the preseason NIT and finished with a sparkling 27-8 record behind the play of Steve Woodberry. Kansas won 27 games again in 1994-95 and also claimed the league championship. Haase, Raef LaFrentz, Jacque Vaughn, BJ Williams and Scot Pollard were the emerging stars.

(By the way, my first impression of Jacque Vaughn came early in his freshman season on a road trip at the preseason NIT in New York. We were standing around in the airport waiting for a departure time and Jacque walked up to me, stuck out his hand, and said, "Hi, I'm Jacque Vaughn." That was a first. No player in any sport ever approached me with a formal introduction. Jacque's first impression was a lasting one. He's one of the best I've seen, both on and off the court.)

As my 50th year of broadcasting approached in 1995-96, I was fortunate to receive some wonderful recognition. During the summer of '95, I learned that I would be inducted into the KU Sports Hall of Fame. Over the summer, I learned the KU athletics department would induct me into the athletic hall of fame. It was a tremendous honor to join a fraternity that includes greats such as Sayers, Chamberlain, Manning, Oerter and Ryun.

Then, the KU Alumni Association awarded me with the Ellsworth Medallion, which is the highest honor the association bestows. I was most grateful for both of those honors.

I thought that everything that could possibly be done for me had been. Then I learned that a "Max Falkenstien cup" was being produced for concession-stand sales of soft drinks at all the basketball games that season. It featured my picture and a resume of my career. That was really just too much, but I will have to say I was flattered. (It was a $3 cup, however, so most of my friends opted for the smaller size.)

The Jayhawk basketball team that season was good. It was another typical Roy Williams team that finished the year with a 29-5 record, the seventh straight season of 25 wins or more. After winning the last Big Eight championship before the Big 12, KU advanced to the Elite Eight for the third time in six seasons. (Syracuse eliminated the Hawks, 60-57.)

Little did any of us know that we were a season away from witnessing one of the biggest heartbreaks in the program's illustrious history.

Chapter 14

Terry Allen: Nice Guys Don't Always Win

When Glen Mason headed for Minnesota after the 1996 season, athletics director Bob Frederick wanted a different atmosphere around Kansas football. Mason, albeit a successful coach, wasn't the best people-person in the world. He made people feel stressed out. Freddie pointed out that he told Mase on several occasions how people around the athletics department were afraid of him.

Golden Pat Ruel and Mike Hankwitz, Mason's offensive and defensive coordinators, both wanted the job very badly. Pat Ruel even called me one night and pleaded with me for an hour to do whatever I could to try to get him the job.

I said, "Pat, you don't have a chance in the world because they are not going to hire somebody who was associated with Glen Mason."

"I wouldn't coach like Mason coached. I would do it entirely different," Pat responded.

Frankly, he would've been great. He was funny, he was great with alums and he had a super football mind. He's gone on to have all sorts of success in the NFL and at the University of Southern California as an assistant.

Other voices from The Hill Bob Davis

One of the stunts Golden Pat Ruel pulled was to sleep in a pup tent on the practice field with Chancellor Gene Budig. I always told Pat, "You've got a hell of a chance to get this job someday because I don't know any coaches who have actually slept with the Chancellor."

Instead of Ruel and Hankwitz, the search brought Frederick to two finalists — Dennis Franchione, a long-time college coach who is from Cherokee,

Kansas, went to Pittsburg State, and later coached the Gorillas; and Terry Allen, a successful coach at the University of Northern Iowa since 1989.

Frederick said he strongly considered Franchione for the job, but several well-respected people in college football suggested to Frederick that Terry Allen was an up-and-coming coach, who was worth a shot. (It probably didn't hurt that his Division I-AA Northern Iowa team had beaten Kansas State during Terry's first year as head coach.) In many respects, Allen reminded Frederick of another coach on whom he took a chance: Roy Williams.

Allen certainly fit the criteria of changing the atmosphere in Lawrence. Without question, Terry Allen is one of the nicest guys you'd ever want to meet. That's the first thing anyone who's ever spent any time around Terry will tell you. It's almost like the guy who's set up on a blind date and all he's told about the girl is that she has "a great personality." We all know how to translate that. In much the same way, hearing that Terry is "a great guy" didn't translate to a lot of wins for Terry and the Jayhawks.

From the beginning, it looked as if Freddie had found another gem. The Jayhawks got off to a pretty good start in the 1997 season, winning four of their first five contests, including victories over Missouri by a score of 15-7 — which happened to be the program's 500th win all-time — and Oklahoma, 20-17. That was as good as it got. The Jayhawks won one more game that season, a 34-24 Homecoming victory over Iowa State. Terry Allen's first season at Kansas, which finished 5-6 overall, wasn't a rousing success but it was far from a disaster.

In the early summer of 1998 I received a telephone call from Bernie Kish, the executive director of the College Football Hall of Fame in South Bend, Indiana. Bernie, a long-time friend and retired military officer, is the son-in-law of George Bernhardt, who had been a long-time assistant football coach at Kansas and elsewhere.

Bernie advised me that I had been chosen to receive the Chris Schenkel Award, which was presented to a broadcaster who had a long and distinguished career broadcasting college football. The award had just been created in 1996, so I was only the third individual to have been selected. The first was Schenkel himself, and the second was Jack Cristil, who for 45 years had broadcast the games for Mississippi State.

Isobel and I flew to South Bend for the ceremonies on August 14th. Many of the big names in athletics were on hand, including George

Steinbrenner of the New York Yankees and coach Eddie Robinson, who gave the keynote address. It was quite a show!

As each of the nominees was presented, he entered from the rear of the room under the glare of a spotlight, and the orchestra played his school's fight song. It was exciting to hear those stirring melodies from Ohio State, Notre Dame, Michigan, Nebraska and others. Unfortunately, there was no "I'm a Jayhawk" that time, although it had played many times before for Sayers, Riggins, Hadl and others.

It was quite an honor to receive the Chris Schenkel Award from the College Football Hall of Fame, and to have the award actually presented by Schenkel himself, who passed away in 2005. —Photo by Dick Wroblewski

Schenkel himself came up on the podium to present me, the last time he was able to do that. Chris was even then suffering greatly from emphysema. (My path had crossed with Schenkel's more than once. He had been to Lawrence several times because he was particularly interested in promoting Haskell Indian College.) After he presented me, I gave a short speech to the huge crowd.

It was an emotional moment for me. I had been nervous thinking what it was going to be like, but when the time arrived, I was surprisingly calm. The audience was warm and appreciative. It was truly a night to remember.

Kish told me, "You will never know how happy this makes me." He might have helped me get the award, but what the heck! Everybody knows somebody important!

I have to tell you one story about Bernie Kish. After he retired from the military, he came to KU to fill a newly created position, one which was designated to promote the sale of football season tickets — always very important in the financial survival of any school's athletics department. Bernie was a prototypical military officer, very detail-oriented and very organized. One of the first things he did at KU was to call retired coach Don Fambrough and ask if he could come out and visit. Fam said sure, so Bernie arrived with his Big Chief tablet and several pencils.

He said, "Coach, thanks for seeing me and for helping me with this project. Now tell me, what is the number one thing in selling football tickets?"

Fam replied, "WIN."

Bernie made due note of that on his tablet, and moved on to his next question.

"Now what is number two on the list of necessary objectives?"
Fam replied, "Go Back to number one!"

Bernie was stunned, and the interview came to a quick end. Probably more truth than fiction to that, don't you agree?

Incidentally, the College Basketball Hall of Fame, which is the counterpart of the fine College Football Hall of Fame, inducted its inaugural class in Kansas City in the fall of 2006.

Things didn't go as well on the field for the Jayhawks to start the 1998 campaign. About three weeks after I received the Chris Schenkel Award, KU opened the season at home against Oklahoma State. If I remember correctly, the game was moved up to September 5 from a later date to accommodate TV. The air temperature that day was 92 degrees, and who knows what it was on the field. But the heat seemed to get to the Hawks — and to the fans. Cowboy quarterback Tony Lindsay threw for 110 yards and rushed for 93, including six yards on a late touchdown run that sealed a 38-28 O-State win.

The next week wasn't any better. Playing at Columbia on a 97-degree day, Missouri's Devin West racked up 319 rushing yards — the most ever given up by the Jayhawks — and two touchdowns as the Tigers won 41-23. KU got its first win of the season the following week, beating Illinois State 63-21 on a 90-degree afternoon. Mitch Bowles and Dustin Curry each ran for 94 yards for the Hawks.

The wildest game of the year, however, came the following week on the road against the University of Alabama-Birmingham. The Jayhawks had shut out the Blazers, 24-0, in the previous season, but this one was much closer. KU held a 10-7 advantage heading into the locker room at halftime after freshman Harrison Hill returned a punt 81 yards for a touchdown with no time left on the clock. UAB actually led late in the game, 21-13, until KU tied it late with a touchdown and a two-point conversion. I was doing the post-game show with Terry then, and so as the end of regulation time approached, I would always leave the booth and go down on the sidelines, which I did that night before KU tied it.

The darn game went to four overtimes! I was down there for an hour before Zac Wegner and Hill connected on a 25-yard touchdown play, and then completed the two-point conversion for the 39-37 win. The game, which lasted 3 hours and 50 minutes, tied an NCAA record with its four overtimes. That also happened to be the first overtime game in KU's history.

Of course, had I known I was going to be spending half the game on the sidelines, I wouldn't have gone down to the field just yet. The rest of the season went downhill. KU won just two of its final seven games and finished the season 4-7. The team's only conference win that year was over 17th-ranked Colorado on Homecoming, 33-17.

I can't say there was a lot of optimism heading into the 1999 season. There was a slightly different feel to the start of the season, however, when KU traveled to Notre Dame to open the campaign against the Irish in the Eddie Robinson Kickoff Classic. It was the sixth time KU and Notre Dame faced each other in football in 61 years, so it was my first time to see "Touchdown Jesus" and the grotto where people would go to pray. The tailgating was amazing, and the little leprechaun in the green suit who ran all over the place exhorting cheers was fun to watch. He was about the only entertaining thing to watch. The game was brutal. The Jayhawks committed turnovers the first three times they had the ball and lost to the Irish, 48-13.

Much like Glen Mason, Terry Allen was a coach who wore his emotions on his sleeve. He got really high with the good and really low with the bad. After they had been blown out by Notre Dame and Colorado (51-17), the Jayhawks crushed Cal-State Northridge, 71-14. Then San Diego State came to Lawrence, and for one of the few times during Terry's tenure here, the Hawks were about a three-touchdown favorite.

Wouldn't you know it, San Diego State quarterback Jack Hawley threw for 343 yards and the Aztecs won easily, 41-13. They killed us. By the time the Hawks scored their first points of the game on a 43-yard touchdown play from Dylen Smith to Hill in the third quarter, SDSU led 31-0.

At the time, we taped the TV shows after the games. After that night game against the Aztecs, we taped at midnight. Just before we went in the studio, Terry sort of did a quick two-step pace and yelled a common four-letter expletive at the top of his voice out of frustration with the way things were going. Then we went in to do the show. I will always remember that.

Unfortunately, times didn't get much better for Terry and the Jayhawks, even though he did have two more years in Lawrence.

But the real downward spiral began early in the 2000 season — in the opener against Southern Methodist, actually.

In the first-ever game at Gerald J. Ford Stadium in Dallas, on a 107-degree afternoon, Kansas just couldn't get it together. SMU scored 24 unanswered points in the first quarter. The Jayhawks made so many mistakes that game, including six fumbles (they lost only three) and a blocked punt. Our special teams just imploded in that game.

It's a shame because if there were a season when we could say that Terry would get it done, 2000 might've been it. Key players — quarterback Dylen Smith, running back David Winbush and defensive backs Carl Nesmith and Kareem High — all were seniors.

The loss to SMU seemed to be devastating because, even though KU beat UAB and Southern Illinois in their next two games, the Jayhawks managed just two conference wins — even if one was against Missouri.

Terry just couldn't get it going. It's especially a shame because he was such a nice guy — so opposite of Mason — that it might have affected the respect he received from his players. *Lawrence Journal-World* sportswriter Gary Bedore remembers a time in practice in 2001 when Terry started yelling in the face of quarterback Mario Kinsey. When Terry turned around, Kinsey just started laughing.

Other Voices from The Hill • Gary Bedore

At the end Terry tried to get tough, but he had been so nice for so long that it didn't work. I remember the week before KU played Texas Tech, which turned out to be one of Terry's last games at KU, Kinsey went home to Waco without telling anyone he was leaving, and missed a practice. He came back two days later. His punishment was that he was suspended for the first quarter of the Texas Tech game. The back-up quarterback Zack Dyer played great in that first quarter, but Terry still brought Kinsey back in.

The Hawks ended up beating the Red Raiders 34-31 in overtime behind Reggie Duncan's 227 yards and four Johnny Beck field goals. But when Terry inserted Kinsey after Dyer had played such a nice first quarter — 30 yards passing and one touchdown — it certainly raised some eyebrows.

Kinsey was one of those players who had a world of talent and athleticism, but wasted it. In addition to winning the starting quarterback job as a redshirt freshman during the 2001 season, he also was a back-up point guard on the Jayhawk basketball team. At least briefly. Roy Williams released Kinsey from the basketball team early during his freshman year. Roy said it was so Mario could concentrate on his academics, but I was quite certain that wasn't the real reason.

Terry Allen, thinking Kinsey might be the person to save his job, tried to build the offense around him. It didn't work. Off the field and court, Kinsey had some brushes with the law. During the 2002 season, new football coach Mark Mangino gave Kinsey his walking papers. Kinsey transferred to Sam Houston State, where he tried football and basketball. Although I'm not sure how he did at Sam Houston, I do know that Mario signed with the American Basketball Association team in his hometown of Waco during the 2006 season.

That overtime win against Texas Tech was Terry Allen's last victory at KU. Midway through the 2001 season, the Jayhawks hit a rough stretch that included six consecutive losses. I believe it was after the Missouri game, a 38-34 loss on October 20, that Terry and his wife Lynn had a party at their house, which was something they did each season. Lynn and Terry both commented that it would be their last party, because they were pretty sure they wouldn't be at KU after the season. And they thanked everyone.

Sure enough, after KU lost to Nebraska, 51-7, in Lincoln, Terry was fired. Going along with the soap opera that seemed to hang over Al Bohl during his time as athletic director, Terry likely knew before the Nebraska game that it was his finale. Supposedly, Al sent Richard Konzem to tell Terry that he was done. Al had asked that Terry not say anything until the following Monday when they'd hold a press conference.

According to Jason King, *The Kansas City Star's* KU beat writer since 2000, Terry mentioned to a few Nebraska assistant coaches before the game that he was done. So, word started circulating around the press box during the game that he would be fired that weekend, with three games remaining. After the game, when someone asked Terry about it, he said, "I don't know what you're talking about."

"You could tell it bugged the heck out of Terry because he was such a good guy," Jason said. "It bugged him so much that he started off the press conference the next day by apologizing. He said that he lied after the game and was asked to say those things."

The Jayhawks were 2-6 after the loss to Nebraska. During his five-year career at KU, Terry finished with an overall record of 20-33, including one fourth-place finish in the Big 12 North, three fifth-place finishes and one last-place finish. Assistant coach Tom Hayes was given the tag of interim coach and led KU for its final three games of the season.

It's tough to pinpoint exactly why Terry wasn't successful. He just never got it going. Really, he was probably overmatched, not really knowing what it took to get the right players and win at the NCAA's highest level of football. He brought his entire staff from Northern Iowa, but he never had any recruiters who knew how to get the players they needed to compete. It was a tough era for Terry at KU.

That's not to take anything away from Terry as a person. Terry and Lynn were great people. They had a couple of wonderful children, and had a third one while Terry was coaching here. Off the field, Terry and Lynn did all the right things. He was active in the community; she was active in volunteer work.

Other Voices from The Hill • Bob Davis

Terry is a quality person and his wife is an absolute peach. We moved into our new house and she came over and helped my wife Linda put the dishes away. I mean, Wow! The head football coach's wife? Are you kidding me? I wish him the very best and hope they're happy.

They were model citizens, but he didn't win on the field. Other coaches have said it doesn't mean anything to do all that kind of stuff in the community, because if you lose you're going to get fired anyway, and if you win you don't have to do any of that stuff. Terry was a great example of that idea, although he and Lynn weren't doing those kinds of things because they had to. That was just their nature. But, he proved that coaching axiom to be true.

After several years as assistant head coach at Iowa State, Allen got another head coaching job at Missouri State in 2006. The year was a rocky one, indeed. It was interesting that Terry had been so close to Eldon Miller, the longtime basketball coach at Northern Iowa. Eldon's son, Ben, was on Roy Williams' staff at KU when Terry was hired. Guess who was on the basketball coaching staff at Missouri State when Allen was hired there? Ben Miller.

Chapter 15

Mark Mangino Raises the Football Bar

Defensive coordinator Tom Hayes finished out the 2001 season as Terry Allen's interim replacement — losses against Texas and Iowa State, and a win over Wyoming in a game that was rescheduled due to the 9-11 terrorist attacks.

It's really a shame that game had to be rescheduled for that time. Since it was the last home game of the season, it was senior day. It was a cold December day and the season was awash, complete with the head coach's departure during the season. It was an absolutely meaningless game. As a result, there seemed to be less than 10,000 people at Memorial Stadium that day. Not an ideal way for those seniors to end their careers.

With the season out of the way, it was time to find a new head coach.

Tom Hayes, who was a great guy with a tremendous football background, seemed to be a viable candidate. He played collegiately at Iowa before an NFL career with the Cincinnati Bengals. After his playing career ended, he had some impressive coaching stops at places including UCLA, Texas A&M, Oklahoma and the Washington Redskins. A lot of KU people were hoping that Tom would be Terry Allen's replacement at Kansas, but Al Bohl saw otherwise. He had his sights set higher, at least in his eyes.

One of the coaches Bohl targeted was Dennis Franchione. Remember, former athletic director Bob Frederick said that Franchione and Terry Allen were the two finalists to succeed Glen Mason.

The other main target of Bohl's search was Mark Mangino, who was the assistant head coach at Oklahoma under Bob Stoops. Mark didn't have quite the same football resume as Tom Hayes, but he was familiar with the Big 12 through a couple of big turnarounds in the conference. Mark worked under Bill Snyder at Kansas State from 1991-98, first as assistant coach and recruiting coordinator, then as the offensive line coach and running game coordinator, and finally as the assistant head coach. He then spent the next three seasons at Oklahoma with Stoops. In 2000, while at OU, Mark won the Frank Broyles Award as the nation's top assistant coach. Of course, both OU and K-State enjoyed wild success while Mangino was on the sidelines. Although I don't know it firsthand, I was told during the writing of this book that KU representatives interviewed Franchione at a neutral, out-of-state location. Mangino was interviewed at a hotel in Oklahoma City around the same time. Bohl liked both men, but he initially offered the job to Franchione, according to Jason King, the KU beat writer for *The Kansas City Star*.

King added that Franchione, whose stay at the University Alabama lasted two seasons, kept asking for more time from Al until Al finally said screw it, rescinded the offer and offered the job to Mangino.

Franchione went so far as to refute a story that King wrote in *The Star*, saying, "This is getting irritating and disruptive for our team and recruiting. ... The story is inaccurate."

Incidentally, Gary Bedore, who covers KU for the *Lawrence Journal-World*, added that Franchione will "deny it to this day that he interviewed for this job but I know he did. I know people who were there."

We do know that Al Bohl worked extremely hard to get Mark Mangino to agree to come. Since Kansas hadn't enjoyed many great victories under Terry Allen, and Mark was in a good situation at Oklahoma — not to mention that there's a perception that Kansas is a "basketball school" — Al was practically doing cartwheels in hopes of hiring Mark. In case the Franchione story wasn't a good enough twist to this saga, there's another one about a time when Tom Hayes was at Al's house having dinner and an informal interview and Mark called. Al, allegedly acting somewhat giddy, said, "I have a phone call here. I've got to go." And he left.

Tom later said, "I knew right then that I had no chance at all to get the job."

Regardless, the hiring committee at KU was impressed with Mark Mangino because he had a precise plan on how to help make KU successful in football. Still, Mark wasn't necessarily impressed yet with KU. In fact, he told me that he really didn't have a lot of interest in the job.

Oh, he and his wife Mary Jane thought Kansas was a beautiful place, their daughter was attending KU, and they liked the fact they'd be close to Kansas City. But, when Al Bohl first called Mark and offered him the job, Mark turned it down. Truth told, he turned it down "several times," as he says. He simply wanted to stay at Oklahoma. The Sooners were winning and he wanted to help Bob Stoops enjoy sustained success there. Not to mention, Mark's family was happy there.

Other voices from The Hill • Mark Mangino

Al continued to sell how they were going to build the program and how they had resources and that the university was committed to doing it. ... It sounded like Kansas wanted to build a football program. Having been a competitor of theirs, I always felt that they were a sleeping giant in football. So I thought about it for another day, and discussed it with my wife and my children and Bob Stoops. I decided that KU really wanted to make a difference ... so, I decided to give it a shot.

Even after Mark got here, I believed that he felt as if KU was a basketball school and nobody cared very much about football. He felt he needed to do whatever it took to change that attitude, even taking relatively minor things to the extreme. I remember walking into the football offices during his first season and it was downright cold in there. He had the air conditioning turned down so low that the poor girls working in there had to wear sweaters and turn on their electric heaters!

Mark had somewhat of a dominating personality. He's fought for everything he's received and he's helped changed the mentality of football at Kansas. As the years have gone by, I've grown to like Mark better and better.

Other voices from The Hill • Robert Hemenway

We need to think of ourselves as more than just a basketball school. We need to think of ourselves as a university that has Division I athletic programs, and try to be successful in every sport that we have at KU. It's an important principle to have, and I think Mark and Bill Self both understand that. They each want the other to be successful. I think Mark has done a good job of articulating the needs of the football program, and with the success we've had on the field and the success we've had raising money for our new facilities, I feel like we're getting close to the tipping point where we're going be able to climb that mountain and really have a terrific football program.

The 2002 season, Mark Mangino's first for the Jayhawks, was everything but successful, at least in terms of wins and losses. The Hawks finished the season with a 2-10 record, with wins over Missouri State in Lawrence and at Tulsa in the fifth game of the season.

In spite of the dismal record, the team seemed to be improving from week to week. On Homecoming against Colorado, KU quarterback Bill Whittemore, a transfer from Fort Scott Community College, racked up 338 yards of offense — 217 yards passing and 121 yards rushing. Unfortunately, Colorado running back Chris Brown ran for 309 yards and two touchdowns in Colorado's 53-29 win.

As remarkable as Whittemore and Brown's numbers that day was something that happened right after the game. Colorado coach Gary Barnett went into KU's locker room to address the Jayhawks. He told them that for a 2-5 team, they showed a lot of heart, and looked to be on the right track. Coaches don't do that often, hardly ever. It showed a lot of class for Barnett to do it, but it also showed that Mangino was starting to change the attitude around his players.

Another game of note from Mangino's first season was on November 2 — the pupil faced the boss when KU hosted K-State in the 100th "Sunflower Showdown." It was the pupil, Mangino, against his former boss, Bill Snyder. The Wildcats' 64-0 victory in that game was the worst whipping either team has laid on the other since the series began between the Jayhawks and Wildcats in 1902. (Including the 2006 season, that loss is also the only time since 1987, when Oklahoma won 71-10, that an opponent beat KU by more than 60 points.)

Only two years later, though, on Homecoming in 2004, Mangino turned the tables and beat his former boss, 31-28. The next year, 2005, was one of the worst games in the rivalry, 12-3 K-State, exceeded only perhaps by the 3-to-3 tie in 1966 that cost KU Coach Jack Mitchell and K-State Coach Doug Weaver their jobs at the end of the season.

The week before KU played K-State in 2002, Whittemore was injured in a loss at Missouri after compiling 269 yards. He didn't play against the Wildcats or in the Hawks' final two games of the season after that. Without Bill at quarterback, none of those three games was close. Besides the 64-0 K-State final, Nebraska beat KU, 45-7, and Oklahoma State won, 55-20.

That was a terrible way to end the season. Coming out in 2003, with a healthy Whittemore, Kansas lost its opener to Northwestern in a downpour in Lawrence, 28-20, in a game that the Jayhawks should've won. Things started to turn around the next week, though.

KU then beat UNLV, 46-24. They went up to Wyoming and won, 42-35. They beat Jacksonville State, 41-6, and then beat Missouri, 35-14, in what was the start of Mangino's dominance over MU quarterback Brad Smith. Smith, as good as he was, had some rough games against Kansas.

After losing to the Tigers in Mark's first season, the Jayhawks beat the Tigers three straight years, 2002-05. Mangino's mastery of MU coach Gary Pinkel and Smith was pretty amazing. Smith did well against almost everyone else, but was ineffective against the Jayhawks. In 2006, however, Pinkel got the monkey off his back in a big way, ruining the season-finale game for the Hawks and keeping them out of a bowl game.

Mark Mangino helped change the attitude toward football at KU when he became the head coach in 2002.

After beating 23rd-ranked Missouri in 2003, the Jayhawks went to Colorado, where they lost in overtime, 50-47. That was a game that glaringly showed what would be KU's weakness all season — defense. The Jayhawks took an early 7-0 lead before giving up 17 straight points in the first quarter.

However, it was another huge game for Whittemore and the Kansas offense. The Jayhawks racked up 586 total yards, including 422 in the air from Whittemore, who helped account for five touchdowns — three by air and two rushing. A fun highlight of the game came right before halftime when Charles Gordon came down with a 41-yard "Hail Mary" pass from Whittemore that gave KU a 35-24 lead at the half.

Kansas beat Baylor the next week for its fifth win of the season. The Hawks needed one more in their final five games to become bowl eligible. KU lost to K-State in its next game, after Whittemore left the game in the first quarter with a shoulder injury. It appeared as if he might be gone for the rest of the season.

His replacement the next week against Texas A&M was Adam Barmann, who took off his freshman redshirt that game and exploded against the Aggies. He threw for a KU freshman-record 294 yards and four touchdowns. It really was a phenomenal game for Adam. However, KU lost to A&M, 45-33. Then, they lost the next two weeks to Nebraska and Oklahoma State.

With KU still needing that sixth win, Whittemore came back in the finale against Iowa State. He picked up right where he left off, accounting for 306 yards as KU beat the Cyclones easily, 36-7, and received an invitation to play in the Tangerine Bowl in Orlando, Florida, to face North Carolina State.

In KU's first trip to a bowl game since 1995, the Wolfpack, behind current NFL quarterback Philip Rivers' 475 passing yards, routed KU, 56-26.

Other voices from The Hill • Mark Mangino

That North Carolina State team didn't belong in the Tangerine Bowl — they were too talented. That was an impressive football team. But it was a great experience for our kids. They hadn't had success for so long. An opportunity for them to play in the bowl game was really exciting and something that they deserved. I've often said about that (Tangerine Bowl) that our kids were so excited to go to a bowl game that we forgot all about winning it. That's the main objective. We learned from that lesson.

Whittemore capped his college career that night against the Wolfpack with 243 passing yards, 84 rushing yards and three touchdowns.

Bill Whittemore is one of the great success stories at KU. A high school "Mr. Football" in the state of Tennessee in 1998, Bill started his collegiate career at the University of Tennessee-Martin. Things weren't working out there, so he transferred to Fort Scott. He came into the KU program at a time when, in addition to not being very competitive, the team often would lay down at the end of the game. The fans loved to watch Bill and for good reason.

During his two seasons at KU, Whittemore took the Jayhawks to heights they hadn't seen in several years. He finished with 4,051 yards on 310 completions out of 568 attempts. His yards and completions put him sixth all-time at the school. He also was one of the school's all-time most athletic quarterbacks. He ended his career with 5,134 yards of total offense, fourth all-time at KU. And, remember, that's in only two seasons!

In 2002, Bill was the Big 12's Offensive Newcomer of the Year. Then, in 2003, while leading the Hawks to their first bowl appearance since 1995, he was one of the top statistical quarterbacks in the nation.

This hasn't happened all that often to me, but after the 2003 season, I got a letter from Bill Whittemore's dad. He wrote: "I just want to thank you for all the nice things you've said about Bill while he played at Kansas. It made it much more enjoyable for all of us and we really appreciate it." That was really a nice thing for him to do. Christian Moody's dad and mom did that after his basketball career. And the Hinrichs, Collisons and LaFrentzes all thanked me, but it doesn't happen all that often.

Without question, Whittemore and Mangino was a good combination. They brought the kind of fire that helped change the tone of KU football fans. In spite of a desire to succeed, both Bill and Mark exude calmness, even with their backs against the wall.

Bob Davis and I sat in the booth after many games and marveled at Mark's composure and lack of apparent irritation at a heartbreaking loss. It's the attitude that no one loss is going to kill us and no one win is going to make us. It's a very admirable trait, especially for a Division I coach. In spite of some tough losses, he's always upbeat and optimistic in his post-game radio interviews.

Other voices from The Hill • Mark Mangino

I just believe that you can't get too high when you win and you can't get too low when you lose. You have to stay the steady course. If your players see you not managing losing well, they won't manage it well. The kids will follow your lead. And that's my job — to lead this program. We have landmark victories or milestones and that type of thing, and those are nice along the way. And, the losses are painful along the way. But when you're in it for the long haul, you have to take the highs and lows in stride, keep focused on the task at hand, and just prepare for the next game.

At least Mark usually takes the high road and stays in stride.

There has been one time when we've seen Mark lose his cool a little. Toward the end of the 2004 season, KU was hosting sixth-ranked Texas. After opening with wins over Tulsa and Toledo, the Hawks had won only one Big 12 game before facing Texas in the next-to-the-last game of the season.

Quarterback Brian Luke had a great day, throwing for 225 yards and one touchdown. The main scoring for KU had come from the leg of Johnny Beck, who had kicked three field goals. Late in the game, KU had the ball and a 23-20 lead. With about 2 minutes left, Luke completed a pass to Charles Gordon at the Texas sideline for what appeared to be a first down. However, the side judge flagged Gordon for pushing off cornerback Tarell Brown. The first down would've clinched the game. Instead, KU punted. Texas quarterback Vince Young marched the Longhorns down the field. The Hawks forced a fourth-and-18, but Young made a spectacular 20-yard run, faking out Nick Reid, one of our best defenders, and got a first down. Then, with three seconds left in the game, Young found Tony Jeffrey for a 21-yard scoring play.

During his post-game press conference, Mark showed some fire. "You know what this is all about, don't you?" he said. "It's called the BCS. That's what made the difference on that call in front of their bench — dollar signs."

Other voices from The Hill • Mark Mangino

Hindsight, we had other opportunities to win the game. We really did. I was proud of the way our kids played. It's a game where basically we were outmanned but we just hung in there and fought with them and competed with them. It just didn't turn out the way we all would have liked. I think we learned from that experience, and got better because of it.

By the way, the Big 12 saw a few extra dollar signs from Mangino. The conference fined Mark $5,000 for his comment.

Other voices from The Hill • Bob Davis

I've looked at that play several times on tape. It should have been a no call. The two guys were banging each other, both pushing off, they came away from each other and then Charles caught the ball, just a great play. I was thinking, Wow, they have locked up the game. But, the Texas coaches just went off. And the official, who I believe is from Dallas, after some delay, threw his flag. Really, I thought both guys equally pushed off after getting tangled up. How could you call that on either side? Well, it was right in front of the Texas coaches.

That was the second rough game with a Texas school in Lawrence that season. In KU's Big 12 opener against Texas Tech, the Hawks had a great first half, scoring 30 points. The defense looked great, forcing four turnovers in the first half alone, and KU led 30-11 at the break. The Red Raiders came roaring back in the second half. Texas Tech held the KU offense to zero points, while scoring 20. The 31-30 loss began a long conference season for the Hawks.

KU finished the season with a 2-6 record in the Big 12 North. The Jayhawks' two victories? K-State by a 31-28 margin on Homecoming. And the season finale at Columbia, a 31-14 win over Missouri.

I will add here that I'm happy to see the KU-MU football game back on the end of the schedule where it belongs. It is so important to both schools that it's a shame to bury it in the middle of the season, as we've seen happen since the start of the Big 12 Conference. In fact, since that 1996 season, Kansas and Missouri have closed out the regular season just three times — 1996, 2004, 2006. For some reason in recent years, Iowa State has been our opponent in the finale. In my opinion, the KU-MU game should be the climax of the campaign for both teams, as it carries huge emotional and bragging rights into the next year.

Even though Kansas ended its season with a 4-7 record, Mark Mangino says he saw a lot of progress in the program. The Jayhawks were starting to come together as a team. And, they were developing a stronger defense, which is Mark's key to building a long-term successful program.

Another key to competing at this level, obviously, are the facilities. In the fall of 2005, the KU athletics department, and the football program in particular, got a huge shot in the arm from former Jayhawk basketball player Tommy Kivisto and his wife Julie, plus long-time supporter Dana Anderson and his wife Sue, who made significant financial pledges to help build a new facility for football.

The project, estimated at $31 million, will give the football team an 80,000-square-foot space with a football complex that will include two practice fields, coaches' offices, a weight room, locker rooms and academic areas, among other features.

Other voices from The Hill • Mark Mangino

It helps level the playing field with most of the teams. One of the good things about KU is that we want to have winning football. We want to compete for championships. We have a firm grasp on it and we have some balance here. But the gifts from the Kivistos and Andersons give KU football a chance to compete at the highest level in the conference. Their generosity is going to have a major impact for years to come on the football program here.

Mark Mangino has done everything you could ask. In his first five seasons, he had three bowl-eligible teams. (The 2006 team won the mandatory six games, but it didn't receive a bowl invitation.) He's the only KU football coach in the program's history to appear in two bowl games in a three-year stretch. More importantly, he's changed the attitude of people around the KU football program and of KU fans.

During the 2005 season, my last of broadcasting KU football, we saw that enthusiasm come out.

After winning their first three and then losing their next four, the Jayhawks put together impressive back-to-back wins over Missouri and Nebraska, 13-3 and 40-15, respectively. The win over Nebraska, which I mention in more detail in the first chapter, snapped NU's 36-game winning streak over Kansas. Then, with an overtime field goal, KU beat Iowa State to close out the regular season and received a bid to the Fort Worth Bowl.

When the Jayhawks went to the Fort Worth Bowl in 2005, where they crushed Houston, 42-13, I don't remember ever seeing so much enthusiasm for KU football. It was beautiful weather for the game and the team played great. Regardless of those things, though, the whole east side of Amon G. Carter Stadium on the campus of Texas Christian University was filled with blue. It appeared as though the majority of the more than 35,000 fans donned KU blue.

For KU football, which has had a latent spirit for years, Jayhawk fans are starting to show off their blue and crimson everywhere, like Nebraska fans with their red, K-State with its purple, and Missouri with the gold and black. It's an uplifting sight to see.

Although I did not broadcast the 2006 season, I watched nearly every game. It was one of the most frustrating seasons for the Jayhawks that I can remember. They were obviously much improved, but they could not sustain leads in games and finished 6 and 6. Actually, they could have, and perhaps should have, won every game on their schedule going into that finale against Missouri, where they were never in the game. What a mystery!

Chapter 16

Bob Frederick and Roy Williams and the Biggest Heartbreak

Roy Williams always used to say, "the thrill of victory is never as intense as the agony of defeat." If ever a season epitomized that, it was 1996-97 in basketball. That season was one of the most amazing in KU's long basketball history.

That team included players that Jayhawk fans have come to know by first names — Raef, Paul, Jerod, Scot, Jacque. In addition to LaFrentz, Pierce, Haase, Pollard and Vaughn, the team also included key players such as Billy Thomas, B.J. Williams, Ryan Robertson and others. Four of the five starters are currently making huge bucks in the NBA. The fifth, Jerod, is the director of basketball operations for Roy Williams at North Carolina.

Coming off a trip to the Elite Eight, where KU lost to Syracuse, 60-57, the '96-97 squad got off to a great start with a fabulous road trip.

Of all the places we have traveled — and that means from Anchorage, Alaska to Miami, Florida, and from Madison Square Garden in New York to the Hawaiian Islands, my favorite spot, by far, has to be the "Garden Island," Maui, in Hawaii. That is the site of the Maui Invitational, a three-game tournament played in the Lahaina Civic Center, a stone's throw from the Pacific Ocean. While my partner Bob Davis was tied up with a KU-Missouri football game, I was sent with the basketball team on a rough trip to California and Hawaii. After the Jayhawks opened with a win at Santa Clara, we headed to Maui, where the team beat LSU, California and Virginia on its way to sweeping the Maui Invitational Championship.

As my friend and long-time Kansas City broadcaster Bill Grigsby might say, winning the Maui Invitational was a "beauuutiful" way to start the season. It also put the team four games into a fantastic 22-game winning streak, which remains tied as the second longest in school history, behind a 23-game streak during 1935-36.

The Jayhawks rolled along until a 96-94 double-overtime loss on February 4 at Missouri.

(When the Jayhawks and Tigers played in Lawrence two weeks later, KU won 79-67 behind Raef's career-high 31 points.)

That was the only hiccup until the NCAA Tournament. The Hawks won the Big 12 Conference Tournament, whipping Missouri, 87-60, in the championship, were No. 1 in all the polls and had truly become "America's team." The guys were exemplary young men, great athletes, and the darlings of the nation. America had fallen in love with these kids; they'd seen them so much on television. Almost everyone expected them to roll to the national title. They beat Jackson State and Purdue in the first and second rounds at Memphis, and drew a bout with Arizona in the first game of the regional in Birmingham, Alabama.

Then it all happened. And, boy, when it happens, it happens with such suddenness.

During the tournament, Haase had developed an extremely sore wrist. He could hardly catch or hold on to the ball. Roy Williams told me during an interview in December 2006 that there's a reason Jerod's wrist was bothering him — it was broken! Literally all season. He broke it against Santa Clara in the season opener, but nothing showed up on the x-ray. But, as KU advanced in the NCAA Tournament, the pain became excruciating.

What could they do? They decided to give him a cortisone shot the day before the Arizona game to see if that would reduce the pain enough that he could play. Roy found out later that something like three or four percent of people develop a negative reaction to the shot. Jerod was one of those. The pain became unbearable. I remember seeing Jerod in the elevator the afternoon of the game, and he was as white as a ghost. He started the game, and on Arizona's first possession, Jerod knocked down a pass on the wing, dribbled down the court and dropped in a layup that gave KU a 2-0 lead. After that he was taken out. He played 14 minutes that game, took three shots and finished with two points and two assists.

Other voices from The Hill • Roy Williams

I remember sitting in the hotel in Birmingham the night before the Arizona game and Jerod was sitting there holding his arm up in the air because that was the least painful position. He had tears running down his face because the pain was so bad. The morning of the game we went to shoot-around and I told him,

"Let me see you shoot a free throw." It fell four feet short. I said, "Son, I'm not saying no, but this doesn't look good. But let's see what it's like to shoot in the pre-game warm up."

I walked out on the court in pre-game warm-up and I said, "All right, let me see you shoot a free throw again." He shot a free throw and made it. But he got this terrible look of pain and sort of doubled over a little bit, and he looked up at me and he said, "Coach, I just want to try." I will never forget that. If you had told me that we were going to lose the game even if I played him, I still would have played him because I've never had an athlete who had given so much and I've never had an athlete who wanted to try so badly.

It was a killer. If we had Jacque and Jerod guarding Mike Bibby, Jason Terry and Miles Simon, those guards weren't going to beat us. Jacque could guard one, but Billy and Ryan weren't quite as experienced as Jerod so they couldn't do it on the defensive end.

The whole game was a nightmare. Pollard had no field goals. He only shot once. Why? And, the Jayhawks trailed by 13 points with 3:30 left in the game, until Robertson and Thomas, who ended with 14 and 13 points, respectively, led KU back.

In the final seconds of the game, with Arizona leading by three, Jacque brought the ball down court, passed up a shot, and fed to Raef in the left corner. Raef dropped back, knowing he had to have a three, and fired. But the ball rimmed out, and Kansas was beaten — America's team was not going to be national champions after all!

After the game, Roy Williams was sitting on the floor outside the locker room. No one was near him. What could you say? I walked over, put my arm around his shoulder and said nothing. It was Heartbreak City!

Bob Davis remembers walking around the locker room, also. He went over to Jacque Vaughn, who was sitting alone, as were most of the players. Jacque looked up at Bob and said, "Are you OK?" That perfectly illustrates the type of kids that were on that team.

And really, they were kids. Bob's sister-in-law was watching the game on TV, which afterwards showed the heartbroken KU players, including one image of Ryan Robertson getting a hug from his mom. Bob's sister-in-law commented, "You know, we see them as great basketball players, but we forget they're still just kids." After that game, we all felt as if we'd just lost our new bicycle or our puppy ran away.

The team returned to the hotel, and all the KU fans, most of them crying, tried to applaud the players who just wanted to get out of there. It's true that the agony of defeat is much more taxing than the thrill of victory.

Other voices from The Hill • Roy Williams

We had six seniors that year. All six of them graduated. Two of them ended up being first-team academic All-Americans. And Jacque was the Academic All-American Player of the Year. Yet at the end of the year, I was destroyed. I never had something that affected me as much as that loss did. To this day, 10 years later when somebody says something about the '97 team and mentions Jacque and Jerod, my first impulse is one of sadness and hurt because I didn't help those guys get to a Final Four. I have never been able to get over that loss. That is the loss that has stuck with me.

Remember how Roy used to argue that a season isn't a failure just because the Hawks don't win the national championship? The loss to Arizona was the impetus for Roy stressing to players, fans and everyone around the University to "enjoy the journey" of the season instead of focusing on the NCAA Tournament.

Arizona went on to win the national championship that season. It was coach Lute Olson's first (and so far only) national title. It's interesting to note that KU has been involved with other high-profile coaches winning their only NCAA championship. Gary Williams, whose Maryland team beat KU in the 2002 Final Four, won it all that year, followed by Jim Boeheim and Syracuse the next season.

For KU fans, though, the 1997 loss stings a little more than '02 and '03. Including the triple-overtime loss to North Carolina in the 1957 national championship game, the loss to Arizona on March 21, 1997, remains one of the toughest in school history.

As difficult as that 1997 loss was for KU, one of the most incredible moments for anyone who witnessed it happened during the 1997-98 season. And, in a way, it brought us back to 1957.

On a warm and terrific January 17 afternoon, as KU played host to K-State, Wilt Chamberlain returned to Allen Fieldhouse for the official retirement of his No. 13 jersey. Again, I was asked to emcee the halftime show, which was shown on CBS. The network interrupted all its other programming to carry this segment. I greeted the big fellow who towered above us all, as you can see in the photo, and voiced the introductory remarks, which led to his emotional talk. It had to be one of the highlights of my broadcasting career. It was a moving sight to see Wilt walk out to center court for the halftime ceremony wearing his letterman's jacket (pictured below) that he'd obviously kept in a safe place and away from the moths. Wilt delivered such an emotional speech that he ended with the stirring words: "Rock, Chalk, Jayhawk."

Near the end of the game, which the Hawks won 69-62, athletics director Bob Frederick told Wilt that he had an escort ready to help get Wilt out of Allen Fieldhouse without being mobbed by fans. To everyone's surprise, Wilt said he wanted to stay and greet the KU faithful. So, KU officials set up a table on the Fieldhouse floor, and Wilt talked with every person and signed every piece of memorabilia imaginable for an hour and a half after the game. It was amazing.

For more than 40 years, Wilt felt the Kansas fans held it against him that the Jayhawks didn't beat North Carolina in 1957 and that he wouldn't be well received if and when he came back. Wilt, who passed away on October 12, 1999, had to have realized when he left Lawrence that day how much Kansas people appreciated and loved him. We are so grateful that the big guy came back one last time.

(Incidentally, about four years after Wilt died, his estate donated

$650,000 to endow two athletic scholarships and one for underprivileged students, and to establish a KU-based Special Olympics clinic.)

I have served as master of ceremonies for dozens of athletics banquets and recognition ceremonies, but none surpassed the Reunion Banquet celebrating 100 years of Kansas Basketball on February 7, 1998. Coach Williams had invited every single living basketball letterman to come back that weekend. And did they come! From all over the nation, from All-Americans to walk-ons. The fellowship was overwhelming! The banquet was on Saturday night, and we were to play Missouri on Sunday afternoon on national television. I told a couple of jokes, Roy and Bob Frederick welcomed the guys, a terrific video was shown and then a representative from each decade spoke.

It was so good, no one ever seemed to care how long it lasted. Plus it was informal. So much so that at one point a couple of the guys from the 1952 national championship team shouted "Sit Down, Smith!" to one of the greatest coaches in the history of the game. There was no undue respect there! Fred Pralle spoke for the '20s and '30s. He was so good. He told about how he and his wife had gotten along so well for over 50 years, because they went out to eat two nights every week! He said, "She went out on Wednesday night, and I went out on Thursday!" That brought the house down! I screwed up the next introduction. Due to a miscommunication I introduced Clyde Lovellette to speak for the '40s. Clyde knew nothing about it, but he got to his feet and started to lumber to the podium, when Roy said, "Max, it's not Clyde! It's Kenney!" So I said, "Stop, Clyde. Go back and sit down. Bob Kenney is going to do it." Clyde was relieved, and everybody else wondered what in the world was happening. Bob Billings represented the '50s, Al Correll the '60s, Roger Morningstar the '70s, Danny Manning the '80s and Jacque Vaughn the '90s.

It was the all-time best night, and so many of the guys told me it was the most fun weekend of their lives. Believe it or not, I introduced every single guy by name during the timeouts throughout the game. Norm Stewart of the Tigers couldn't have been more gracious, and KU won, 80-70.

The whole 1997-98 season seemed fitting for a 100-year celebration. In spite of injuries to key players Raef LaFrentz (wrist) and Billy Thomas (shoulder), the Hawks cruised through most of the schedule with very few close games in their 35 wins, which tied a school record. They also took home the Big 12 regular-season and tournament championships, and only three losses, all on the road — Maryland, Hawaii and Missouri.

As KU headed to the NCAA Tournament, Raef and Billy were in pain. Roy felt that if his team could survive the first weekend, they'd be in good shape.

After an easy first-round match with Prairie View A&M, which KU defeated, 110-52, Kansas ran into Cuttino Mobley and Rhode Island. Behind Mobley's game-high 27 points, Rhode Island, which shot 50 percent from the field, upset KU, 80-75, in Oklahoma City. As Roy said of the loss nearly 10 years later: "It just eats your gut out."

Raef finished his college career that night with a double-double, 22 points and 14 rebounds.

The 1998-99 season wasn't as good as some of the other seasons, as KU finished with a 23-10 record.

One funny incident happened on February 22, when Oklahoma State came to Lawrence. Very early in the game, the KU student body noticed something strange, and started chanting: "Shorts on backwards." Sure enough, Doug Gottlieb, the Cowboys starting guard and one of the team's stalwarts, had put his game shorts on wrong, and the students let him know about it in a very loud way. Oklahoma State called a timeout, the team huddled around Gottlieb at the bench, where he dropped his drawers and reversed his apparel before play resumed. It truly was one of the funniest incidents that I can recall, right along with the time when KU Coach Ted Owens bent over and split the backside of his slacks.

Incidentally, Gottlieb, who's now a popular basketball analyst on ESPN radio and TV, had nine assists in that game, which KU won, 67-66, in overtime. Gottlieb went on to become the Big 12's all-time assists leader with 793. As most KU fans know, though, Aaron Miles later shattered that mark with 954 assists during his time with the Jayhawks.

In the second round of the NCAA Tournament, after beating Evansville, the Hawks had a meeting with Kentucky. The two teams had faced each other early in the season at the Great Eight tournament in Chicago, where the Wildcats handed it to the Hawks, 63-45.

The NCAA Tournament game was a lot closer. In fact, had Kentucky made just one more bucket, KU would've won. (Yes, you read that correctly.) The Hawks held a 79-76 lead with less than a minute to play. Kentucky's

Wayne Turner drove to the basket and put up a shot that missed. But, the ball was tipped to UK's Scott Padgett inside the arc. He dribbled, took a step back and hit a 3, tying the game with 20 seconds left.

After Turner knocked the ball loose from Jeff Boschee on KU's ensuing possession, Ryan Robertson picked it up and drove the lane. Instead of taking a shot, Ryan flipped the ball over to an open Kenny Gregory. Even though Bob and I thought Kenny might go in for the dunk, he pulled up for a jumper. Missed it. Kenny never was the best shooter on the floor but he almost always was the best jumper. He could jump out of the building. The game went into overtime and Kentucky went on to win, 92-88. Ryan Robertson, playing in his final game, scored a career-high 31 points. Boschee, a freshman, finished with 18. So, that remains the game that's made us say, if Kentucky scores, KU wins.

I hosted Roy Williams' weekly television show the entire time he was here. I remember soon after he arrived I drove him to Tonganoxie on a hot summer day to have barbecue. We wanted to discuss the kind of show he wanted, and what he desired to feature. The air conditioner there was broken. Some guy came up to him and said, "Ain't you the new basketball coach at K.U.?" Wow — what a change 15 years wrought!

Anyway, we had a lot of fun doing the show. Coach never wanted to rehearse anything, or know any of the questions I was going to ask him. I was pretty good on timing, etc., and so for over a dozen years we only had to do one retake as I recall, and that was because I had a score wrong or something like that. First Mike DiNitto, then Mike Lickert produced the show. They both were really good and developed some terrific features, like when the athletes interacted with Special Olympians, or shopped for needy families at Christmas, or told us about their moms and dads. More than once, Roy and I both shed tears as we recorded the program.

After Roy's 12th year here, the KU administration decided to do away with the show. They said the audience was too small to justify the expense of airing it, and that people had seen the games on television and didn't want to see the highlights again. I personally thought that was a big mistake, because true KU fans throughout the Midwest felt like they knew the players so much better from the exposure the guys received on the program, and I thought it strengthened an already dine-a-mite product.

When Bill Self arrived, the coaches' show was revitalized. Bill had done one at Illinois and wanted to do one here. I was not invited to host it, and I have to say it hurt my feelings after all those years, but I understood that some perhaps thought things shouldn't be just the same as they were with Roy.

When KU rolled into the 1999-2000 season, the team featured three freshmen – Nick Collison, Drew Gooden and Kirk Hinrich. Each of the three saw their fair share of time in the starting lineup. It became more obvious throughout the season that they were going to be a special group.

The Hawks finished similarly to how they did the previous season, 24-10, but they lost in the Big 12 tournament to Oklahoma State.

The Hawks drew an eight seed for the NCAA Tournament. After playing well against DePaul in the opening round in Winston-Salem, North Carolina, KU faced old foe Duke, a No. 1 seed, in its next game.

Kirk got off to a great start in the game on his way to a season-high 12 points. But he picked up his third foul in the first half.

The game went back and forth late, until KU missed a shot on one of its final possessions and started fouling. Duke went on to win the game, 69-64. It was the third straight year that KU lost in the second round of the tournament.

During the offseason, the day many KU fans had dreaded throughout the 1990s came. At the end of June, North Carolina coach Bill Guthridge announced his retirement. Bill, who's a K-State guy, had been an assistant under Dean Smith for 30 years and succeeded Smith in 1997. Even though Roy was not asked to replace Dean, everyone knew he would be asked to take over for Guthridge.

Sure enough, Carolina officials got approval from Bob Frederick to talk with Roy.

Other voices from The Hill • Bob Frederick

I made a decision at that time that we weren't going to put any pressure on him. And we weren't going to say, oh, we'll do this or we'll do that. I thought the best thing for him was to let him think through this. I got a lot of criticism for that from alleged fans and some media, saying we should be offering him more to stay.

I said we didn't do anything to put pressure on him, but one thing we did do when he was on his way back from Chapel Hill, I asked (assistant athletics director) Pat Warren to have Joanie Stephens, Roy's secretary, print every e-mail message that he'd gotten. They put them in one pile, stacked on his desk. So, when he went back in the office, he'd see that pile of e-mails. He told me later that he was overwhelmed at the outpouring of affection by the people here.

The decision was tearing at Roy. He told me that he and Wanda went to Wild Dunes, South Carolina, walked the beach and went back and forth on his decision. One second he'd say the North Carolina job is the job he'd always wanted, so he was going to accept it. The next second he'd say he couldn't look his KU players in the eyes and tell them that he was leaving.

It didn't help that while he was in the Charleston area trying to clear his head, residents were lobbying for either Kansas or North Carolina. Roy says several people put UNC flags outside their homes. A couple others had Jayhawk flags outside.

Obviously fans back home lobbied much harder. Jason King, the KU beat writer for *The Kansas City Star*, remembers "shrines" that fans had built around Allen Fieldhouse. Incidentally, that was Jason's first week covering KU.

On July 6, one week after Guthridge retired at Carolina, Williams decided to stay at Kansas, much to the shock of college basketball "experts" around the country. Sitting next to Bob Frederick in the football locker room, Roy simply said: "I'm staying," to the roar of more than 15,000 fans sitting inside Memorial Stadium, watching the press conference on the Jumbotron. He later added: "If we have another press conference like this it will be either when I'm retiring or dying."

Other voices from The Hill • Bob Frederick

Earlier in the day, we went up to meet with the Chancellor and when we came back down to the parking garage, there were a whole bunch of media. At that point he was ready to say he was going to stay. We split up so he could try to sneak out and avoid the media. While a few guys were interviewing me, someone spotted Roy and everyone ran like crazy trying to catch him. They didn't catch him before he slipped into the locker room. He called my office from the locker room and said, "Bob, can you come down here?" When I went down there he said, "I definitely made a decision to stay here, but here's what I want to do." And he told me he wanted to have a press conference. We finally decided to have it in the stadium to accommodate the people.

As Roy looks back, he says one of the big reasons he stayed is because of a promise he made to Nick Collison when he was recruiting Nick against Duke. According to Roy, Duke coaches told Nick that if he went to Kansas, Roy wouldn't be there for his entire career — he was going back to North Carolina. Roy assured Nick that wasn't the case. "I'll be here longer than you are going to be here," Roy said.

Other voices from The Hill • Roy Williams

Anybody who followed college basketball, including my coaching peers, were all saying that I was going to leave Kansas and go back home. But two things I never could come to grips with – what I was going to say to Nick Collison. I know that sounds corny, but I told that kid that I was going to be there throughout his career. And so I've got that emotion on one side and on the other side I've got the emotion of going back home and coach Smith wanting me to come back to North Carolina.

It came down to the fact that I was very happy where I was. And I didn't want to trade being happy and having those kids and having the support from the administration and Nick Collison for the unknown.

With the announcement, a huge sigh could be heard from Garden City to Atchison. The worrying — by Roy and by KU fans — was over. Coach Roy would forever be a Jayhawk. "(Williams) just seemed so relieved and at peace with his decision," said Jason King. "At that time I didn't know him, but I thought there's no way this guy can ever leave now."

The emotion of Roy's announcement, coupled with the fact that the KU lineup featured incredible talent in Gregory, Collison, Hinrich, Gooden and Boschee, gave many fans much more optimism than usual heading into the 2000-01 season.

As the season moved along, indeed, this looked like a team that could make a run in the NCAA Tournament. The Hawks won 17 of their first 18 games, including their first six in Big 12 play. By the time they headed into the NCAA Tournament, Kansas had put together a 24-6 season.

After beating Cal State Northridge in the opening round, KU destroyed 17th-ranked Syracuse in the second round, 87-58. Gooden finished the game with a double-double, 17 points and 15 rebounds, and Collison added 13 rebounds as the Jayhawks outrebounded the Orangemen 56-23.

In the Sweet 16, KU's first trip there in four years, the Jayhawks faced fourth-ranked Illinois at the Alamodome in San Antonio.

Other voices from The Hill • Jason King

Drew Gooden was one of my favorite players to interview because he would say the funniest things. Leading up to that (Illinois) game, we asked Drew if he knew anything about the Alamo, since they were going to be playing in San Antonio. He said, "All I know about the Alamo is that Ozzy Osbourne got kicked out of the state for urinating on it."

A couple years later, the night the Memphis Grizzlies picked Drew in the NBA draft, we asked him if he was going to visit Graceland, Elvis Presley's home. He said, "I didn't know Elvis was from Memphis. I thought he was from Tennessee." Then someone asked him what he was going to do with all of the money he'd be making. He said, "I'm going to build a big house in Lawrence with a white picket fence around it to keep the media away."

Drew was always a happy guy. I would be surprised if Drew Gooden has many enemies.

That season, Illinois was coached by Bill Self, whom I knew from his days as a player and assistant at Oklahoma State, and then got to know better during the 1985-86 season when he was a graduate assistant at KU for Larry Brown. At the Alamodome, the Jayhawks had their allotted time for practice (closed to outsiders) right before Illinois. I was lingering around when the security guard approached me and advised that I, in my KU shirt, would have to leave the arena because Illinois was about to use its practice time. Bill happened to overhear that and shouted to the guard, "It's O.K. It's Max. He can stay." I thought that was a pretty nice gesture. It wasn't as if I knew enough about basketball to pose any kind of a threat. But it was just a nice thing to do.

Too bad Bill's team wasn't nearly as nice to the Jayhawks. Illinois, a very physical team, won the game, 80-64. Frank Williams led the way for Illinois with 30 points, the most any player scored on the Hawks that season. The game, though, was never really close. The Illini jumped out to a 41-29 lead at the intermission. The closest KU got after that was five points with about five minutes to play, but there didn't seem to be a feeling that KU would be able to overtake Illinois.

About a month after KU's basketball season ended, we found out we'd have another interesting off-season. On April 26, Bob Frederick announced that he was resigning as the school's director of athletics.

Bob's decision came almost eight weeks after he announced that the school was eliminating the men's swimming and tennis programs because of budget cuts. According to reports at the time, keeping the programs would give KU a debt of $650,000 heading into its next fiscal year. Instead, the university would save more than $3.5 million over the next five years.

Bob hated cutting those, but it was a business decision. Doing so put tremendous pressure on both Bob and Chancellor Hemenway from fans, the current tennis and swimming participants (and their parents), and even from a former athletics director.

Monte Johnson, Frederick's predecessor, led a group of about 75 protesters in front of Hemenway's house. If that wasn't bad enough, Monte said publicly that the cuts "wouldn't have happened if I was there."

Being one of the nicest, most loyal guys you'd want to meet, Freddie absorbed the criticism from Johnson and others. He worked hard to find ways to save the programs, but it just didn't work out.

"I made a number of mistakes during my time as athletics director, like everybody else does," Bob said. "But we did a lot of good things, and I'm proud of those things."

I think for Freddie, the biggest perk about being the AD was that he could spend time with the student-athletes. He genuinely cared about each student-athlete. Since resigning, he's received that joy through teaching at the university's School of Education. As he says, "Life is great."

On June 28, Al Bohl, who had been the AD at Fresno State, was introduced as KU's next director of athletics. He was selected over three other finalists: Kathleen DeBoer, a Kentucky assistant athletics director; East Carolina AD Mike Hamrick; and Saint Louis AD Doug Woolard. It was apparent at his initial press conference that improving football on the field and in the stands was going to be Al's biggest project.

From the outset, Bohl seemed to be basically a nice fellow. But, with his sights set so closely on football, he did some things that made people wonder about him. The most controversial came in early November when he fired football coach Terry Allen after the Nebraska game with three contests remaining on the schedule of an already disappointing season.

Two days later, during his weekly press conference, Roy Williams called the firing of his friend Allen "unjust."

Al Bohl, not one to sit back quietly, said in an article by Jason King for *The Kansas City Star* on November 8: "I'm running this program. I'm not asking Roy for permission to do things. It's a new era here. I'm going to run this program like a CEO would run a company. There's going to be no confusion over who's in charge."

From that moment on, I felt there was a lot of friction between Roy and Al. Frankly, I don't think Roy cared for Al, period.

Roy relayed a story about one time when Drew Gooden was going down to the athletics weight room to work out. The strength coach who was supervising the room made Drew leave, saying that only football players were allowed to use the weights at that particular time.

Of course, all of this is happening when the Hawks are starting their 2001-02 season in what promised to be another terrific season. We started off in Hawaii at the Maui Invitational. The tournament was played before air conditioning was installed in the Lahaina Civic Center, and several KU players went down with leg cramps in the Ball State Opener. Shockingly, Ball State beat KU in the season opener, 93-91, in spite of Gooden's 31 points and 10 rebounds. But the Hawks came back and won their next 13 games.

During that streak, KU played North Dakota University up in the beautiful arena in Grand Forks. Coach always tried to schedule at least one game in every player's career as close as possible to his hometown. Jeff Boschee was from Valley City, North Dakota. He is KU's all-time leader in three-point field goals with 338. He could really shoot the rock! Boschee was such an icon in North Dakota that radio stations in the state joined the KU Sports Network to carry the Jayhawk games.

So, in 2001, Kansas played up there right before the players were going to scatter for Christmas break. They had all kinds of video on the board saluting Jeff, and it was quite a night. KU won easily, 108-77, behind (appropriately) Jeff's game-high 23 points.

But when we came out of the arena after the game, a blizzard had started. We bussed to the airport, but were told no flights would depart until at least the following morning, if then. Roy laughed about the prospect of even flying the next morning. Based on the conditions, he was in no mood for flying. Did we want to wait, or see if we could get a bus and start for Lawrence? The players voted, "Let's go," and off we went. Slipping and sliding with poor visibility.

We picked up a fresh driver in Fargo and headed south. We watched two movies, with the loudest sound tracks I have ever heard – one about boxing, the other about the Chicago mob with plenty of gunshots. It was like warfare in there! I said after the din had subsided, "Personally, I would rather have seen OLD YELLER."

The next morning, we pulled in to the Kansas City airport around 5:30, just in time for Drew to catch his Christmas flight to California. We then rolled into Lawrence around 7. What a night to remember!

The team's 13-game winning streak ended at UCLA. But then the Hawks put together a fantastic string of victories, including back-to-back wins over sixth-ranked Oklahoma State in Stillwater, and then at home against No. 5 Oklahoma. They also blew out No. 22 Missouri, 105-73, and beat Texas in overtime, 110-103, in Austin. Boy, there were some great games in that streak. KU finished undefeated in Big 12 play at 16 and 0.

After losing only one more game before the NCAA Tournament — in the conference tournament — the Jayhawks got an opening-round scare in St. Louis against Holy Cross. During that 70-59 win, Kirk Hinrich sprained his ankle. Initially, it looked like he could be lost for a couple weeks at least. Doctors certainly didn't think he'd be able to play two days later against Stanford.

I watched as the team went down the stairs to their postgame meal after the Holy Cross game. Hinrich couldn't even walk. The trainers and managers had to carry him down the stairs. I said to myself there's no way he can play. Two nights later KU played a very good Stanford team. Late in the first half, Roy inserted Kirk into the lineup! I couldn't believe it. He went on to play the remainder of the game. It just demonstrated, as we have later learned even more dramatically, what a tough guy Kirk Hinrich was and is. I love to watch him play. And now he's a multi-millionaire!

Other voices from The Hill • Roy Williams

Our whole thing before that game was that we wanted to win so we could play the next weekend when Kirk could play. The night before the game I told the team that we had to play our tails off so Kirk could come back. We didn't want the season to end like that.

Then, we had Stanford 18 to 0 and Kirk was over there bugging me to death. Wouldn't get out of my way. Standing up all the time. And so he said he felt better. He said, "Coach, I just want to play in this kind of game. I want to play." And I put him in and he played well.

Next up for KU was a trip to Madison, Wisconsin, to face Bill Self's Fighting Illini again. This time, though, we were a No. 1 seed and they were a No. 4. During the game, Kirk and Nick sat quite a bit on the bench in foul trouble. But freshmen Wayne Simien, Aaron Miles and Keith Langford picked up the slack, combining for 35 of KU's 73 points as the Hawks won by four.

In the Elite Eight, the Hawks took on a tough Oregon team that featured the two Lukes, Ridnour and Jackson, and Freddie Jones. Despite Jones' 32 points, KU did a great job keeping the Lukes in check, holding the pair to a combined 19 points. The Jayhawks, playing one of their best games of the Tournament behind Nick's 25 points and Langford's 20, cruised past the Ducks, 104-86.

KU was headed to the Final Four for the first time since 1993. Heading to Atlanta, out of the four teams including Maryland (KU's opponent), Indiana and Oklahoma, I felt the Jayhawks were the best team.

Other voices from The Hill • Roy Williams

We weren't playing the best. Maryland was playing the best and they had that focus. They had been to the Final Four the year before. And they had played better, I thought, down the stretch, than anybody else, but it was almost like the leadership of their team had decided we are going to win regardless of what happens. We got off to a great start, but we were taking bad shots. They were just going in. We had them down at the start of the game, but I didn't feel very good because we were in such a rush that we were taking bad shots. It was a little sort of like fool's gold.

Maryland had a senior-laden team. Much like Roy, Gary Williams hadn't won a national title. With some extra motivation and composure, the Terrapins came roaring back and took control of the game. Boschee, who was the lone prominent senior, rallied the Hawks for a late push, but KU couldn't quite catch up. Sure enough, Maryland held on for a 97-88 win. Still, that was a great KU team. (The Big 12's other team at the Final Four, Oklahoma, also lost that night.)

PowerGroup
Companies

Chapter 17

The Two-Year Battle

Talk about talent. Even without two integral players in Jeff Boschee, who graduated, and Drew Gooden, who left a year early for the NBA, from a Final Four squad, the 2002-03 version of the Jayhawks was loaded. Nick and Kirk returned for their senior seasons. Keith, Wayne and Aaron had their freshmen seasons behind them — and they experienced the pressure of playing in the Final Four. Not to mention good role players coming off the bench in Michael Lee, Jeff Graves and Bryant Nash.

After opening the season with a couple of easy wins in the Preseason NIT, the Hawks headed to New York's Madison Square Garden to face Matt Doherty's North Carolina team. Although they struggled mightily the year before, the Tar Heels took care of the Hawks, 67-56. Then, two nights later, in their final game of the NIT, the Jayhawks lost to Florida by 10 points. Suddenly, thanks to a 2-2 start, along with injuries to Kirk and Wayne, some people started questioning the talent on the team and Roy's ability to coach.

But, after losing to the Oregon Ducks in Portland in one of those "hometown" games for Aaron, and dropping their record to 3-3, KU put together a nice little stretch of 10 straight wins. In early January the Hawks went up the road to Kemper Arena in Kansas City to face UMKC. Even though the game was never in doubt, during the first half, Simien went up for a jam and dislocated his shoulder. He fell to the court in pain, and a pall fell over the crowd in more or less a meaningless game. Wayne had so many injuries and illnesses that forced him to miss 32 games — basically a season — and kept a great career from being even greater. Unfortunately, that pattern has followed him into the NBA. That's too bad. Wayne is too good a young man to have these things always happening to him.

The weekend of January 25 and 27, 2003 brought two unbelievable games to Allen Fieldhouse. On Saturday, Kansas and Arizona hooked up in a national headliner. The Wildcats laid it on the Jayhawks, 91-74. Two nights later, powerful Texas came to town with the Big 12 early lead on the line. The Jayhawks held on for a 90-87 win, but the real story was Nick Collison. He was absolutely spectacular in that game, scoring 24 points and grabbing 23 rebounds. Near the end of the national telecast on ESPN, as Collison left the court, sportscaster Dick Vitale (never one to shun the limelight) stood up and applauded Nick personally. It made quite an impression on everyone. That was something terrific.

Although Dick Vitale never is one to avoid the spotlight, we all echoed his sentiments when he stood up and applauded Nick Collison's performance against Texas in 2003.

Speaking of impressions, one certainly was left on me that season on senior night, March 1, when KU played host to Oklahoma State. It was the last home game for Nick and Kirk. KU was on its way to the league championship. Near the end of the game, which KU was going to win, O-State coach Eddie Sutton left his bench, walked down to the KU bench, and personally shook hands with both Nick and Kirk. Eddie's gesture made a tremendous impression on me personally, and on all the KU fans.

The Hawks lost to Missouri in the Big 12 tournament eight days later, but survived an opening-round game in the Big Dance against Utah State and then cruised past Arizona State. That set up a meeting with Duke in Anaheim, California, in the West Regional.

As much excitement as there was on the court, there was an equal amount of drama behind the scenes in the KU athletics department. The day before KU played Duke in Anaheim, North Carolina ended its disappointing 19-16 season in the NIT with a loss to Georgetown. (Keep that in the back of your mind.)

The discord between Roy Williams and Al Bohl continued to escalate.

Other voices from The Hill • Roy Williams

I felt like every day I went to the office, I was having to fight a battle. Every coach was coming in from the other sports and talking to me about how bad things were for them. I was the sounding board for everybody and it was difficult. I hate to just point down at Al Bohl, but it wasn't a good mix. That's the bottom line. I didn't feel comfortable. I didn't feel appreciated. I felt like we were being pushed aside to take care of everything else.

He had in his mind so much that he had to get football going that he didn't care about anything else. I even felt like he was hoping I would lose because I was too powerful. To go through that for two years was hard.

I don't know that the disagreements reached a point where those of us who were spectators felt one of them would be gone soon, but it was getting close to that. Coincidentally, in Chapel Hill, there were rumblings about the future of coach Matt Doherty. (Of course, with those rumors came the questions from some about Roy's future.)

According to Drue Jennings, who served as the interim athletics director when Al eventually was fired, Chancellor Robert Hemenway approached him about taking over for Al before the Hawks went to Anaheim.

Other voices from The Hill • Drue Jennings

I knew Roy personally, but I wanted the Chancellor to ask Roy if he could embrace the concept of an interim athletics director while the school looked for a permanent one. And, number two, if so, would I be acceptable to Roy as somebody he knew he could work with. And the team was playing in one of the regional tournaments in Anaheim, California. So the Chancellor went out to the tournament that weekend and called me late Sunday night. He said he had finally cornered Roy, who said yes on both scores.

That was comforting to me because I needed to know that Roy was at least content that he could run his basketball program and know that we were moving things in the right direction and that some of these distractions he'd had were not going to affect his coaching status and his attention to his recruiting and so forth.

One other little catch to this story is that while people were whispering Roy's name as a possible replacement for Doherty, who was still Carolina's coach, UCLA was courting Roy.

Distractions aside, the Hawks had an important weekend of basketball ahead of them. Behind a wonderful game by Nick Collison — 33 points and 19 rebounds, KU beat Duke, 69-65, and reached the Elite Eight and a rematch with Arizona.

The Wildcats had spent most of the season ranked No. 1. This time it was the other senior, Kirk Hinrich, coming up big for KU. Playing 39 of 40 minutes, Kirk had 28 points and blocked Arizona's last shot of the game, preserving the Jayhawks' 78-75 win. That also happened to be the 1,800th win in KU's history, good for third-most in NCAA history. Kansas, for the second straight year, was going to the Final Four.

It was odd at the time, but I was walking with Roy and his wife Wanda while we were in California and they were talking about how they wouldn't want to live in Southern California and fight the traffic every day.

Even at that time, Roy says that he thought he'd coach another 10-15 years at KU and then retire to the mountains of North Carolina and play golf everyday. That idea was reinforced when Roy and Wanda got home from Anaheim.

Other voices from The Hill • Roy Williams

We got back from that great, great trip to Anaheim and Matt Doherty had called and said, "Coach, I'm sorry you had to put up with all the speculation, but we've had some meetings here and everything is going to be fine." After I got the message, I told Wanda, "That's great. I am so happy for him. I'm calling UCLA tomorrow and telling them that I am not coming there because this made me realize that I could never leave Kansas for anywhere except North Carolina." So I called UCLA the next morning and told them that I would not talk to them then or ever because I've decided the only job that I would have ever considered leaving Kansas for was North Carolina. And so that week, with Matt's message, I'm thinking it's great because I'm going to be at Kansas for the rest of my life now even more so. Three days later, UCLA hired Ben Howland.

On Tuesday, April 1, two days after KU beat Arizona, Matt Doherty resigned under pressure. With impeccable timing, Roy said North Carolina athletics director Dick Baddour called the next day.

Roy said: "I told him, 'If you have to have an answer right now, the answer is no.' I did not want to leave Kansas."

Of course Matt's firing — as Roy calls it — fueled more than enough speculation later that week when KU, Marquette (the Jayhawks' semifinal opponent), Syracuse and Texas arrived in New Orleans for the Final Four.

Marquette featured a phenomenal player named Dwyane Wade, who is having a wonderful NBA career. In the semifinal game against KU, he scored 19 points and was one of the few bright spots for a good Marquette team. The Jayhawks, with a pregame challenge from Roy to be aggressive, came out on a mission and didn't look back.

Other voices from The Hill • Roy Williams

I didn't look at the clock a single time in the first half. But I knew we were playing pretty doggone well. I remember walking off the floor at the Superdome and looking up at the clock and we are up 59-30 at half. I knew we were playing pretty well, but I didn't know it was that big of a margin. I had watched the tape of Marquette's game against Kentucky, and Dwyane Wade looked like Michael Jordan. So I told (assistant coach) Ben Miller, "When you cut out the clips to show the team, don't cut out any of Wade's clips from the Kentucky game." He looked phenomenal, like he was unstoppable. I helped coach the Olympic team a few years later and the first thing Dwyane Wade said to me was, "Here's the coach that beat me to death."

KU crushed Marquette, 94-61, in the fourth-most lopsided win ever in the Final Four. Five Jayhawks scored in double figures: Langford (23), Hinrich and Miles (18 each), Michael Lee (13) and Collison (12).

Up next was Syracuse and its super freshman Carmelo Anthony. Even though he scored a game-high 20 points, "Mello" wasn't the player that gave KU the most fits. Freshman Gerry McNamara hit six three-pointers for the Orangemen. Syracuse went up by as many as 18 in the first half. At halftime, trailing 53-42, Roy says he "promised them that we would be there at the end of the game and that we'd still have a chance." Sure enough, the Hawks fought and fought. And even with their woeful 12-for-30 from the free-throw line, they were close. Down three with less than a minute to play, Michael Lee put up a three-pointer that Hakim Warrick blocked, sealing the championship for Syracuse, 81-78.

Kansas fans thought they got a good glimpse into the future immediately after the game. During the interview with Roy on CBS — the obligatory talk with both coaches outside their locker rooms — Bonnie Bernstein asked Roy the typical questions about the game. Then, she asked what everyone wondered: if he had any interest in the North Carolina vacancy. At first, Roy shrugged it off.

"Bonnie, I could give a flip about what those people want," he said. "You have to ask that question. I understand that. But as a human being ... all those people that want that answer, to know right now, they're not very sensitive."

She asked again. Big mistake.

"As a journalist, I understand why you have to ask that question," he responded. "The guy in your ear that is telling you to ask that question is not a nice person. I could give a s--- about North Carolina right now."

Not many people have said things like that on national TV.

But that was on many people's minds as much as the games themselves. During the weekend, Andy Katz interviewed me on ESPN. He asked me if I thought Roy was leaving for North Carolina.

On national TV I said, "No, Roy Williams will not leave Kansas because he can't look those players in the eyes that he recruited, and tell them that he won't be there any longer."

After all, when he announced he was staying on that July night in 2000, with thousands of fans at Memorial Stadium, he said that he was staying until he was fired or until he died. But, of course, we both were quite wrong.

Other voices from The Hill • Robert Hemenway

Frankly, I was thinking a little bit like that. I felt Roy made a very strong statement about his planning on staying at KU. Circumstances changed. ... But his fans and I were pretty upset about it. I really regretted it, too. Roy Williams just reached the decision that he wanted to go home to North Carolina to pursue his career. Roy Williams was a fantastic basketball coach, who had been with Kansas for a very long time. I was always under the opinion that we should all thank Roy for his service and appreciate what he'd done for KU. … I was as happy for Roy as anybody was when he finally won that national championship for North Carolina in 2005.

Chancellor Robert Hemenway and I had some good radio interviews throughout the years.

Maybe in an effort to help salvage the situation and make Carolina less tempting for Roy, though, two days after the national championship game, on Wednesday, April 9, Chancellor Hemenway fired Al Bohl, who was less than two years into his five-year contract. It didn't help with Roy. Less than a week later, Roy did care about North Carolina.

Other voices from The Hill • Robert Hemenway

I think Al is a person who enjoys being around people and tries hard to be friends with people. It just never quite worked out here. Before very long during Al's tenure as athletics director, I began to receive calls and complaints about him. We tried to work through some of these things. In the end it was an obvious decision that Al just didn't have the kind of support you need in order to be an effective athletics director.

Bohl's firing wasn't a complete shock. But, what happened over the next few hours only fittingly continued the Al Bohl saga. He wanted to address the media at the John Hadl Auditorium at Allen Fieldhouse, but Hemenway denied him that privilege, saying he was no longer an employee of the University of Kansas. So, Al Bohl announced that he would have a press conference on the driveway of his home. Much to his neighbors' delight, I'm sure, all the big TV trucks pulled up to Bohl's house.

Al stood there and read from a statement he had written, that was directed as much toward Roy and the basketball program as it was toward anything else. It was then that Al made his famous statement: "I believe the Kansas basketball coach had the power to hold his athletics director in his hand like a dove. He had the choice to either crush me with his power of influence or let me fly with my visions for a better total program. He chose to crush me."

He also said: "I strongly believe the mandate for my dismissal reverts Kansas back to the pattern of great men's basketball teams with other sports barely surviving."

Oh, boy.

Al was a gregarious guy. Intrusive and extreme extrovert are good words to describe him. He always wanted to be very visible. I'll never forget the time in St. Louis when Don Green and I were in a restaurant after a game. Al came in and shouted in a loud voice: "Are there any Jayhawks in here?" Don and I tried to make ourselves inconspicuous, so nobody would see us.

There was another night before a game when I looked over at the KU band, and there was Al, in the trombone section. Not actually playing; just being goofy. You just never knew where Al Bohl was going to show up. His heart was in the right place. He just was not the right guy at the right time for KU athletics.

There was a lot of speculation about how much Al Bohl's presence played into Roy's considering, and ultimately taking, the job at North Carolina. As we look back now, one can't help but wonder if Roy would've stayed at Kansas had Al been fired sooner, say in January or February.

Other voices from The Hill • Roy Williams

I don't know if I can say it like that because we don't know, but chances would have been much, much greater. If I had been as happy at Kansas as

I was during Bob Frederick's tenure, I never would have left. There is no question in my mind. I loved the University of Kansas and I still love the University of Kansas.

When I said no to North Carolina the first time in 2000, I never looked back. I never one day thought I would ever be the coach at North Carolina. And it didn't bother me.

If my situation had not changed during that two-year period, there is no question in my mind I would never have left Kansas for North Carolina or anywhere else because I felt like it was my program. I felt like it was a team. I felt like everybody in the athletic department was pulling for each other. I felt like that was my second home. I had said no to the Los Angeles Lakers twice. I had said no on two different occasions to UCLA. I had said no once to North Carolina. And so other than Kansas and North Carolina, UCLA or Kentucky would have to be the top of college basketball. I was going to stay at Kansas forever. But in that two-year period, each and every day I felt like I was fighting, and the only time that I was happy was when I was on the court with my team.

I've also wondered if Roy would still be at Kansas today if Al had been fired earlier. But after talking with Roy during the writing of this book, I'm convinced he didn't have his mind made up during the season as some people have suggested. Roy told me that after the loss to Syracuse, a small group of close friends, including coach Smith, and some golfing buddies, were in his room at the hotel. Not one word was mentioned by anyone about North Carolina. In the end though, I just think he was so beholden to Dean Smith that if Dean told Roy that North Carolina needed him, he would go back. I had the feeling that right after Roy made the decision, he must have felt that he'd just made the biggest mistake of his life. That's the way he looked to me. But he said not. He said, "I didn't look back." Painful as it might have been. He certainly seemed to me to be in pain – mental pain, that is.

Other voices from The Hill • Drue Jennings

I know he was really torn between the life he had fashioned here and just the worship that he deserved here as part of our community, and his allegiance to Dean Smith and to Carolina. Most of us would hope we were never confronted with that kind of a decision. It's like choosing between your wife and one of your children.

A lot of people have a bitter taste about Roy, but I have nothing but the highest of regard for him and what he did for us here, the kind of person he was and the kind of kids he recruited — the way they made you feel. I used to sit there when I was still active in business and say I hope I can perform under pressure the way these kids do. Roy taught those young men an awful lot about things that would carry them through their lives. And I think as a community of KU loyalists here, we have to be forever grateful for that. And then you can't quarrel with the results of the basketball program. But I'll tell you something — Bill Self is every bit the man.

With Al Bohl gone, Drue became the interim athletics director. Drue had played defensive back for Pepper Rodgers' first team at KU. He was coming off a very successful career as the Chief Executive Officer and Chairman for Kansas City Power and Light when the Chancellor called him.

Bob talked with Drue about taking the job on a full-time basis, but the timing wasn't right for Drue. His wife had died of cancer a few months before that, so Drue says he didn't have the energy level to immerse himself in 12-14 hour days. Plus, he didn't have a background in athletics. But, he was a good choice to help smooth the road before the new AD came in.

Other voices from The Hill • Robert Hemenway

I went to Drue and explained what was going to happen to Al and asked him if he would be willing to step in as the director of athletics. Drue is a person with integrity, so everybody knew that if Drue was involved, it was going to have to be done right. He's also a person who understands that when you're in charge of an organization, you've got to keep the employees happy and help them stay focused and on task. He did all those things extremely well. He provided great advice and support to me. He was a tremendous help to KU.

Evidently, the athletic department needed help at the time. Of course, everything blew up in Drue's face from the outset. According to Drue, he saw that the people working in the athletic department were extremely devoted, but "their work habits were poor. ... The discipline in running the organization, I thought, was lacking."

Then, on top of the organizational issues, the school's highest-profile coach had left. Drue went to Chancellor Hemenway with a plan for finding a new basketball coach.

Other voices from The Hill • Drue Jennings

I told the Chancellor we couldn't deal with a big search committee. I said, "We have got a squad of about 12 or 13 young men down there who right now are hurting anyhow because they had just lost to Syracuse and now they have lost their coach." We had to keep that team together. I told him, "We've got to attend to these kids and how they feel right now. They have lost their coach. They have lost the national championship. We have got to focus on them. We've got to do it quickly, right now, as fast as we can. … So we can't put together some big Noah's Ark search committee. You are just going to have to trust me on this. We have got to go out and get a great coach and get him quickly because we don't have weeks to sit here and go through the process." He agreed with that.

I promised him that we would be prudent in terms of the economics and the financial arrangements we would make. I promised that he had to be involved every step of the way, but that he needed to give us some freedom to do things at odd hours and to go out and talk with people and to consult resources that we needed. So, I asked him for the freedom to let me, Doug Vance and Richard Konzem and him, the Chancellor — a committee of four people — get out and start beating the bushes immediately.

Bob and Drue agreed in that meeting that they needed to move as quickly as possible. If that wasn't stress enough for Drue, he also had to deal with the annual basketball banquet and the brewing controversy over whether Roy should be allowed to attend. Many people were vehemently opposed to Roy being permitted back. But, as Drue made clear to those people, this was Roy's team. Those were his kids, and their collective run to the national championship game. Although Drue's decision wasn't popular, there never was any doubt in his mind that expecting Roy to return to Lawrence was the right decision.

With the exception of one guy who loudly voiced his opinion — but quickly was put in his place by Dave Collison, Nick's dad — the evening was a great success.

Chapter 18

Bill Self Ushers In A New Attitude

It's funny how things work out sometimes. Did you know that if it weren't for former Missouri coach Quin Snyder, Bill Self might not be at Kansas today? In April 1999, when Norm Stewart retired from coaching, Bill, who was coaching at Tulsa, was a finalist to be his replacement. Missouri athletics director Mike Alden had Quin and Bill in different locations at the Kansas City Marriott Hotel. Alden spoke with Quin first and asked him if he'd be interested in taking the Tigers job if asked. When Quin replied, "Absolutely," Alden went to the coffee shop where Bill was waiting and told him that they'd decided to go with Quin. And, as they say, the rest is history.

We never really dreamed that Roy Williams would leave KU, especially after the big announcement when he first turned down North Carolina in 2000. Still, we sometimes would say, "If there is ever a chance Roy would leave, it would be terrific if we could get Bill Self."

I had always liked Bill Self, as a player at Oklahoma State, and then as a graduate assistant at Kansas for the great 1986 team. He was basically the same age as the players then. He had so much fun that year. He banged around with R.C. Buford. They stayed at Larry Brown's house. R.C. did things such as clean up the house after the dogs were left alone by Larry for three days. (And now he's the General Manager for the San Antonio Spurs.)

We're lucky Bill Self didn't get that job offer from Missouri.

Other voices from The Hill • Bill Self

If I had gotten that job, I would've missed out on three important things:
1. *Having the greatest season in Tulsa history that next year (1999-2000).*
2. *Coaching at Illinois and helping the Illini win two Big Ten championships.*
3. *Coaching at Kansas. None of those events would've happened to me if I had gotten the job at Missouri.*

My path crossed Bill's a few times as his coaching career moved along, but I think the most meaningful occasion, at least to me, was the story I mentioned in chapter 18 from the NCAA Midwest Regional at San Antonio in 2001, when Bill told the security guard it was OK for me to stay at their closed practice.

That season, Illinois beat Kansas 80-64, reaching the Elite Eight for the second time in Bill's career. He had taken Tulsa that far in the Tournament the previous year. He was a young, successful coach with ties to Kansas.

So, when Roy took the North Carolina job, confidence was high for everyone around Kansas that Bill Self would be one of the main candidates. The committee of four felt the same way. Once they identified a short list of candidates to replace Roy, they contacted the athletics directors at those schools. One of the first calls they made was to Ron Guenther at the University of Illinois, seeking permission to contact Bill Self.

After receiving about 35 phone messages every hour or so — because that's all his phone would hold — during the previous 24 hours from everybody except KU's four-man committee, Bill got the call from KU on his first day of vacation with his family at Fisher Island, off the coast of Miami. By the time he finished visiting on the phone with Drue, Doug Vance and Richard Konzem, even though he hadn't made a decision about whether he'd want to leave Illinois, he says "I knew the KU job was something I wanted to definitely look into."

Besides the interview the committee conducted the night of the basketball banquet, they did three other telephone interviews. Drue Jennings, the interim athletics director, said that Bill's interview, by far, was the best. The committee liked the other three, but Bill quickly jumped to the head of the list because of his roots and the success he enjoyed at Illinois, where he was 78-24 in three seasons.

Other voices from The Hill • Drue Jennings

We did everything by telephone. The economic conditions of his contract, at least the main part, were resolved in probably the first 15 minutes. There was never a question of what we were going to pay him to come here, in my mind or in Bill's. He wasn't looking for a bigger contract. He wanted to come to KU.

If he could get the KU job, the money wasn't the issue. At the same time, as badly as he wanted to make that next leap in his own career, his conscience was so torn in dealing with the kids he had recruited to Illinois and the community that he had become a part of up there. You know, when you watch him struggling with his conscience that way, you know you've got the right guy. I mean, this is Phog Allen type stuff — to get his shot at something that had been a dream of his, but he's debating whether to take it because of his sense of responsibility to Illinois. I knew from that that Bill was the guy we wanted.

Bill was in a great situation at Illinois. His teams were successful and he was very popular. When KU approached him about becoming the head coach, it had to be a tough decision based on his success at Illinois, not to mention that KU didn't have a full-time director of athletics yet. Still, the following Saturday night, he decided he was going to become the eighth men's basketball coach in KU history.

The official announcement would come on Monday, exactly two weeks after the Hawks lost to Syracuse in the NCAA national championship game. With all that had happened, though, it felt more like a month since that night in New Orleans.

Other voices from The Hill • Bill Self

Yes, I was at a great place at Illinois. And the timing was not right for me personally to leave there. The timing is never usually perfect. We could have stayed in Illinois and been very happy there, I believe, but over time I would have wanted to get back closer to my area. And, the fact of the matter is how many jobs of Kansas's caliber open up? So, even though short-term it was difficult to leave Illinois because the timing wasn't great, in the long-term the timing was the best.

A couple great stories of Bill's hiring surround the hours leading up to the press conference introducing him as the next head coach at the University of Kansas. Great cloak-and-dagger kind of stuff.

On Easter morning, April 20, six days after Roy announced he was leaving, Drue flew in a private jet to Illinois to pick up Bill and his family and Norm Roberts — who had been an assistant coach with Bill — and fly them back to Lawrence. Even though pretty much everyone assumed Bill was the man for the job and would be announced soon, Drue felt rightly so that it was important to wait and make the official announcement at the press conference on Monday morning. He definitely didn't want the media that had been camped out around Allen Fieldhouse nearly around the clock since Roy's departure to see Bill.

Since the media stopped Drue every morning at 6:15 as he went into his office, he felt he had a good idea where they'd be on Easter morning. So, everyone except Drue got out of the car at a back door. Then, Drue arrived at his normal spot alone. Meanwhile, someone drove the Self family and Norm to where they'd be staying until Monday.

There was one minor detail to finish before the press conference in Hadl Auditorium — the terms of the agreement. The parties had the critical terms written on a sheet of paper, but it wasn't the full contract. To avoid any embarrassing glitches, about 30 minutes before the press conference, Drue and Bill faxed everything to Bill's attorney in Oklahoma City to review. Then they signed everything before the press conference in front of an estimated 300 fans and media.

Rumor had it that around the time Bill took the job — that day or the next — Larry Brown called Bill and said, "D--- it Bill, you took the job that I wanted." As with most rumors, that's not exactly how it happened.

Other voices from The Hill • Bill Self

What really happened was that when we took the job, before the press conference, I called the three living coaches that had coached at Kansas: Ted Owens, Larry Brown and Roy Williams. I told them how excited I was and what an honor it was to sit in the same chair that they sat in. Of course, Larry said, "Well, Bill, you know that's the job I wanted." I said, "Coach what job haven't you wanted?" I love Larry. I learned a ton from him when I was here. He's done an awful lot to jumpstart my career. And I'll forever be indebted to him.

With the hiring of a new basketball coach done, the next big task was finding a full-time athletics director to replace the fired Al Bohl. The search led the committee to hire Lew Perkins from the University of Connecticut in June 2003.

At first glance to some, Lew wouldn't belong at a Midwestern university. After all, he's from Massachusetts, he had been the director of athletics at UConn since 1990, and was the AD at Maryland before that. Lew, however, has some good Kansas roots.

He played basketball at the University of Iowa for KU grad Ralph Miller and he was the athletics director down Interstate 35 at Wichita State during 1983-87.

If you asked him today, Lew would tell you that he learned more about life and about who he is and what he is from Ralph Miller. Lew, who loves history and tradition, was intrigued, even at that time, by Phog Allen and the mystique of Kansas. In fact, he says that in the back of his mind, there were only two AD jobs that could lure him from Connecticut — Iowa and Kansas.

So, even though Lew had helped turn the UConn basketball teams into national powers, was seeing a revitalization of football, influenced six national championships and oversaw the construction of a new football stadium, when the KU committee contacted him, he was eager to listen, even though it took somewhat of a sales job to get him here.

Other voices from The Hill • Lew Perkins

I knew the history and tradition about KU and how proud they were about a lot of things, especially the athletic program. But I think over the four or five years before I got here, there were a lot of issues that took away from that great tradition, that great pride. I think everybody began to feel inferior. I didn't realize until I got here just how much they had lost their swagger. We've spent a lot of time and effort to try to rebuild that. I think we've made some tremendous progress, but we still have a long way to go.

Therein explains largely why Lew would leave a successful situation at Connecticut and come back to the Midwest — he loves challenges, he loves to work. He's not a "caretaker."

As I mentioned in the first chapter, when KU hired Lew, friends and colleagues were warning me about Lew coming in and cleaning house.

The paranoia is often warranted with a new athletics director, because they like to be surrounded by their own guys, just a like a new coach. In Lew's case, though, that wasn't the case.

On the contrary, besides enhancing my final season as a broadcaster, Lew didn't have a strong desire to change coaches. "Nothing's broken," he said, "so my job is to enhance everyone around here and to make them better and to help them."

Lew has been a great addition to the university. Teams across the board are improving and we're seeing improvements to the existing facilities or development for new ones. Additionally, he really loves the student-athletes. He wants everything to be first-class for them. He also expects them to call him Lew instead of Mr. Perkins since, as he says, the athletics department is there for the student-athletes.

In the summer of 2003, I received a call from the Naismith Basketball Hall of Fame in Springfield, Massachusetts. They told me I had been chosen to receive the Curt Gowdy Award for excellence in broadcasting and they wanted me to come back for the ceremonies that fall!

That was really a stunner for me. I learned that of all the broadcasters who had been previously honored, only one other in the award's history had been a college broadcaster – the late Cawood Ledford of Kentucky. All the others were national figures — Bob Costas, Jim Nantz, Dick Vitale and Billy Packer. (Cawood, incidentally, had broadcast NCAA Tournament games nationally on radio.) And now, Max Falkenstien was going to join that list??? How could it be? I thought it must be pretty important when KU's new athletics director, Lew Perkins, bent and kissed my ring the next time he saw me.

As we were with the award from the College Football Hall of Fame five years earlier, Isobel and I were off to another big banquet. As soon as we arrived, I found myself in a reception with Dr. J! Julius Irving. What a nice guy! Ray Meyer, the 90-year-old legendary coach of DePaul, plopped down in a chair beside me. Meadowlark Lemon of the Harlem Globetrotters introduced himself to me. I was like a 5-year-old kid in a candy store! So many of the greatest names in the game, and I'm right there visiting with them all. And you know what? Everyone I met could not have been any more friendly.

Our names were up in lights in the rotunda, we were interviewed on national television, I gave a little talk and said whereas James Naismith had come from Springfield TO Lawrence, now I was returning to Springfield FROM Lawrence, so maybe we closed the circle. It was two days to remember, that's for sure!

Although Kansas had its new director of athletics, and the football team was heading for a berth in the Tangerine Bowl in 2003, the great anticipation for KU fans was the annual "Late Night" opening of the basketball season. People were excited about Bill Self as the new coach. Of course with that, many wondered about Bill's traditional physical style of basketball as opposed to the up-tempo game of Roy's teams.

Some of the players who had been successful under Roy were a little slow to buy into the Bill Self system. After all, they had been recruited to play a certain style and a certain way, which wasn't the style for which Bill's teams had become known. To make matters worse, he was implementing his style — of coaching, of teaching, of practicing, of playing — with a team that was six months removed from the NCAA national championship game.

Other voices from The Hill • Bill Self

You have to coach within your personality and your own system. The system they had here was great, but it wasn't me. Certainly, I think some players benefited more than others from the coaching change. I know Wayne Simien would be the first to tell you, being first-team All-American, he benefited from this. But then Keith Langford, who was more involved in an up and down type of game, probably benefited more from the prior regime. You have to play within what your personnel allows you to play. And we thought that this gave us the best chance to win the way we played. I think it did, as evidenced by that first year.

Behind a core that included Simien, Langford, Aaron Miles and J.R. Giddens, the Hawks got off to a quick start that season with wins over UT-Chattanooga, Michigan State and Texas Christian. It was such an exciting time that I remember while we were doing the post-game show after the win over Michigan State at Allen Fieldhouse, Norm Roberts came in and said, "Man, I thought we had some great crowds at Illinois, but I've never seen a crowd with the enthusiasm of this one."

Along the way, KU lost an early-season game to Stanford at the Wooden Classic in California and then lost at Nevada four games later.

One thing I remember in particular from that season was something that happened away from the court. After the Hawks beat Colorado in Boulder on January 5, we were stuck in the Denver airport while we waited for our plane to show up. Keith Langford, who was a junior at the time, and I hadn't bonded at all. In football it's tough to get to know the players because there are fewer games and more players. In basketball, we're around a dozen or so kids 30-40 times a season.

We were sitting in a room with this huge spread, and everybody ate all they could, so some guys were sleeping against the wall or off listening to their headphones. Langford was messing around with a deck of cards. I went over and said, "Keith, you want me to show you how to play blackjack?" "Yeah, man," he said, "that would be great."

So we spent about 30 minutes playing blackjack, just the two of us, and from that point on we were really good friends.

Incidentally, our plane back to Lawrence finally left around 4 a.m.!

One of the most disappointing losses of the nine the team suffered during the 2003-04 season came on January 22 at home against Richmond, 69-68. That snapped KU's home streak of wins against unranked opponents at 52 games. It also was the first loss at Allen Fieldhouse since the Arizona game on January 25 of the previous year. Although it snapped a streak, Bill said it's a game that "got our attention."

About three weeks later, losing just once in their next five conference games, the Hawks suffered back-to-back road losses to Oklahoma State and Nebraska. The 80-60 loss to the Cowboys came just two days after KU blew out 19th-ranked Texas Tech, 96-77, at home. That loss in Stillwater also marked Bill's first trip back to his alma mater as coach of the Jayhawks. As much as he loves Oklahoma State and Eddie Sutton, Bill was not a happy camper that night.

But then KU won five of its next six games, including the regular-season finale at Missouri when David Padgett hit a line-drive jumper from the corner with two seconds left. The 84-82 KU win was the final game at Missouri's Hearnes Center. It was nice to get that win, especially since they dedicated the court to former coach Norm Stewart and had many ex-players on hand for the game's festivities. It took us a long time to wrap up our broadcast, and an hour after the game a lot of Missouri fans were still sitting there. It was such an unbelievable loss for them and such a heartbreak. Who knows, maybe they just didn't want to fight the traffic.

Once Kansas reached the NCAA Tournament, Bill and his Jayhawks got wins over Illinois-Chicago and Pacific before meeting Alabama-Birmingham — coached by current Missouri coach Mike Anderson — and their "40 minutes of hell." The Hawks turned the tables and gave Anderson's team 40 minutes of hell while running the Blazers into the ground with a 100-74 win behind Simien's 30 points. In spite of an overtime loss to Georgia Tech the next game in the Elite Eight, it was a great first year for Self.

During the offseason, Lew Perkins did something that still hasn't settled well with many fans when he announced that starting with the 2004-05 season, basketball seats for men's season tickets at Allen Fieldhouse would be based on a point system. Under the plan, people would accumulate points based on monetary giving, season tickets purchased for other sports and tenure as a season-ticket holder. Many fans — especially longtime season-ticket holders — were livid with Lew and the new system.

Even though it ticked off a lot of people, the point system has helped generate additional revenue for the athletics department, and helped the budget creep up toward those of some of the other schools in the Big 12.

Other voices from The Hill • Lew Perkins

I could have waited about three years after I came to implement that and I think it would have been better for everybody -- everybody except the athletics department and the student-athletes. We were hurting so badly financially that we couldn't wait. Once we educated people, people began to understand that this was good for everybody. What's interesting is we have very few people talking about it right now. The most important thing of all is we have given our coaches and our student-athletes the opportunity to be successful because we are giving them the resources. We weren't trying to upset people. We needed money. Still, we are probably 20 years behind the times. We were doing this at Connecticut and Maryland 15, 18 years ago.

Even though we are part of an academic university, we are a business. We are self-sufficient and we have to raise our own money. But we can never lose sight of the fact that we are part of an academic environment, and we can't lose those values and the things that are important in an academic community.

My goal is to put Kansas in the position to be in the higher echelon of the Big 12 in whatever way we have to do it.

Since Lew has been at Kansas, by the way, the athletics budget has gone from $27 million to $40 million — thanks mainly to fundraising efforts and the new points plan.

The 2004-05 season brought about a great and unlikely streak and a heartbreaking end, as would the next season.

The Hawks rattled off 14 straight wins at the start of the 2004-05 campaign. Besides four Big 12 wins in that stretch, the streak also included an overtime win at home against Georgia Tech, after KU trailed by 16 points in the first half, on New Year's Day. Then, a 65-59 win versus Kentucky at Rupp Arena. Not many teams win at Rupp.

During that game, as Christian Moody was leading KU in scoring with 11 points and tying for the team-high in rebounds with seven, television analyst Billy Packer was tabbing Christian on CBS as the greatest walk-on in college basketball history. That might've been a slight exaggeration of Christian's talents at the time, but there's no arguing the great game he played. There's also no exaggerating what a great kid he is.

Making that streak even more impressive is the fact that All-American Wayne Simien hurt his thumb against South Carolina and missed the next four games, including the contests against Georgia Tech and Kentucky.

On January 22, we traveled to Philadelphia to take on Villanova. That was a nightmare of a trip. First and foremost, Villanova won 83-62, handing Bill one of his worst losses ever. But, while we were getting beat inside, outside is a blizzard. There were about two feet of snow on the ground when we made it back to the bus after the game.

The buses somehow trudged through five miles of snow drifts to get to the airport. Then, just as we were ready to board, they closed the airport! We had to turn around and head back downtown because we weren't going to be able to take off.

On Sunday morning, we made it to the airport about 7:30. That day the Eagles were hosting an NFL playoff game. Cars were lined up for a mile or so to get into the football stadium's parking lots, while workers tried to clear the snow from the lots. Talk about dedicated fans!

KU won its next six games, including Missouri and K-State, but then the Hawks lost three in a row – at Texas Tech in double-overtime on a controversial call, at home against Iowa State in overtime, and at Oklahoma. Things didn't look too good for the team. Besides the losses on the court, the complete team just wasn't healthy. Christian got hurt against Texas Tech and missed the next few games. Langford got hurt and missed the Oklahoma State game in the Big 12 tournament, and then he basically missed the NCAA Tournament.

In the first round of the tournament, facing Bucknell in Oklahoma City, the Jayhawks played a bad game and lost, 64-63. They ended the season with a 23-7 record. That game marked the end of the collegiate careers of Simien, Langford, Miles and Michael Lee. Afterwards, Bill was kind enough to give me a radio interview in what had to have been one of the lowest times in his coaching career.

Other voices from The Hill　•　Bill Self

That was a down time. It wasn't an embarrassing time, which a lot of people wanted to portray it to be, because we knew without Keith, Bucknell had good enough players and could play with us. We thought it would be a very tough game, and it was. They made a hook shot from 12 feet from in front of the rim to go up one, and then our best player, Wayne, had a good look from 15 feet and missed it. That's the difference between winning and losing in the Tournament. It was a sad way to see four quality seniors end their careers.

Although things looked bleak with the first-round loss to Bucknell and the departure of four key players, Bill had a terrific recruiting summer. Bill and I were on our way to Topeka to play golf late that summer. He was talking to Brandon Rush on the phone, assuring him that Kansas would be a great place for him. "Everything is going to be great. We're looking forward to having you play for us," Bill said. In a recruiting coup, KU got him.

Other voices from The Hill　•　Bill Self

Brandon gave us a shot of adrenaline when our program needed it. We were one player short and Brandon kind of fell into our lap, so to speak. In recruiting terms we worked him, but it didn't take the normal year and a half process to convince him to come. And of all the guys that I've recruited, I would say he's been as pleasant of a surprise as anybody.

The terrific recruiting class also included Mario Chalmers and Julian Wright. With sophomores Sasha Kaun and Russell Robinson, the main five

Jayhawks heading into the 2005-06 season — my 60th and final behind the microphone — were going to be extremely young, but incredibly talented. Early in the year, they played as one might expect a young, inexperienced team to play: inconsistently. The Hawks opened with a win at home against Idaho State before returning to my favorite travel destination in the world — Maui, Hawaii — for the Maui Invitational. Not a bad way to begin my final basketball season.

Basketball-wise, it wasn't so great. The Hawks lost to two good teams, Arizona and Arkansas. Otherwise, it was as great as ever. Walking on the beach under moonlit skies, and all that stuff. Seeing my good friend, Wayne Duke, who had hired me to do the Big 8 Television Game of the Week when he was commissioner. He later went to the Big Ten, and after retiring was director of the Maui Tournament. He was succeeded by Dave Gavitt, former commissioner of the Big East Conference, who said something I remember, and certainly agree with: "The NBA has the best players, but college basketball has the best game." The shot clock is too quick in the NBA, and at least to me, all the games seem alike. Well, back to Maui.

Jim Marchiony and I hung around together. Our wives didn't make the trip, so we sort of paired up. We dined at "Cheeseburger In Paradise," and twice we lunched with Jaime and Larry Keating at the Plantation Golf and Country Club, right off the 18th fairway and green. It was so beautiful. The flowers were unbelievable. Plantation is where the PGA Tour plays its first tournament in January of each year.

One afternoon, Jim and I started for a sightseeing drive past the Plantation. We thought we would see a little of the countryside. Thank goodness, Jim was driving. We went on and on, the foliage was getting ever thicker, the mountains were getting ever higher, the road was getting ever more narrow! After awhile, there was no place to turn around, so we kept going. The valleys were breathtaking, and so were the turns in the road. If we ever met a car, one would have to stop. Occasionally, we would come to a little village of eight or ten houses, and we wondered how they could ever get to the grocery store. After about two hours of 20 m.p.h. or less — blind hairpin turns, boulders in the road, you name it — we finally made our way down and found ourselves in Lihue, the site of the Maui airport, clear across the island from Lahaina. We then checked the map that we had received from the rental car office, and the road which we had just traveled was marked in red, with the notation, "Rental cars are not to travel on this roadway!" Oh well, no one ever knew the difference, and we had a great time, a lot of laughs, and some unforgettable scenery.

Oh yeah, KU did win the last game in Hawaii — against Chaminade — and then lost at home to Nevada, and lost to Saint Joseph's in New York.

But then the Hawks started to play better. They won seven straight games, including a 73-46 blowout of Kentucky at Allen Fieldhouse. But then, two games later, the unthinkable happened. At least the unthinkable in recent years. On January 14, Kansas State came to Lawrence and beat the Jayhawks, 59-55, ending KU's domination of the Wildcats that had covered 31 games. The last time K-State had beaten KU was on January 17, 1994, also in Lawrence.

As impressive as that streak is KU's dominance over K-State in Manhattan. Going into the 2007-2008 season, the Wildcats haven't beaten the Jayhawks in Manhattan since January 29, 1983! Strictly a coincidence, but that was Ted Owens's last season coaching the Hawks. That means that Larry Brown and Roy Williams NEVER lost in Manhattan.

Other voices from The Hill • Bob Davis

That's one of the most amazing stories in KU history. How can you explain that? Obviously KU has had better teams many, many of those years, but throughout the streak we have seen double-overtime, we've seen last-second wins, we've seen come-from-behind wins, we've seen blowout victories. How do you go into your in-state rival's building all these years, 24 years now, and not lose? It's unbelievable.

In case losing to K-State at home wasn't bad enough for the young Jayhawks, two nights later, Kansas went to Missouri and lost in overtime, 89-86. KU held a three-point lead with a few seconds left when Thomas Gardner hit a long 3-pointer for the Tigers. Then, with 0.4 seconds left, senior Christian Moody went to the free-throw line with a chance to give the Hawks the win, but he missed both shots. That loss put the Jayhawks at 1-2 in the Big 12.

Bill and I sat in the locker room, ready to do the post-game show and he said, "Max, this is the lowest I've been in my coaching career." It's easy to understand. Losing to Kansas State and Missouri in a span of three days would have to be tough for any KU coach.

Thinking about the situation Christian was in — tie ballgame, on your rival's court, with no time left, and they clear the lane for you to shoot free throws — gives me butterflies to this day. With the exception of that moment, Christian really had an amazing career. He came to Kansas to be a walk-on. He didn't come to start; he came just to be part of the history and tradition. But, because of circumstances with injuries and such, he got a chance to play a little down the stretch of his sophomore year. Then, he played more, including some starts, his junior year. Finally, he played a key part of the team's success during his senior year.

Other voices from The Hill • Bill Self

The thing that was frustrating as a coach was that we had to keep telling Christian he was good. We had to convince him that he deserved to start at Kansas and be labeled the "greatest walk-on in college basketball history." In his mind, he was just a guy here having a good time. And that was neat, because he came to school for all the right reasons. He came to become a doctor. And then, who would have thought that his performance determined if we won or lost basketball games? That was a unique deal for him. But he handled it beautifully.

That night at Missouri, I think he probably felt like he let so many people down. That situation was probably about as tough a situation that a guy could be in during a regular-season affair. At the time I told him that I had confidence. "You've been in these situations, you're a senior, go do it." You know what? If I had to do all over again, I guarantee you to this day it wouldn't bother me a bit to have him on the line.

The back-to-back losses seemed to serve as a wake-up call. The Hawks won their next 10 games and joined the top-25 list for the first time of the season at No. 22. The ninth win of the streak was a payback game against Missouri. This time, heroics weren't necessary. Eleven Jayhawks scored in their 79-46 rout of the Tigers. A week later, Kansas went to Texas and lost to the seventh-ranked Longhorns, 80-55, and fell a game behind Texas in the Big 12 standings.

Looking back, Self says that loss, and the game not being close, was a great thing for the Jayhawks. Even though they had improved drastically throughout the season, they didn't realize what it took to compete against the nation's "elite" teams.

Indeed, the Hawks went on to tie for the Big 12 regular-season championship with a 13-3 record, and then the Big 12 tournament title after beating Texas, 80-68, in Dallas. When they beat Texas that day behind five players scoring in double-figures, I thought they could beat anybody. Well, almost everybody.

KU was disposed of again in the first round of the NCAA Tournament against a team whose school started with the letter "B": Bradley.

Bradley turned out to be a good team, but the Hawks just didn't have their best stuff that night. They made a ton of mistakes and seemed to feel the pressure of the NCAA Tournament atmosphere. That was a stunner of a game.

The season, though, showed us those freshmen were pretty darn good. Plus, Russell Robinson improved during the year.

Hard to believe that from that 3-4 start we roared back to be co-champions of the Big 12 Conference and champions of the conference post-season tournament. As good an improvement in one season as you'll probably ever see. Well, maybe we have to mention again the finish of 1988! You can look it up!

As teams such as Bucknell and Bradley have proven in recent years, college basketball is so competitive and the tournament so unpredictable that it's impossible to say whether the Hawks will win another championship. Shoot, by the time you've read this book, they might've won one. They're certainly in capable hands as long as Bill Self is here.

I've been asked if I think Bill would leave Kansas for his alma mater, Oklahoma State. Unlike the North Carolina blue cloud hanging over Allen Fieldhouse while Roy Williams was here, with the thought in the back of many people's minds that he one day would leave for Chapel Hill, I don't believe it's the same with Bill and O-State.

Bill has told me many times that the year he was here as a graduate assistant was the happiest year he ever spent. He remembers nothing but the good days in Lawrence. And then, of course, I think he realizes that Kansas is one of the three or four best basketball schools in America. So, I don't get any sense at all that Bill would ever leave Kansas. But things change. You never know. For now, the future looks great with Bill Self at the helm.

Chapter 19

A Contrast in Greatness

Reflecting on my 60 years of broadcasting KU basketball, there is no way for me to pick a favorite coach with whom I've worked. Each coach has had unique mannerisms, styles and personalities. In a way, each one has been a favorite.

Certainly, though, Phog Allen has to be near the top of the list. Besides being a good coach and highly competitive, Doc had a wonderful way with words.

Whenever someone would ask Doc if his current team was the greatest he'd ever coached, he would skate around the question by saying, "Let's wait 20 years and see how these young men turn out." Sure, with that statement he was stressing education and the character of his players away from the court. But that also was his way of avoiding the question and keeping everyone happy.

Ever since Bill Self took over for Roy Williams, people have been comparing the two, on and off the court. I'm often asked about the differences. I generally want to take the high road — and Doc Allen's approach — and say let's wait until Bill's been here 15 years before making a comparison.

After all, Roy and Bill are both good friends of mine. They're both great coaches with amazing success. Both are intense competitors and will chirp at the officials from time to time. Both place a huge emphasis on defensive play, and both are unbelievable recruiters.

Former KU football coach Pepper Rodgers once told me, "I can coach good players; I can't coach bad ones." Roy and Bill both know that, all too well.

Roy called Raef LaFrentz every Sunday night at exactly 9:00, within the framework of the NCAA rules, for 52 weeks and he got him. There are no better kids than the three Roy got from Iowa: Raef, Nick Collison and Kirk Hinrich. Their families are tops, as well.

On the other side, Bill is an amazing salesman. One of the best stories, I think, is that of Julian Wright, the terrific player from Chicago Heights, Illinois. Bill and assistant coach Kurtis Townsend visited Julian and his family and made their great pitch for the Jayhawks. Julian had never been to Lawrence, Kansas. After they visited with Julian and his family in Chicago, Bill and Kurtis drove away, hoping they had made a good enough presentation that Julian would come to KU for a visit. A few miles down the road, Bill's cell phone rang. It was Julian's mother, Gina. She said, "Coach, I think you better come back."

After Bill hung up he said to Kurtis, "You don't think he'd be willing to commit now, do you?" Kurtis replied, "I don't know, but I know one thing — we've got to go back."

They returned and were told: "Julian wants to come to KU." How about that? A McDonald's All-American commits to the Hawks, without ever seeing a game at Allen Fieldhouse. That's some pretty terrific recruiting!

As I mentioned earlier in the book — and Bill said in an "Other voices from The Hill" — a big difference between Roy and Bill is on the court with the style of their teams. A trademark of Bill Self's teams at Illinois was their physical play. In 2001, when KU played Illinois in the Sweet 16, they just destroyed us physically. They won the game, 80-64, which the Hawks avenged a year later in the same round of the NCAA Tournament. But Bill's teams always had those bruisers at every position. Roy's teams, on the other hand, have always focused more on finesse and running. I always felt Roy's teams loved to run the other team down until their tongues were hanging out.

The on-court differences don't end there. I have known Roy, on more than one occasion, to take all five players off the court when he was displeased with the way the game was going. That way, no one individual was singled out, but it was obvious coach was ticked off. On the other hand, if a player messed up his individual responsibility, coach would leave him in for a few additional minutes before replacing him. Roy told me that way the fans and media would not know of the error, but Williams would waste no time on the bench reminding the player of what he'd done.

On the other hand, Bill doesn't hesitate to use the hook immediately when a player messes up. He can't wait to get the player out of the game and let him know what he's thinking!

Another big difference between Roy and Bill is that Roy would hold his timeouts. He wanted to save them. I've seen Bill call a timeout 5 minutes into a game.

Subtle differences, maybe. But great results for both.

I had the feeling as the years went by that Roy was enjoying less and less his dealings with the media. He did what he had to do, but I don't think he ever really had much fun doing it. Frankly, I'm not sure if he really wanted to get that close to the media. Since Bob Davis and I weren't really seen as the media, we got along great with Roy and ate together somewhat regularly during the season.

Traveling with Roy was kind of an interesting experience because always on the road we'd have shoot-around, and then Roy would almost always go with a few of us, usually the broadcast crew, out to lunch somewhere. I remember this place, a real dump, in Waco, Texas, called Buzzard Billy's. Roy always liked to go there for lunch. There's a barbecue joint in Grapevine, Texas, where we went at least twice, and Roy just loved it. There was this guy there who sliced the brisket of beef by holding the meat in one hand while using his other hand to slice that stuff. It was a miracle he didn't cut his hand. But it was always fun to travel with Roy because he was always taking a few of us out to these kinds of places. Places that you might say had "atmosphere."

Instead of grabbing a meal after shoot-around, it's my perception that Bill's more inclined to watch video of that night's opponent — a video he's already watched 100 times.

However, Bill does seem to enjoy his time with the media.

When his weekly press conference is over, usually around noon, after they've had their formal recording session, he'll go into the media room with all the guys and sometimes sit there for more than an hour, just shooting the bull and letting his hair down. It's kind of like that Las Vegas commercial: "What happens in Vegas stays in Vegas." Same with Bill and these bull sessions. It's understood in that setting, everything is "off the record."

Other Voices from The Hill • Chris Theisen

Practice starts between 4-4:30. I've told him that we could do the press conference at 3, go until 3:30, and then I'll get the players on the court by 3:45.

But coach insists, "No, we have to eat lunch with the media." Then, he sits there, with no recorders on, and just talks. He's a baseball genius, so they'll talk about baseball. He'll throw his opinion out and the media people seem to love it.

When a member of the media or someone else like that is trying to get in touch with coach, he'll tell me, "Chris, just have him call my cell." I'm in my third year and he has yet to change his cell phone number.

Even today, amazingly, Bill is pretty much the same guy that he was when he worked as a graduate assistant at KU under Larry Brown in 1985-86. The difference now is that he is really a major player on the college basketball scene. He is just as comfortable in his own skin as anybody I've ever been around. The great thing about Bill is he can be talking to the president of the university or the janitor who's doing the floor and be equally comfortable with both of them and they with him.

Roy is so precise and so organized in everything he does. Bill is a little more laid back. Bill is more inclined to let others handle some of the details; Roy is not. Bob Davis and I had to chuckle one time when we were on the team bus going from the airport to the hotel, and Bill said to nobody in particular, "What hotel are we staying at here?" Roy would have known not only the name of the hotel, but also the name of the catering manager and exactly what time the evening meal was going to be served. That's not to say one is right and the other wrong. They're both great!

Other Voices from The Hill • Jerry Waugh

Randy Towner, a local golf pro, was one of Roy's very good friends. He said the difference between Bill and Roy was that Roy would call him and ask him to play golf. If they said they'd play at 4:00, Roy would be in the parking lot at 3:58, grab his clubs and head straight to the tee. After they played a round of golf, Roy was gone. He had other things to do. Bill will call and say, "Hey some of the guys want to come out, can you play with us? We're going to be out there around 4:00 or so." Around 4:20 they show up. Then, after they finish the round, Bill will stay and talk to everybody that comes by.

If there's one thing that's remained constant with Roy and Bill, though, it was our time together doing the postgame interviews. And in the way they handled my sometimes less-than-perfect questions. Mind you, I have always enjoyed doing the postgame interviews with the coach, after which we would usually visit "off the air" about the game.

We always did Williams's interviews in the John Hadl Auditorium in front of the television cameras and the media, while Self prefers to do his live radio report from the coaches' locker room, with no one else in attendance, after which he then goes and meets publicly with the media. Once in a feature in the basketball program, coach Williams was asked, "What's the best thing about coaching basketball at the University of Kansas?" I'm sure, with tongue in cheek, he said, "Doing the postgame show with Max Falkenstien."

Our postgame interviews usually went on without undue notice, unless I said something stupid, at which time the newspaper guys in the room had a field day and the radio audience got a good laugh. Fortunately, this only happened a couple of times that I can remember.

Once in talking with Roy, I mentioned something in KU basketball history that took place in the early 1960s. I said to Roy: "You remember that, don't you?" To which he replied, "Dadgummit, Max, I was only 6 at the time." I was embarrassed!

And then during the 2005-06 season, my last on the air, I mentioned to coach Self that, "Jeff Hawkins had a career night tonight, hitting a record seven three-pointers and a total of 19 points." Bill looked at me with a twinkle in his eye and said, "Max, did you take mathematics in school?" How stupid was I? Jeff had 19 points alright, and seven baskets, but obviously, not seven three-pointers.

That happened to be the same night that a reporter from the Lawrence Journal-World was following me all day to get a story on what game day was like for me. The accompanying photographer snapped the picture while Bill — and I to a lesser extent — were laughing. It graced the front page of the sports section. I was embarrassed again! Oh well, win a lot, lose a few!

With these two coaches, even with different styles and personalities, more often than not you definitely can count on winning more than losing.

Chapter 20

Bob Davis: A Terrific Announcer and An Even Better Friend

During my 60 years with KU, I had a chance to work with some great radio partners, such as Gerry Barker, Bob Fromme, Al Correll, Jerry Waugh and Jim Fender.

Gerry Barker had been one of the all-time athletic greats at Ottawa University. Bob Fromme was a K-State grad, but became a great KU fan, and was an associate of mine at WREN. Al Correll, who was the first black captain of a KU basketball team in 1963-64, was very articulate, and did a great job on the radio. Jerry Waugh was an assistant basketball coach for Dick Harp and the 1957 team that played for the national championship. Jim Fender was a wide receiver on the KU football team. I had great fun traveling and working with each of these gentlemen.

But in 1984 I moved from the play-by-play chair over to color analyst when Bob Davis came to Lawrence from Fort Hays State University, where he'd been an announcer for many years.

When I was invited to serve as a color commentator to Bob's play-by-play description, I had many reservations. It wasn't going to be easy going from telling what was going on, as I had done for about 38 years, to why it was happening. (Frankly, being on both sides, I think play-by-play is easier.)

But Bob made it so easy for me that we soon settled into a pattern that fans really seemed to enjoy. First of all, Bob had listened to me for years and I think he respected what I had done. Secondly, he was not burdened with the big ego that is so common in our business. He and I just settled into a conversational pattern. He would say what was happening, and I would remember things from the past and relate the close relationships and confidences I had with the players and coaches.

Most importantly in the long run, we laughed a lot and had fun. Bob has a GREAT sense of humor and is very quick-witted. Thousands of people told us that whenever a game was on television, they would mute the sound and listen to "Bob and Max" on the radio. They liked hearing the same guys on every game, not different announcers who didn't know the people nearly as well as we did.

One of my phrases was "Don't Make Me Laugh," because Bob would start telling a story, and we would laugh so hard that I would become hoarse, which made doing the game that night more difficult than it might have been. After many years, one or the other of us would start a story, and everyone in the group would remember it, and jump to the punch line, and then we all would laugh. We saved a lot of time that way!

Our partnership of 22 years is probably one of the longest pairings in college sportscasting history. Of course, just up the road, Denny Matthews and Fred White called Kansas City Royals games together for 25 years. Partnerships at the college level, however, tend not to last as long. Dick Vitale named us as a pair to his Sweet Sixteen of basketball broadcasters in the nation, the only twosome from one school in the whole country.

Looking back at that picture in chapter 11 from 1984, Bob and I haven't changed that much in 22 years. OK, maybe a little.

There are so many great stories from our time together, it's impossible to remember all of them. And, frankly, some probably are best forgotten. But there are a few memorable moments that pop into my head immediately.

On January 26, 1986, the Hawks played at Colorado in a great game when Calvin Thompson hit a last-second shot and we beat the Buffaloes, 70-68. The team was going to fly on a little charter to Ann Arbor, Michigan, for a nationally televised game the next day against the Wolverines. There wasn't room on the charter for our two-man radio crew, so Bob and I had to drive back to snowy Denver to catch a commercial flight to equally snowy Detroit, late on Saturday night. Bob enjoys this story so much that I'll let him tell the rest.

Other voices from The Hill • Bob Davis

About midnight, we were trudging out in the snow in Detroit to rent a car to drive to Ann Arbor. Dead tired after this long day, Max and I were the only two guys on the rental-car bus headed over to where they parked the cars. The bus driver had this long, beautiful, wavy blonde hair. Max, who's always pretty friendly with people and doesn't really know a stranger, says from the back of the bus, "Honey, how far is it up to Ann Arbor?" The bus driver turned around — showing a great big, blonde mustache — and said in a deep voice, "About 30 minutes." Max and I had many great laughs over the years, but I had to enjoy that one all by myself.

Then, there was the morning of the 1992 Aloha Bowl on Christmas Day against BYU. Bob and I were enjoying a pregame Hawaiian-style brunch at Aloha Stadium before anchoring in our booth for the broadcast. A few of my travel buddies saw an opportunity to have some fun at my expense and asked the Aloha Bowl queen, dressed in a sarong, to sit on my lap. They pointed in my direction with the instructions, "Go over and sit in that old guy's lap." Well, she came heading my direction and decided that Bob more aptly fit that description. She settled in his lap, and we all took pictures. Bob didn't seem to mind being the "old guy."

Other voices from The Hill • Bob Davis

Hema Heimuli, who later played in the NFL, was BYU's star running back that year. Since it was Christmas and a bowl game, they had all sorts of festivities with cartoon characters on the field, as Max and I talked on the air about all the Christmas in Hawaii stuff. With the game's opening kick in the air, I said, "Mele Kalikimaka," which, of course, is Merry Christmas in Hawaiian, "and Hema Heimuli at the goal line ... and he's going to take it all the way." Sure enough, he returned it for a game-opening touchdown. After they kicked the extra point, we broke for a commercial. Max leaned over and asked me, "Who scored that touchdown?" I said, "Hema Heimuli." He said, "Oh, shoot, I thought you said 'Merry Christmas and Happy New Year." So, that's how we started that bowl game.

Other voices from The Hill • Bob Davis

I remember one time at a ballgame in the mid-1990s, the Hawks had a fast break, three-on-two, with Jacque in the middle, Paul Pierce on one side and Jerod Haase on the other, and they are flying down the court. Jacque makes one of his no-look passes to Paul, who stuffs it. Allen Fieldhouse just erupted. I am trying in some way to describe that play and I looked at Max, who said, "Do you ever watch the Discovery Channel?" I said, "Well, once in a while I flip by it. Why do you ask me that right now?" He said, "The speed of that fast break reminded me of that impala running through the jungle being chased by a cheetah."

I said, "Boy, you're talking about some speed there. What happens when the cheetah catches the impala?" And Max said, "I don't know. I always flip the channel right before that happens."

Bob and I always had fun on trips. We liked the same kind of food. Home-cooked style, mostly. Greasy was okay. We always joked that if our wives wouldn't go into a place, it probably would be perfect for us. Once, when we stayed at a beautiful resort, The Inn At South Mountain, in Phoenix, Bob and I would walk out to our rental car and drive a couple of miles to eat at the Waffle House.

The Jayhawk football team opened the 2000 season with a night game in Dallas against Southern Methodist University – the opening of the

Mustangs' new stadium. Bob, doing his baseball duties of calling games on TV for the Royals, had been in Tampa for a series. He flew to Dallas on Saturday morning. Richard Konzem, Janay Leddy and I picked him up and headed for lunch.

We always liked to find the little local places, the holes in the wall, in the different towns we visited. This particular trip we went to a local hamburger place. As we sat there, I started to look around and noticed that there were a lot of couples — friendly couples. However, Janay was the only female in sight. So, we all nudged a little closer to Janay. At that point we were ready to just eat and leave. We were sitting there quietly eating our hamburgers until I decided to speak up: "You know, these are pretty good hamburgers." SMU beat KU, 31-17, that night, so the hamburger joint turned out to be the highlight of the day.

Those are the kinds of things we remember more than the games. One of Bob's great lines is, "This would be a great trip if we didn't have to do the games."

One of the funny incidents of many happened during the 2002 NCAA Tournament. The Hawks were in Madison, Wisconsin, for the Midwest Regional, where they played Illinois and Oregon. Bob, his wife Linda and I went out to dinner one night at a nice restaurant that someone recommended.

Verne Lundquist, who is one of the nicest guys in the whole business, was there with his CBS-TV partner Bill Raftery and a couple other guys. As we were being seated, we saw the group and waved to each other.

The waiter came by and said, "The silver-haired gentleman over there would like to buy you folks a drink."

Bob said, "Well, thank you. Please thank Mr. Raftery, but tell him we are a couple of tee-totaling Kansans over here. But we appreciate the offer."

A few minutes later, the waiter came back and said, "Mr. Raftery wants to know if you'd rather have the money instead." (Of course we said yes!)

Other voices from The Hill • Bob Davis

One other great moment happened shortly after KU signed the new zillion dollar deal with Nike. There was so much hoopla about the new uniforms for the sports. The first home basketball game the team is playing in these beautiful new white uniforms. All of a sudden, in the middle of the game,

Max says, "What's that little checkmark on their shirts?" I said, "Well, that's the Nike swoosh that they've spent about a billion dollars on." And Max said, "Oh, yeah, yeah, yeah. I know about that."

Over the years, Bob and I have walked to breakfast through the icy cold of Anchorage, Alaska. We've eaten dinner in Maui, Hawaii, as the sun has seemingly set into the Pacific. And we have lined up at Joe's Stone Crab Restaurant in Miami. While there, Kansas State Senator David Wysong saw us at the end of a long line of those waiting to get in. He left for a few minutes to talk to the maitre'd. In a few moments he came back and said, "Follow me," and the maitre'd announced, "Governor Wysong's party" next. We always figured he slipped the maitre'd $50 or so. But from that moment on, Dave has always been "Governor Wysong" to us.

Bob and I like to go to zoos. We have visited many to kill time on game day. We have visited the Richard Nixon Presidential Library in Yorba Linda, California, and the George Bush Presidential Library in College Station, Texas. Bob is well-versed in history and has a great memory. He seems to know the words to every country-western song ever written, yet he almost always listens to sports-talk radio while in the car. Not me. I get tired of hearing the same jerks express the same opinions over and over.

You can probably tell that Bob and I laughed more often than we can count. Although I had some apprehension about going from play-by-play to color — only because I didn't really know if I could do it — when he came to KU in the fall of 1984, working with Bob for the final 22 years of my broadcasting career couldn't have been more enjoyable.

As more and more honors fell my way, it seemed that Bob was always the guy to emcee the event or to introduce me for the award. He always did a terrific job. Surely he must have gotten tired of that, but I never sensed it, and he was always gracious and complimentary to me. There are not a lot of guys around like that, so I will always be indebted to him. I was pleased that he was inducted into the Kansas Broadcasters Hall of Fame in 2006, and I am sure many more awards will come to him in the future.

KU MEDICAL
CENTER
The University of Kansas

THE UNIVERSITY
OF KANSAS HOSPITAL
——— KUMED ———

Chapter 21

That's a Wrap

As I've worked on this book, it's reinforced to me how lucky I was to spend 60 years broadcasting KU games. Sure, I witnessed some great games and wonderful teams. But, really, for me it's been more about the people. The coaches, the student-athletes, the athletics department staff and the fans.

It's gratifying to know the feeling is mutual. When a sportswriter was interviewing people on the occasion of my retirement, I was pleased when I heard what Chris Piper had to say.

"Max is not the media," Pipe told the reporter. "All of the players always regarded him as a friend."

The mug shot for my 60th and final season behind the microphone.

After all the celebrations and recognitions of my 60th and final season, the spring and summer of 2006 came along. Although nothing seemed different to me because I wouldn't have been broadcasting games that time of the year anyway, the word "retirement" seemed to have struck a chord with fans. Everywhere I went, people congratulated me, thanked me, and inevitably asked me, "How do you like retirement?" At first I started to explain that really nothing was any different, but then I just resorted to, "It's O.K."

And finally, it came! The first KU football game in 60 years where I had nothing to do. It was a strange feeling, indeed. I went to the stadium early, as I always had done, but what should I do? There was a nice seat in the press box assigned to me, alongside my friends Larry Keating and Jim Marchiony. I went to the athletics director's suite and visited with some alumni, and enjoyed some nice food. I didn't have any spotting charts to prepare, no need to acquire and study statistics on the Hawks and the opposition, no need to line up a halftime interview, no need to visit with Bob Davis about other Big 12 teams we would be talking about in the pre-game show. In fact, just plain nothing! So I sat there and watched the game.

My buddies were doing other things, so for the most part I was all alone. It felt very, very strange.

In the football press box, you sit behind closed glass. The only windows that are open are little ones at the top. Consequently, you don't hear the crowd, you don't hear the band. All you hear is the inside press box announcer calling out the plays and the yardage. I felt like I was at home watching the game on television. In all my years, we always did football through open windows, no matter how hard it rained or snowed, or how hard the wind was blowing. And you could hear everything. We felt like we were in the game. I didn't have that feeling sitting in the press box that September 2006 afternoon.

In the fourth quarter, my friends showed up and said, "Let's go down on the field." So we went through the locker room and ended up by the scoreboard at the south end. While there, the video board director apparently spotted me, because they flashed my picture on the huge video board and I got a big cheer from the crowd. After that, I slipped out early, got in my car, and drove home. As I pulled in the driveway, they were just wrapping up Coach Mangino's post-game interview. I figured I got home at least an hour earlier than I would have last year.

As nice as that was, it felt odd.

On the day of the second game my son Kurt said, "Why don't you come and sit in the stands with me? I have a great spot on the east side right on the 50-yard line." So I said OK. There were a lot of great KU fans there. They cheered and they cussed. They cheered the players, they cussed the coaches and the officials. AND on every good play, everybody stood up — and I couldn't see a damn thing! I told Kurt at the half that I'd had enough. I was going back to the press box! See how spoiled I had become in 60 years?

The third game was on the road at Toledo. I didn't go, but listened on the radio. David Lawrence had taken my place in the booth, and Nate Bukaty was the sideline reporter. Bob, David and Nate did a nice job, I thought. I also didn't go to Iowa State, but I flew with the team to Baylor, where we lost a one-point heartbreaker — too typical of the 2006 season.

Before the game, Lew Perkins asked me if I would like fly on KU's jet to College Station after the game to watch the volleyball match with Texas A&M that night. Sounded great to me.

The flight was only about 20 minutes, and we arrived at the arena in time to see most of the match. Then we flew back to Lawrence in the KU jet and were home by about 10 p.m. I was thinking, "This is a pretty big-time way to travel!"

My wife, Isobel, and our children, Jane Hart and Kurt Falkenstien, who have spent many hours listening to me on the radio or television. They might consider themselves my No. 1 fans. Actually I am their No. 1 fan.

The student Homecoming Committee had asked me months before if I would be willing to serve as Grand Marshall of the Homecoming Parade in early October. It is not as big as it used to be, but it was fun never-the-less. I sat on the back of a convertible as we wound across the campus, and I waved at a lot of people who waved back and shouted nice things. (I think.) The alumni magazine later showed a colorful chalk drawing on Wescoe Beach in which I was featured, with a microphone and the words MISSING MAX.

The football season concluded with a game at Missouri on the same day KU's men's basketball team played No. 1-ranked Florida in Las Vegas. In the KU jet, "KU100," we left Lawrence at 7:55 a.m., flew to Missouri and watched a disappointing finale loss to the Tigers. We then got back on the jet, flew to Lawrence to drop off Chancellor Hemenway and Mike Maddox, and after refueling, headed for Las Vegas. We got there at 6 p.m., two hours before tip-off, and watched the Jayhawks put together a spectacular performance to beat the Gators in overtime.

We then caught a few hours sleep in Vegas and flew back to Lawrence on Sunday morning. It was quite a weekend. Started with a huge disappointment, ended with an exhilarating win. It is still fun for me to be a part of it, although a very different part. I will still travel some with the teams, although probably not when they are scheduled to arrive home after 2 a.m. I've had enough of that! But, let's face it, flying on one of KU's jets to see a volleyball or basketball game on the same night as a football game, is pretty nice. Maybe this title of special assistant to the director of athletics isn't half bad.

Mascots and Traditions

I want to take a little precious space in this book to tell you about mascots and traditions. After all, they are part of what makes college athletics so different and so much fun. We'll have to restrict it to the Big 12, otherwise there is no place to stop.

I'm going to make one exception right off the bat. One of my top favorites in the whole nation has to be The Hawk of St Joseph's of Philadelphia. This noble bird flaps his wings continuously for the entire game, never stopping even once. You think that guy isn't in shape? Try that yourself for even five minutes.

In the Big 12, I love Texas A&M. When their corps of cadets marches on the field before the game, it gives me goose bumps. Their military band is great, their mascot Reveille XI (or whatever number it is now) is a beautiful collie dog, and the whole stadium is the 12th man. When they start swaying, the entire stadium structure, holding 80,000 fans, sways as well. It's quite a feeling! We all remember the awful tragedy of the bonfire casualties, another proud tradition which has been scaled way back.

Nebraska's Li'l Red is my favorite mascot, by far – some guy is in this helium-filled suit, which I guess is supposed to be a Cornhusker. He can bounce, jump, stand on his head, turn himself inside out and upside down in the most hilarious moves you can imagine. So much fun to watch.

Colorado has Ralphie, the real buffalo. Usually Ralphie is a "she." So, she (or he) storms out of the tunnel before the game and second half, and does a race around the stadium perimeter behind a quartet of handlers, all of whom look like they are simply hanging on for dear life. One time they came so close to one of our star running backs who was warming up, he had to leap backwards to avoid injury. I wouldn't want to be hit by a charging buffalo!

Baylor has its beautiful live bear! He is washed, combed, and is indeed a handsome rascal. Two or three students keep him company at the end of the field. Last time we were in Waco it was so hot that the bear sat down in a tub of ice water. What a life!

Oklahoma has the Sooner Schooner. It's a covered wagon pulled by a team of miniature horses, and driven by a crew of students. It, too, storms out of a tunnel periodically during the game. Okay, but not near the top of my list.

Texas Tech has the Red Raider, a mysterious kind of guy with a mask, riding a black horse. Makes a pretty imposing combination. I wouldn't want to meet them in a dark alley.

Kansas State doesn't have a live Wildcat. At least, I don't ever recall seeing it. But everything, and I do mean everything, is purple. Nobody does the Wabash Cannonball as well as they do it, and their pom-pon girls and cheerleaders lead the league.

Iowa State is called the Cyclones! What can you do with a blast of air? They have Cy the Cyclone. Not too impressive.

Oklahoma State has that damn Pistol Pete. He's dressed up like a Cowboy, with a plastic head. And every so often he fires that frigging pistol, usually when you least expect it, and makes you wonder if you should have gone to the bathroom.

Texas has Bevo, a truly handsome Longhorn Steer. Again, he is coddled and brushed and treated like a king. He is SO lucky that he didn't end up at Burger King.

And then there's Missouri. They don't even have a live Tiger! And in spite of what Don Fambrough says, I don't really believe that border ruffian William Quantrill was a graduate of MU.

Then we come to Kansas. Since the Jayhawk is a mythical bird, it has to be a costume. We have Big Jay and Baby Jay, and they are good at entertaining the crowd, and especially at shooting t-shirts from an air gun high into the stands. Sometime watch what fools people make of themselves signaling how much they would like to have a shirt! The best things about Kansas are the "Waving Of The Wheat" at the football games, and the spine-chilling and hypnotic "Rock Chalk Chant" which is heard near the end of a successful basketball conquest.

Oh yes, I wish Texas Christian was in the Big 12 Conference. Then we could have a bunch of Horned Frogs running around our league.

During the basketball games at Allen Fieldhouse throughout most of 2006-07, I could be found a few seats down from my old spot. But, again, it was different — not preparing for a game, not interviewing Bill afterwards, and, of course, not traveling with Bob and the team.

Bill Self has invited me into the locker room and told me, "Travel with us; make any trips you want to make." Lew said the same thing. He said, "Any time you want to go to a game, you can sit wherever you want to or go on any trip that you want to make — you're part of the travel party." It's different now, though.

To be honest, my first season away from the microphone after 60 years wasn't this great, relaxing time. Really, I was lost like a fish out of water because there was nothing for me to do. And so I simply went — and will continue to go — to the games as a spectator, most likely in the press box at Memorial Stadium or on press row at Allen Fieldhouse. I made it a point not to go into the football radio booth. They asked me a couple of times to be on the air and I told them I just really would rather not at this point.

Looking back, as I mentioned in the first chapter, Lew was probably right about the way I should end my 60 years. Instead of my plan to wait until March and then say, "Next week I'm gonna wrap it up," and that be the end of it, Lew had the great idea of having a "farewell tour." I realize now how much I would've missed if I'd done it my way. Not that I'm big into recognition, even though that was spectacular, but the way we did it gave me a chance to thank people I've gotten to know throughout the years around the Big 12. Indeed, I would've missed a ton if I'd done it my way.

And, of course, wonderful fans seemingly everywhere I go still say they miss me and that the broadcasts aren't the same without me. Then, when I walk into Allen Fieldhouse, the student section yells: "HEY MAX!" All of that makes me feel good.

I do miss broadcasting. I suppose I always will, but that's OK.

After all, I still get a chance to be around many of the people who helped make my 60 years in broadcasting a remarkable experience. They, along with our school's wonderful history and tradition, make me proud to be a Jayhawk.

Afterword

Max Falkenstien and I became friends in 1985-86 when I was hired to be a graduate coach at Kansas under Larry Brown. In my eyes, Max was already a legend. He treated everyone, especially a young kid from Oklahoma State, with great interest and kindness. That year was as much fun as a young coach could have and Max was a big part of that.

After leaving Kansas and going back to Oklahoma State as an assistant, I always found a way to stay in touch with Max. It was an automatic to spend some time together in Lawrence or Stillwater when the Hawks and Cowboys played. He has always followed my career and when I was named Coach at KU, Max was one of the first to make me feel welcome.

I have always enjoyed being around great story tellers and Max is one of the best. He has a unique way to put a spin on every story in a positive way. I love sitting around and listening to Max tell Doc Allen, Larry Brown and Roy Williams stories.

Every player that comes through here feels a connection to Max. He loves the kids, as he puts it. They all respect and understand that in his world of broadcasting, Max Falkenstien is a legend. I felt so honored to be the Coach at Kansas on Senior Day 2006 when we honored our seniors, including the greatest "senior" of them all, Max Falkenstien.

Although Max has retired, I hope he will still be my partner on the golf course! I hope he comes to every game, and I hope he continues to impact each kid's life like he did mine. I know you have enjoyed this book and all of Max's stories from the All-time Greatest Ambassador for the University of Kansas.

— Bill Self
Kansas Men's Basketball Coach

About the Authors

Max Falkenstien spent 60 years behind the microphone calling University of Kansas football and basketball games before retiring at the end of the 2005-06 basketball season. His long career included all but one of KU's Final Fours in basketball, including two national championships in 1952 and 1988, plus Jayhawk football appearances in two Orange Bowls and others. Max has been honored with numerous awards and citations including the Ellsworth Medallion, the highest award of the KU Alumni Association; the Chris Schenkel Award for broadcasting excellence from the College Football Hall of Fame; and the Curt Gowdy Award from the Naismith Basketball of Hall of Fame. At the conclusion of his 60th year of following the Jayhawks, the KU Athletics Corporation presented Max with its first ever Lifetime Service Award. He was honored by Resolutions of Commendation from the United States Senate, the United States House of Representatives, the Kansas Governor's Office, the Kansas Senate, and the Kansas House of Representatives. His mythical jersey (Number 60) was retired in Allen Fieldhouse, next to all the great KU athletes who have been so honored. On the business side, Max spent a long career in the banking industry, retiring as a Senior Vice President of Douglas County Bank in Lawrence. He currently serves as Special Assistant to Kansas Athletics Director Lew Perkins. Max and his wife Isobel have two children, three grandchildren and one great-grandchild.

Matt Fulks, who started his journalism career while attending Lipscomb University in Nashville, Tennessee, when his baseball career was cut short by a lack of ability, spends his time as a free-lance writer, editor and broadcaster. He is a regular contributor to various publications, including kcmetrosports.com — the Web site for Kansas City's all-sports TV station Metro Sports, *The Kansas City Star* newspaper and the Royals *Gameday magazine*. He is the author/co-author of 11 other books, including *Echoes of Kansas Basketball, More Than the Score: Kansas City Sports Memories, The Road to Canton*, co-authored with NFL Hall of Fame running back Marcus Allen, and *Good as Gold: Techniques for Fundamental Baseball*, with Royals legend Frank White. More information is available at www.mattfulks.com. Matt resides in the Kansas City area with his wife Libby and their children, Helen, Charlie and Aaron.

Doug Vance is in his third year as Executive Director of the Kansas Recreation and Park Association in Topeka and previously spent 20 years in the University of Kansas Athletics Department, serving as Assistant Athletic Director of Media Relations and Associate Athletics Director for Communications. He has co-authored two KU sports books — (the original) *Max and the Jayhawks: 50 Years of KU Athletics with Max Falkenstien* and *Beware of the Phog: 50 Years of Allen Fieldhouse*. He also serves as a free-lance writer for both *Lawrence Magazine* and *Topeka Magazine*. Vance was named to the College Sports Information Directors of America (CoSIDA) Hall of Fame and is a former president of the organization. Doug and his wife, Sue, along with two Golden Retrievers — Sassy and Phog — reside in Lawrence and are the parents of two sons, Cory and Stuart, and have four grandsons, Cade, Skylar, Kole and Eli.